CHOCOLATES ON THE PILLOW AREN'T ENOUGH

CHOCOLATES ON THE PILLOW AREN'T ENOUGH

Reinventing the Customer Experience

JONATHAN M. TISCH
WITH KARL WEBER

BICENTENNIAL
1807
WILEY
2007
BICENTENNIAL

John Wiley & Sons, Inc.

Published by John Wiley & Sons, Inc., Hoboken, New Jersey.
Published simultaneously in Canada.

Wiley Bicentennial Logo: Richard J. Pacifico.

For general information on our other products and services or for technical support, please contact our Customer Care Department within the United States at (800) 762-2974, outside the United States at (317) 572-3993 or fax (317) 572-4002.

Wiley also publishes its books in a variety of electronic formats. Some content that appears in print may not be available in electronic books. For more information about Wiley products, visit our web site at www.wiley.com.

Library of Congress Cataloging-in-Publication Data:

Tisch, Jonathan M.
     Chocolates on the pillow aren't enough: reinventing the customer experience / Jonathan M. Tisch with Karl Weber.
        p.   cm.
     Includes index.
     ISBN 978-0-470-04355-4
     1. Hospitality industry—Customer services.   2. Hotels.   3. Customer relations.   I. Title.
     TX911.3.C8T57   2007
     647.94′068—dc22

                                         2006036647

Printed in the United States of America.

10 9 8 7 6 5 4

CONTENTS

ACKNOWLEDGMENTS

IN AUGUST OF 2004, MY DAYS WERE FILLED WITH EXCITEMENT, TREPIDA-tion, and just a bit of fear. In just a few short weeks, my first book, *The Power of We*, would be shipped to bookstores all over the country, and the preorders at web sellers like Amazon.com would start to be filled.

Over the next four months, I had a variety of hard-to-get TV inter-views planned, commencing with *The Today Show* the first week of September and including sit-downs with Larry King, Charlie Rose, Harry Smith, and the nationally syndicated radio host, Joan Hamburg. And I was fully prepared for the grind of a 12-city book tour and speaking engagements that would take me from Toronto and Chicago to Seattle and Los Angeles.

But everything changed with one phone call.

Bob Tisch, my father, and the man who, with his brother Larry, created what is today Loews Corporation, had been diagnosed with a stage 4 brain tumor.

Like every family that is touched by the dark shadow of cancer, we grew closer than ever as we dealt with my father's diagnosis, prognosis, and care.

Over the next 15 months, my father was afforded the chance to live, experience, and love, thanks to a dedicated team of physicians, nurses, and caregivers. And during this period, he never complained or whined.

Of course, I offered to scale back my commitments to my day job and the book tour, but my father wouldn't hear of that. He was pleased that I had fulfilled my dream of putting some of my thoughts into writ-ing, and he insisted I go on the road and talk about *The Power of We*.

On October 1, 2004, when the book hit the *Wall Street Journal*'s best-seller list, he was as proud of me as I had ever seen him.

On November 15, 2005, exactly two years to the day after his brother had passed away, my father lost his battle with cancer.

Three weeks later, amid the first snow storm of the year, some 2,500 people from all over the world gathered at Avery Fisher Hall in Lincoln Center, to pay their respects to Preston Robert Tisch, or, as many referred to him, PRT.

The service was a celebration of a life well lived. In addition to my brother, sister, and me, the speakers included New York's Mayor Michael Bloomberg; Beverly Sills, the famed opera singer and a childhood friend of my father's from Brooklyn; and my dear friend, Tiki Barber, the great running back of the New York Giants. We heard from other individuals whose lives my father touched, such as Evelyn Houser, a housekeeper at the Loews Regency Hotel, and Sammy Arthur, from Ghana, who came to work as my father's driver in 1986, and quickly became one of his closest friends and confidants. And our spirits were buoyed by musical performances from Michael Feinstein, Brian Stokes Mitchell, Ronan Tynan, and Steve Tyrell, all backed by a 50-piece orchestra and a choir of some 30 students from New York University.

Perhaps a few sentences from my remarks that day will give you a clear sense of who Bob Tisch was, and how fortunate I have been to have him in my life:

> Bob Tisch was not only my father, he was my mentor. And for the boy who idolized his dad and followed in his footsteps, nothing could have made me happier. I was able to learn the great art of hospitality from one of the industry's founders and pioneers. And while the business of hotels has become much more complex over the years, the hotel business has remained the same.
>
> At its core, it's about making people feel welcome and comfortable. And nobody did that better than Bob Tisch. Whether you were a guest in his hotel, an employee, or a friend, Bob was the embodiment of hospitality. He could walk into any room, of any hotel and know the names of everyone who worked there. He knew to follow the basics and not be swayed by the trends. He had a laser like focus on the bottom line, but it was his natural understanding of the human side of the business, that really set him apart.

And what I learned from my father really became the starting point for much of what we write about in this book. Hence its dedication to his life and memory.

Through these difficult months and years, I have been blessed to have my family available to provide love, support, and encouragement. My mother Joan, my brother Steve, my sister Laurie, and their families have been remarkable during this time of loss and change.

And the same is true of my kids, who are always there for me, and who I hope will forge a life based on generational values, hope, and caring for others. Laura and Stafford, I thank you for all your assistance in this part of life's journey.

With the publication of my second book, I can't hide behind the notion of making rookie errors any more. Fortunately for me, most of the individuals who supported me so well a few years back are involved in this book as well, starting with my cowriter, Karl Weber, a man of intelligence, humor, and fine literary style. Our second collaboration was an effort of pleasure and one that hopefully the reader will find interesting and helpful. Thank you, Karl, for your hours and hours of research, writing, and editing.

Jeffrey Stewart, the senior vice president of communications and public affairs for Loews Hotels and a dear friend, was once again there with me every step of the way, offering insights and counsel, and making the writing and editing process fun.

And my agent, Wayne Kabak, from the New York City office of The William Morris Agency, has been invaluable with his guidance, knowledge, and support.

So many individuals and organizations have provided partnerships, like those that I wrote about in *The Power of We*, which have enabled me to spend time on this book. They include my cousins Jim and Andrew Tisch, with whom I am fortunate to share the responsibility of managing Loews Corporation, as well as the superb team at Loews Hotels, headed up by our president and COO, Jack Adler. Also, as part of my team in New York City are two people who help hold my crazy life together—my assistant Vicki Alfonzetti and her assistant, Susan Shannon. And then add to that the 7,500-plus individuals who make me so proud every day at Loews Hotels—my colleagues who make staying at a Loews Hotel a memorable experience for thousands of guests every year.

Also, I want to thank the team at John Wiley & Sons, including my publisher, Joan O'Neil; my editor, Debra Englander; my production manager, Mary Daniello; Peter Knapp and all the hard-working people in marketing and events; and to all others who contributed to this book. My thanks also to Mark Fortier who did a superb job of promoting my first book and with whom I'm pleased to be working again, as well as my good friend Don Epstein and the wonderful group at Greater Talent Network, who help me spread the message to groups of all kinds.

Thanks, too, to the people who shared their insights, stories, and experiences with us as we researched and wrote this book. And thanks to Alex Kassl of New York University, who helped us with background research on many of the organizations profiled in these pages.

Finally, my thanks to Lizzie: I deeply appreciate your listening to my whining, ravings, and crazy ideas . . . and thanks for the constant support through it all.

In the hotel industry, our goal is to turn customers into guests. My hope with this book is that, whatever you do with your life, you will be able to arrive at a similar place, touch people in a positive way, and create personal success for yourself and the people in your lives.

J. M. T.

CHOCOLATES ON THE PILLOW AREN'T ENOUGH

The Hotelier's Secret

WHEN MY FIRST BOOK, *The Power of We: Succeeding Through Partnerships,* was published in 2004, the reception it received was very gratifying. The book sold well around the country and the world, and appeared on national best-seller lists. To this day, I get calls and e-mails from readers eager to tell me how much they enjoyed learning about the power of partnerships from the book. They also share their stories about how they've put some of the ideas into practice in their own lives and careers.

Perhaps most enjoyable for me, the publication of the book gave me the opportunity to speak before a wide range of audiences. The traditional author tour, which some writers describe as an ordeal, turned out to be great fun. As the CEO of Loews Hotels, a midsize chain of luxury hotels that is a subsidiary of Loews Corporation, I was invited to speak to many organizations and individuals involved in the hospitality and travel industries—airlines, restaurants, travel agencies, tour operators, cruise lines, and my fellow hoteliers. But even more interesting, I had the chance to speak with thousands of people from many other lines of work, from bankers and teachers to retailers and service professionals. I gave talks before groups of concrete manufacturers and suppliers of rubber hose, and at companies like Microsoft and Amazon. Employees and leaders of not-for-profit groups invited me to speak with them, as did many people connected with government agencies large and small. And countless students, both in business schools and in undergraduate colleges and universities, wanted to know how they could apply the lessons I had learned to their own work lives.

Naturally enough, most of the stories I told in *The Power of We* and during the book tour that followed were drawn from my experiences as a hotelier. At the start of my tour, I was a little concerned: Would audiences from varied walks of life find my tales of the hotel business interesting and meaningful or would they seem boring and irrelevant? To my delight, I received an amazing response. It turned out that people like hearing about the adventures, challenges, and triumphs of a hotelier, and they find the lessons I've learned over the years not only relevant to their own work but extremely useful.

There are probably several reasons for the widespread interest in the hotel business. One factor is that everyone knows (or thinks they know) the hotel business: we've all stayed in hotels, experienced great and not-so-great service in them, and developed strong opinions about what we like and don't like. Another is the intimate nature of the services hotels provide: hoteliers get to know and cater to some of the most personal needs of their clients, which creates some daunting challenges (and generates some colorful stories). People come to hotels for many of the most important moments in their lives, from bar mitzvahs, sweet-sixteen parties, weddings, honeymoons, and anniversary celebrations to crucial business meetings, family reunions, and once-in-a-lifetime vacations. The sheer drama of what goes on in a hotel makes the life of a hotelier inherently interesting.

However, there is another more basic reason why my work in the hotel business is interesting, and perhaps even important, for people in many walks of life.

In today's world, organizations of every kind—not only businesses but also government agencies, cultural institutions, and not-for-profit groups—are experiencing huge difficulties in attracting and retaining clients. Competition is intensifying, consumers are becoming more demanding, and old ways of creating customer loyalty have lost much of their impact. And with the communications media becoming ever more interactive and fragmented, it is becoming harder and harder for organizations to convey a strong and convincing message to the general public.

In this difficult environment, offering a good product or a useful service is no longer enough. Today's consumers are looking for something more—a relationship with an organization that will truly enrich their lives. As a result, organizations are discovering that the only sure way to establish strong and lasting connections with their clients or customers is by providing them with experiences that are unique, memorable, delightful, comfortable, and deeply rewarding. *And this is exactly what the best hoteliers have always specialized in doing.*

Just consider a few of the unusual characteristics of the hotel business:

- Whereas most organizations address a single, often narrow human need, hoteliers are responsible for their clients' total well-being—physical, emotional, psychological—from the moment of check-in until the visit ends. We have to find ways to make everything about our guests' stay enjoyable, which calls on a wide range of skills, talents, and processes.

- Unlike most organizations, a hotel is open for business 24 hours a day, 365 days a year. There are no down times for retooling our systems or recharging our batteries; changes and adjustments to the business must be handled on the fly, even as more customers are arriving to be cared for. Being a hotelier may not be quite as demanding as, say, being the chief physician of a busy emergency room or president of the United States—but believe me, it has its moments.

- Hoteliers must nurture people who are in a vulnerable situation. They are on the road, far from their homes and often from their families, totally dependent on the hotel for safety and security as well as basic physical needs: a fine meal, a good night's sleep, a well-appointed bathroom. People literally put their lives in our hands, which is a sobering, daunting challenge.

- Hotel guests bring an incredible range of expectations to their encounters with us. For the business traveler, a state-of-the-art service center with high-speed Internet access, a conference room, and the availability of specialized services like language interpretation may be the most essential requirements for a successful stay. For a honeymooning couple, a magical atmosphere of romance, indulgence, and privacy may be the key. And a vacationing family may need a concierge with the local knowledge to suggest a week's worth of fun activities for everyone from a grade-schooler to an octogenarian.

Driven by these customer requirements, we in the hotel business have developed a unique expertise in the art of creating great experiences—not just now and then but consistently, over and over again. Call it the hotelier's secret. And in today's ever-more-demanding, ever-more-competitive arena, this secret is not just relevant but potentially extremely valuable for leaders of every kind of organization.

This book is my opportunity to offer insights into the art of creating great customer experiences based on my years in the hospitality business as well as to share stories and lessons I've gathered from my colleagues and mentors here at Loews Hotels and around the industry. However, the ideas in these pages extend far beyond the hotel business. My coauthor, Karl Weber, and I have sought out examples and stories from many industries as well as from the worlds of nonprofit and government work to illustrate how great organizations of every kind are discovering powerful new ways of forging lasting customer connections. We also depict the challenges and pitfalls they've encountered along the way.

Leaders and aspiring leaders of organizations everywhere are invited to draw on the lessons in these pages and to share with us your ideas, experiences, problems, and experiences as you seek your own ways of providing customers with unforgettable experiences. Here's hoping you'll enjoy exploring the ideas in this book as much as we've enjoyed developing them for you.

PART ONE

The Problem and the Solution

CHAPTER 1

What Happened to My Customers?

IT IS PROBABLY NORMAL FOR PEOPLE TO ASSUME THAT THE PROBLEMS they face are tougher than those encountered by past generations. Perhaps it is a way of consoling ourselves for the difficulties we encounter and of fortifying ourselves psychologically for the challenges to come.

It is an especially tempting attitude for those of us who help to run organizations. We look back at the business world our parents participated in a generation ago—or, for that matter, at the worlds of education, health care, social engagement, or politics—and we wax nostalgic. Those were simpler times, we think, when the United States was on the rise, cities and neighborhoods were safe, incomes were growing, families were strong, and technology seemed to promise endless progress. By contrast, today's world—troubled by terrorism, international discord, increasing social and economic inequality, and hyperpartisan politics—feels like a much less friendly, secure place.

Pessimism isn't my thing. I've always been a great believer in the opportunities available to all of us, not just here in the United States but increasingly throughout the free world. Having seen how my own family rose from modest working-class status to success in the world of business through hard work, creativity, attention to the needs of others, and a bit of good luck—and having seen many others achieve just as much or more—I remain a partisan of the American dream. And being an optimist who believes that people armed with determination can overcome almost any difficulty goes with that territory.

Nonetheless, as a hands-on manager of a business (the Loews Hotel brand), as an active participant in the direction of that business's parent (Loews Corporation), and as a deeply engaged leader of one of the world's largest and fastest-growing industry sectors (travel and tourism), I've been well placed to see the changes that the past two to three decades have brought to the business world and, more broadly, to the relationship between organizations of all kinds and the people they serve. And what I've seen has convinced me that, in some ways, today's business world is perhaps the most challenging in recent history.

Don't misunderstand me, we have plenty to be grateful for: the spread of economic and political freedom around the world in the wake of the collapse of the Soviet empire; the technological advances that have made both business and daily life far more productive, varied, and enjoyable than our parents could have imagined; the expansion of opportunity to American women, young people, and racial, ethnic, and religious minorities; and the steady increase in innovation that has created many kinds of new businesses, not-for-profit groups, and political and social organizations, all working to expand individual choices and advance human welfare. In many ways, the early years of the twenty-first century are an incredibly exciting time to do business.

But this is also an extraordinarily difficult time, filled with the challenges that come from change. In fact, some of the remarkable, positive developments mentioned in the previous paragraph are contributing to the strains that most organizational leaders are experiencing as they try to adjust to life in a rapidly evolving environment. Change is good, especially when it creates new freedoms. But change is also stressful.

Most leaders will quickly recognize the symptoms of the organizational stresses that have been caused by the economic and social dislocations of recent decades. They include:

- *Shrinking brand loyalty:* A generation ago, iconic American brands—from Coca-Cola, Ford, and Levi's to Sears, Zenith, and Kellogg's—ruled the world and commanded the lifetime loyalty of tens of millions of consumers. Today, customers seem to be ready to jump to the competition at the click of a mouse.
- *Increased price sensitivity:* Brand loyalty once commanded a price premium: Customers were willing to pay a little more for the

higher quality they associated with their favorite goods and services. Today, trained by years of price wars and discounting, customers are exerting intense, unyielding pressure on their suppliers to meet or beat competitive prices or lose the business.

- *Heightened competition:* Globalization, new media, technological and strategic innovation, and a global flood of capital seeking investment opportunities have spurred the emergence of new competitors in almost every business sphere from around the country and around the world. New kinds of competitors have multiplied—for example, if you run a local hardware store, you are now competing not just against other hardware stores but against Internet web sites, big box retailers, giant discount outlets, and individual sellers on eBay.

- *Increasing customer knowledge, skepticism, and power:* Today's consumers are more sophisticated than ever before. Raised in the world of Ralph Nader, *Consumer Reports,* and the Internet, they are accustomed to comparing products and prices, scrutinizing quality claims with a jaundiced eye, and demanding satisfaction when products or services fall short. And these attitudes aren't applied only to business. Citizens have become just as demanding and hard-nosed (some might say cynical) about government, social and civic organizations, and not-for-profit institutions.

As a result of these trends, it is getting harder and harder for businesses, not-for-profits, and government agencies, to understand, attract, satisfy, and retain their customers.* In fact, the basic connections between organizations and customers—once relatively powerful, long-lasting, and mutually beneficial—are increasingly breaking down. This disturbing trend is making itself felt in a host of ways.

---

* Those who are served by not-for-profits and government agencies are commonly referred to by terms such as *clients.* Throughout this book, however, I use the word *customers,* no matter whether for-profit businesses or other kinds of organizations are being discussed.

Desperate Companies: When the Old Connections Break Down

Launching successful new products has always been difficult. But the evidence shows that in recent decades it has become more challenging than ever. An authoritative 1991 survey by the Product Development and Management Association found that just 1 in 11 serious new product ideas is developed and brought to market successfully.[1] A more recent study by the respected Doblin Group, a Chicago-based firm that is a leader in innovation strategy, found that some 96 percent of all attempts at innovation fail to meet their companies' target rates for return on investment.[2] Thus, meeting your organization's growth objectives is no longer a relatively simple matter of developing a few spin-offs from already successful products or launching an exciting new brand. With store shelves already overflowing with thousands of goods and service offerings that jockey for attention, it is getting harder and harder to break through the new-product clutter.

For generations, organizations turned to traditional techniques of advertising and marketing to connect with customers. Now those tried-and-true business tools are losing their potency.

Not so long ago, if you were launching a new product or a new ad campaign, you could run a 30-second commercial on any of the three major television networks and be assured that you'd reach a huge swath of the national consumer market. Those days are long gone. With the proliferation of cable networks and the fragmentation of the mass audience, "you'd need to advertise on 92 channels to reach that same audience today," says one media consultant.[3]

After years in denial, today even executives at leading ad agencies are speaking about the crisis their industry is experiencing. Douglas Atkin, a partner and chief strategy officer at Merkley + Partners, speaks gloomily about the waning power of advertising and the growing complications in reaching out to customers:

> I used to be a brand manager at one of the most famous brand marketers of all time. In fact, they would claim that they invented brand marketing—Procter & Gamble. There was a time when there were just very, very simple ingredients to how you create a brand: You develop the best possible product; you have a great visual identity; you advertise the

hell out of it; you get distribution and the right price; and it works. The consumer saw the brand in advertising, bought it at the store, and used it in the washing machine. Nowadays, the brand is communicated everywhere through word of mouth, through the impression in a retail store, through advertising, through guerrilla activity. In fact, actually the biggest stimulant for someone to buy something is word of mouth. Advertising is increasingly retreating as a persuasive media.[4]

Even as advertising retreats, other forms of communication are growing in importance. Unfortunately for leaders, they are often forms that organizations have little or no control over. Blogs—those interactive Internet web sites that anyone with a personal computer (PC) and a web browser can set up in just a few minutes—have now acquired the power to make or break brands and even companies overnight. Take a blog like *Gizmodo*. It's a popular guide to new high-tech gadgets and toys that boasts 1.5 million visitors every month. A reviewer on Gizmodo endorsed the company DiscHub, which makes a simple yet ingenious soft neoprene gadget for safely storing CDs, DVDs, and similar items. Almost immediately, hits on DiscHub's web site increased from 20 to 10,000, and today the company founder Jonathan Bruck credits Gizmodo with making the firm successful. Similar success stories have been attributed to blogs such as *MoCo Loco* (which reviews modern design and architecture), *Dailycandy* (which features clothes and cosmetics), and *Treehugger* (which covers environmentally friendly products).[5]

When an organization runs afoul of the blogosphere, the results can be disastrous. In September 2004, a maker of bicycle locks named Kryptonite was blindsided by a series of postings on blogs frequented by bike lovers that claimed certain models of Kryptonite locks were vulnerable to picking simply by using a plastic pen. At first, the company disregarded the furor ("It's just a few techies, no big deal"). But soon Kryptonite found its products being pulled off the shelves of bike stores and its sales plummeting.

Kryptonite has since recovered, introducing a new line of locks with the design flaw remedied. And they have also made monitoring of the blogosphere—and participation in blog forums about biking—a regular part of their public-outreach efforts.

With advertising in decline and consumer-driven communications growing in stature, some marketing professionals are waving the white flag. Martin Puris, founder of Ammirati & Puris, one of Madison Avenue's most venerable agencies, is among many advertising executives who are defecting to nontraditional media. Puris spent 30 years driving huge sales through great TV advertising based on simple, powerful slogans; he's the man who dubbed the BMW the "Ultimate Driving Machine." Today he calls TV the "dead zone." In partnership with John Bernbach, another pro with deep roots in advertising history (his dad helped found the legendary Doyle Dane Bernbach agency), Puris has launched a new company called Not Traditional Media (NTM) to focus on everything *but* traditional advertising. NTM is linking clients to customers through such innovative—sometimes untested—channels as light boxes in subway tunnels, product samples given to guests at extended-stay hotels, even TV programming targeting bedridden patients in hospitals.

Many organizations are testing the new nontraditional marketing and advertising channels that consultants like NTM are flogging. Some are giving consumers the power to create their own advertising. The Converse sneaker company has created the Converse Gallery, a web site where thousands of fans have posted 24-second video clips lauding the company's footwear. Some of these amateur films have been chosen to appear in Converse's TV ads. Many consider these do-it-yourself advertising programs a new and promising way of connecting to the passion that customers feel for their favorite products.

But they may also make organizations vulnerable to embarrassing mishaps. During the 2004 presidential campaign, the Republican National Committee (RNC) created a web site titled "Make Your Own Campaign Poster." It was a great way to tap the political passions of an election year—but the RNC was forced to shut it down when Democratic partisans raided the site and created snarky ads for the Bush/Cheney campaign with satiric slogans like "Ending our nightmare of peace and prosperity."[6] Giving customers the keys to your company may be a tempting notion in an era when company-driven communication is losing its power, but it also reflects the increasing fear of being out of touch with customers that many organizations are feeling.

Other organizations are trying techniques that are supposed to capture and harness the magic power of word of mouth that traditionally has been generated spontaneously through enthusiastic, self-motivated consumers. Now, however, word of mouth supposedly can be produced systematically and deliberately. One of the first to travel this path was automaker Toyota. In 2003, it launched its new Scion brand, aimed at a hip young audience of 20-something drivers, using a marketing campaign designed primarily to generate word of mouth. Sales reps in goatees and sunglasses were dispatched to bohemian neighborhoods in cities like New York and San Francisco to distribute Scion-branded music CDs, clothing gift certificates, and copies of alternative lifestyle magazines like *Urb* and *Tokion*—all to induce young people to take a test drive and talk about Scion with their friends.[7]

Toyota has retained and expanded this edgy marketing approach. When it introduced a new Scion model—the boxy Scion bB—in December 2005, the company initially pretended it was launching a new MP3 player to compete with Apple's iPod. Flyers and stickers implying as much blanketed urban neighborhoods to fuel rumors. Toyota even outfitted salespeople at 54 HMV music stores in Japan with shirts and bags carrying the bB logo. The truth didn't come out until the car was unveiled on December 26 at a Tokyo club—complete with a new pop single that a local band dedicated to the vehicle.[8]

Now Scion is going even further to generate buzz—into what online gamers call the *metaverse*. In July 2006, Toyota announced that the new Scion xB was being "released" for sale in Second Life and Whyville, two popular online fantasy communities—the first automaker to infiltrate these worlds. *Avatars* (online personas created by real-life, game-addicted humans) who "live" in these worlds can buy Scions, take out loans to help pay for them, customize their vehicles, and take their virtual friends for rides around cyberspace. Not a single *real* dollar (or *clam*—the official currency of Whyville) ever enters the coffers of Toyota from these fictitious sales. But the company hopes the strategy will generate even more talk about their brand . . . and, perhaps, real-world sales.[9]

Other organizations have taken notice of Toyota's word-of-mouth gambits and are experimenting with similar programs. There is even an entire company—Cambridge-based BzzAgent—that exists solely to create not-so-spontaneous grassroots word of mouth for paying clients, turning curious consumers into what BzzAgent calls "trained and managed volunteer brand evangelists."[10]

Will these new techniques for connecting with customers produce lasting results? Who knows? The only thing that's for sure is that what used to work doesn't work any more; hence the search for something, anything, to take its place. Organizations are trying every established technique—and a host of new ones—to break through the commercial and communications clutter and reestablish meaningful connections with people.

The retail world is another arena where the current upheaval is being felt. More and more companies that once relied on traditional retailers, distributors, and marketers to bring their products and services to the world are now trying to bypass those middlemen. Companies want to connect with and sell to customers directly. The now ubiquitous phenomenon of e-commerce is a huge part of this trend. Almost every company has an Internet portal where customers can buy their products or services without having to visit a mall or downstore store (and perhaps being tempted by a rival company's wares). This isn't a risk-free strategy. Online selling direct from the maker has led to increasing channel conflict, as retailers who resent being cut out of transactions scramble to make up the lost revenues by downplaying brand-name merchandise in favor of their own branded products or no-name knockoffs that are "just as good" as the brand-name stuff.

Even more striking is the proliferation of branded stores highlighting the merchandise of a single manufacturer—sometimes just a few yards from a department store, big box retailer, or other outlet where the same products are also on sale. One of the first manufacturers to take this route was Coach, the maker of fine women's handbags and other leather goods, which opened its flagship store in Manhattan in 1981—just a few blocks from Bloomingdale's, the trendy department store that was one of Coach's best customers. The experiment proved to be successful for everyone: During the first year after the Coach store opened, sales of Coach goods at Bloomingdale's actually increased, thanks to strengthened brand awareness. Today, Coach has over 200 stores of its own, and these outlets account for fully 75 percent of its $1.7 billion in annual revenues.

In the years since Coach broke the ice, many other manufacturers have opened retail outlets.[11] Some have been enormously successful, including the chic, high-tech Apple stores, the Lacoste sportswear shops, and the Lego "concept stores" where kids can experiment with the plastic building toys to their hearts' content (more on these in Chapter 3). Now more and more companies—from Sony and Dell to Eddie Bauer and Levi's—are launching their own strings of retail outlets, from conventional stores and kiosks located in leading malls to theme-based concept stores like "Niketown."

Yet some entrants in the own-brand retailing arena have flopped badly. Warner Brothers opened a string of stores to sell movie-themed merchandise linked to all the company's most famous franchises, from Batman to Bugs Bunny; the stores were shuttered after four years of disappointing sales. Similarly, Gateway Computer, after years of success in direct selling via phone and the Internet, found that its 322 Gateway Country Stores were nothing more than a costly drain on profits. Establishing a link to customers via direct retailing is not a cure-all for what ails today's struggling businesses.

Failures of the old customer connection paradigms are driving still other forms of business innovation. As fears of being out of touch increase, organizations are scrambling to revamp their market research programs, searching for clues to what drives the new and increasingly fickle breed of customer.

Traditional methods of monitoring consumer attitudes are losing their credibility. For example, more and more people are refusing to participate in polls and surveys, feeling fed up with a constant barrage of phone calls and direct-mail questionnaires from marketers eager to pick their brains. According to one market research expert, survey participation rates under 10 percent are now increasingly common. As a result, fully half of all survey responses are coming from less than 5 percent of the population—"professional respondents" who answer every survey they're sent. This narrow slicing means that the survey results—once relied upon by organizations to provide sound guidance for future strategies—are becoming less and less meaningful.[12]

Or consider the growing dissatisfaction with focus groups. For decades, they've been a staple of marketing efforts—an effective research window into the interests, needs, values, and preferences of consumers. But in today's volatile markets, more and more companies are finding the insights generated by focus groups increasingly unreliable.

In 2004, Pepsi tested a new cola called Pepsi Edge using focus groups. Consumers in the groups seemed to like the idea—a drink that tasted like Pepsi and had half the calories—and Pepsi launched the product with high hopes. But real-world consumers were confused about the drink's identity: Was it a diet soda? A regular cola? Some weird hybrid of the two? Why should they switch to it from the drink they now preferred? There were no clear answers, and the product flopped, costing Pepsi millions. Now instead of using focus groups, Pepsi is testing new product ideas with online panels of consumers whom they contact via instant messaging programs.[13]

Some of the new techniques for getting inside the minds of customers are almost goofy. Chrysler has hired Organic, an online marketing agency, to help it figure out the mind-set of what it believes—or hopes—are typical customers for its cars. As part of the process, Organic has created "persona rooms" that are supposed to capture the essence of fictitious individuals who exemplify Chrysler buyers. The prototype owner of a Jeep Compass is "Jenny," a seller of pharmaceutical products who lives in Atlanta, Georgia. Jenny's persona room is littered with artifacts of her busy, completely fictional life: a pet fish in a bowl, a copy of *Elle* magazine, a yoga mat, a *Sex and the City* DVD. "Roberto" stands in for all the buyers of the Dodge Caliber hatchback. His Boston apartment contains a generic pizza box, a glass stolen from a bar, and posters for the movies *Fight Club* and *Akira*.

Marketers from Organic and Chrysler huddle in these and other persona rooms, trying to channel the spirits of their customers and divine the proper marketing tools to reach them. Will it work? Who can say?[14]

As the changes in customer behaviors and attitudes spiral on, companies are behaving in increasingly desperate ways. Some are trying to imitate the power of grassroots communication (now often called *viral marketing*) by creating corporate web sites designed to look like fan sites. Coca-Cola developed a fake "unauthorized" web site to promote a spin-off drink called Vanilla Coke. Dubbed vclounge.com, the site purported to be written by an insider at Coca-Cola to reveal the company's "insidious plan for world domination."[15] The hoax was quickly exposed, making the company appear less than hip, and Vanilla Coke was soon discontinued due to lack of customer interest.

More recently, a series of wildly popular video clips appearing on the YouTube web site has been revealed as a hoax orchestrated by a pair of Marin County filmmakers in an effort to find an audience—and ultimately a distribution deal—for their new movie. Millions of fans became obsessed with "lonelygirl15," who posed her moody musings on YouTube in the persona of a repressed home-schooled teenager eager to find friends in the larger world. In one sense, the hoaxsters achieved their goal: "Lonely Girl" became famous, and the chances of a movie deal have certainly improved. But is tricking customers a sustainable strategy or simply an invitation to backlash? As one technology column noted, "Whether fans, whose disbelief in lonelygirl15 was not willingly suspended, but rather teased and toyed with, will embrace the project as a new narrative form, condemn it, or simply walk away, never to be fooled again, remains to be seen."[16]

Then there's the story of America Online (AOL), the once-dominant online service now struggling to retain customers and practicing policies seemingly designed to make it difficult for disgruntled customers to cancel their memberships. Cancellation requests are handled by "retention consultants" who receive bonuses based on their ability to talk customers out of quitting. This reportedly has led to many customers who continue to get billed even though they are convinced they have canceled their service.

In 2004, the company signed an agreement with the Federal Trade Commission to stop making it hard for customers to quit; a year later, it reached a similar agreement with New York State's then-district attorney (now governor) Eliot Spitzer and paid a $1.25 million fine to the state. Nonetheless, complaints keep coming, including a famous blog posting by 30-year-old Vincent Ferrari of the Bronx, who posted the audio file of his 21-minute struggle to cancel AOL online, embarrassing the company. This is the mark of a company desperate to keep its link to customers alive while behaving in ways that only increase the alienation.[17]

A Fresh Start—Getting Back to Basics

There's no use longing for the return of the good old days. The new world of electronic information and global competition is here to stay. Customers will no longer simply gravitate to the brands, products, services, and organizations their parents trusted. Instead, they will continue to experiment, change, talk back, and exercise their new-found freedom of choice in ways that make life for organizational leaders increasingly challenging.

In response, we need to learn new ways of creating stronger, longer-lasting ties with our customers. It is no longer enough to manufacture fine products or provide good services. We need to help our customers improve their lives—one experience at a time. After all, that's what made them try our products or services in the first place. And that's what will make them loyal customers again—provided we learn how to do it right.

The truth is that today's rapidly changing world, which is making life so difficult for those of us who run organizations, is also making life hard for our customers. We are not the only ones who find the twenty-first century stressful. In a world that is:

- Increasingly hurried,
- Painfully insecure (especially post-9/11 and post-Katrina),
- Physically and mentally exhausting,
- Socially and economically fragmented, and
- Psychologically and emotionally demanding.

Millions of people are desperately in need of opportunities to feel:

- Free from time pressure,
- Safe and secure in their surroundings,
- Pleasantly stimulated, physically and mentally,
- At peace with themselves and others, and
- Ready to be open-minded, creative, and productive.

Organizations that can provide such opportunities by reimagining the customer experience—whether they are businesses, nonprofits, or government agencies—will attract an enormous number of customers in the years ahead and keep them coming back.

The ability to create comfortable, intimate, exciting, and rewarding life experiences for customers is the crucial organizational skill for our time. Many of today's smartest companies are already acting on this insight, finding innovative ways of getting inside the minds of customers and responding to the needs and desires they discover there.

Take Procter & Gamble—the great company that Doug Atkins once worked for, whose traditional formula for success has lost its potency. By the 1990s, Procter & Gamble's sales growth had stagnated. Spin-offs of the company's great brands were cannibalizing other product sales instead of driving impressive growth. Even when the goods were of high quality—which they usually were—advertising alone wasn't attracting the attention of shoppers.

To adjust to the new reality, Procter & Gamble has had to change its attitudes and its approach to business. Patrick Whitney, director of the Institute of Design at Illinois Institute of Technology, describes the old mind-set: "P&G had the best chemical engineering and marketing operations in the country. It didn't care about the user experience." But by the 1990s, the company had recognized the need for change: "It had to create new products, and to do that, P&G had to get closer to the consumer."[18]

To their credit, the leaders of Procter & Gamble didn't use Internet hoaxes, make-believe word-of-mouth programs, or attempts to force customers to keep buying from them. Nor did they simply create persona rooms to help them understand imaginary customers. Instead, they launched a major effort to live with, talk to, and observe real customers around the world.

Procter & Gamble sent designers and consultants to homes in Europe, Asia, and North and South America to watch people cleaning their bathrooms, mopping their floors, and doing their laundry. They noticed how the products people used worked well, how they didn't, and what frustrations and irritants were built into these everyday experiences. Based on these studies—almost anthropological in their depth—Procter & Gamble designers created prototype products and brought them into still more homes for testing in real-world settings. It wasn't enough, they knew, to design products with great attributes. Those products had to deliver results that people would appreciate, even cherish.

The results have included such successful innovations as "Mr. Clean MagicReach," a hand-operated cleaning tool for bathroom walls and showers with a detachable four-foot pole; "Tide Buzz," an ultrasonic wand that uses Tide cleaner to remove stains from garments; and the "Swiffer" electrostatic floor sweeper that has become Procter & Gamble's newest billion-dollar brand. Company CEO Alan G. Lafley deftly summarizes the new wisdom that is driving Procter & Gamble's reinvention: "People remember experiences. They don't remember attributes."[19]

Other companies are following a similar path. Kimberly-Clark, maker of Huggies diapers and other baby products, found its sales slipping. To reverse the trend, the company resorted not to traditional focus groups or surveys but to an innovative technique to get inside the customer experience: They mounted a camera and microphone on a pair of glasses for parents to wear as they cared for their babies at home. The system allowed Kimberly-Clark researchers to see and hear what customers saw and heard, and it soon unearthed an unmet need. Moms, it seemed, were struggling to open packages of wipes and pour out lotions while holding babies and diapers awkwardly on beds, floors, and tabletops. The company responded by redesigning their product containers for easy grabbing and dispensing with one hand.[20]

This new wave of customer-centered innovation isn't occurring only in the packaged-goods arena. In my own field of hospitality, Marriott, a longtime pioneer and industry leader, has developed new design concepts for the lobbies of its Marriott and Renaissance Hotels with input from a team developed by IDEO, Inc., the well-known design consulting organization. IDEO sent seven consultants—one an anthropologist—on a 6-week, 12-city tour to watch travelers interact with public hotel spaces, from lobbies to cafés to bars. They noted what was good about the customer experience and what was not so good; for example, few lobby spaces were comfortable for conversations, reading, small meetings, or private work sessions. As a result, the new lobby areas that Marriott is creating will include "social zones" for informal meetings and semiprivate work areas with plenty of room for laptops, papers, and coffee cups.[21]

You don't have to employ an anthropologist to develop meaningful insights into the customer experience. It helps if you are a customer yourself. As a hotelier, I approach every travel experience in the spirit of research. When I stay in one of our Loews Hotels (or when I visit a city where no Loews Hotel is currently available), I take detailed mental and written notes about the quality of the experience, from my interaction with Loews coworkers at check-in or meals right down to such details as the water pressure in the shower, soundproofing in the bedroom, and colors in the living room that are conducive to a relaxing evening. The other executives from Loews' home office also act as customer surrogates; in fact, we have a checklist they use for rating every element of each hotel they visit. They offer the results to the general manager and operations manager of the hotel for them to consider and learn from. These notes often become the basis for our next hotel restyling or, perhaps, for a simple upgrade of the amenities in a single room or suite.

I also encourage everyone who works at Loews to take seriously any input we receive from customers about their experiences with us. You don't have to be an anthropologist (or a CEO) to have powerful insights about the customer experience, you just need to be human.

Creating great customer experiences is a challenge that hospitality industry leaders have long understood. Now it is one that leaders in every arena need to focus on. It is the only real solution to the crisis of change that is battering almost every kind of organization in our fast-paced world—and the only way to reestablish and maintain powerful connections with the customers who make our work possible, meaningful, and profitable.

CHAPTER 2

Engineering the Total Customer Experience

IN TODAY'S ULTRACOMPETITIVE WORLD, THERE'S ONLY ONE WAY THAT ANY organization—whether a for-profit business, a government agency, or a nonprofit group—can attract and retain customers, clients, or other followers; and that's by becoming truly *customer-centric*. Such an organization realizes that it is providing not just a product or service but a total experience, beginning with the first moment that a person considers becoming a customer and extending through the months or years until the experience has become a memory.

This means that the leaders of the organization must learn to examine the customer experience as a totality, understanding the importance of every touchpoint, empathizing with what clients need and want at each one, and then designing the organizational structure to provide it.

This complex series of tasks calls for an array of skills and concerted, continual effort by all your people—not just those who are formally charged with customer care (such as sales reps and service personnel) but by everyone whose work affects customers. And that, for all practical purposes, means everyone. In practice, then, being customer-centric also means paying close attention to your relationship with your employees—how you select, train, motivate, and reward them. If the members of your team are unhappy, it's likely that your customers will be unhappy, too.

The following organizations have succeeded beyond all expectations primarily because they found ways to make the total customer experience unusually rich, memorable, and satisfying. Each one offers lessons that extend well beyond the specific field in which they operate.

"The Real Deal"—A Fast-Food Experience Even the Critics Love

In some industries, there's an 800-pound gorilla—a company so big, powerful, famous, and dominant that it makes competing and surviving problematic for other firms. In discount retailing, it's Wal-Mart. In consumer software, it's Microsoft. And in fast foods, it's McDonald's. With its 30,000 stores in 118 countries, nearly 50 million customers every day, annual revenues of over $20 billion, and hundreds of millions of dollars to spend on television advertising, it's hard to fathom how any rival chain can hope to outcompete the Golden Arches—especially when the rival's menu is based on the hamburger, the same classic American staple that McDonald's has always featured.[1]

Mission impossible? Maybe—but don't tell the people at In-N-Out Burger. This family-owned fast-food chain is outgrowing McDonald's in the American West using the simple formula of ultrafresh burgers, fries, and shakes. Their secret: A customer experience that can't be matched by McDonald's, Burger King, Wendy's, or any other competitor. It has made fans out of such unlikely patrons as the late *doyenne* of French cuisine, Julia Child (who had In-N-Out burgers delivered to her hospital bed while recovering from surgery), chef Thomas Keller of the famed restaurants French Laundry in Napa Valley and Per Se in New York City, and actress Angelina Jolie, who confessed that she left the 2003 Oscar ceremony early for a quick bite at the nearest In-N-Out.[2]

Even Eric Schlosser, author of the muckraking book *Fast Food Nation,* which turned McDonald's into Public Enemy Number One for a generation of hip, health-conscious young adults, has kind words to say about In-N-Out Burger: "I think they're great. It isn't health food, but it's food with integrity. It's the real deal."[3]

How has In-N-Out spawned a cultlike following that other organizations would die for? On the surface, the chain's 200+ outlets look much like other fast-food stores, with a drive-through lane, an indoor seating area, a few outdoor picnic tables (to take advantage of the sunny weather with which most In-N-Out locations are blessed), and a menu featuring burgers, french fries, and shakes. But a deeper probe reveals the unique qualities that differentiate In-N-Out from McDonald's and virtually every other fast-food place.

One of these qualities is ultrasimplicity. Check out the menu board posted by the drive-through window and you'll see four main items listed: cheeseburger, hamburger, french fries, and shakes. A small sidebar lists a few varieties of soda, milk, and coffee. That's it. No pizzas, tacos, salads, chicken nuggets, roast beef sandwiches, sundaes, pies, or any of the many other items that rival chains have added to their menus in a desperate effort to retain bored customers and stem declining growth. In-N-Out has had virtually the same menu since the first store was founded in a Los Angeles suburb by Harry and Esther Snyder in 1948. (By contrast, McDonald's has added 37 items to its menu since 1955, as well as many other dishes on a limited trial or promotional basis.[4])

Changing and expanding your product and service offerings as customers evolve is often a necessary strategy, and in Chapter 12 we'll look at some organizations that have done this successfully. But In-N-Out Burger illustrates how a simple, unvarying array of offerings can be equally attractive—so long as the entire customer experience remains fresh, pleasurable, and satisfying. The classic simplicity of the menu means that people know exactly what to expect from In-N-Out. If they want burritos or egg rolls or a chef's salad, they'll go somewhere else. But if they love hamburgers, they know that In-N-Out is their sort of place.

Of course, if you stake your business essentially on one product, you'd better make sure it's fantastic. This is the second key to In-N-Out's success. The burgers, fries, and shakes they serve are all made from superfresh ingredients. The company's own butchers prepare the ground beef in the company's own processing plant; potatoes are sliced for fries in each store daily. There is no freezer in an In-N-Out store since no frozen meat or other frozen products are ever used; there is no microwave or heating unit since no food is prepared until a customer orders it and nothing is ever reheated.

The lack of prepackaging means that individual meals can be customized to fit personal tastes. And that leads to the third, and perhaps most important, key to the brilliance of In-N-Out: the famous "secret menu" that has spawned dozens of dedicated web sites and made the chain the subject of countless rumors and urban legends among its fans.

The secret menu isn't really a menu, since it doesn't represent a selection of dishes devised by the company's chefs. Nor is it secret—a quasi-official version is available on In-N-Out Burger's corporate web site, and expanded listings can be found all over the Internet. It's an array of variations on In-N-Out's classic items, mostly invented and named by the customers themselves, and spread through word-of-mouth. Secret menu items include:

- *The 4 × 4:* A burger that includes four meat patties and four slices of cheese.
- *The 2 × 4:* Two patties and four slices of cheese. (Actually, a customer can order any combination of patties and cheese slices by number: 6 × 3, 2 × 5 . . . you get the idea.)
- *Animal Style:* A burger patty fried in mustard and served on a bun with pickles, lettuce, tomatoes, extra sauce, and grilled onions.
- *Flying Dutchman:* Two meat patties, two slices of melted cheese, and nothing else—no bun, no lettuce, no nothing.
- *Protein Style:* A burger wrapped in lettuce instead of a bun.
- *Fries Well:* Extra crispy, longer-cooked fries.
- *Animal Style Fries:* Topped with two slices of cheese, sauce, and grilled onions.
- *Neapolitan Shake:* A shake combining all three flavors (vanilla, chocolate, and strawberry).
- *Pepperbeer:* A Dr. Pepper mixed with root beer.

The secret menu gives In-N-Out customers the fun experience of being insiders. (The fact that In-N-Out does virtually *no* advertising enhances the feeling—people learn about the chain by word of mouth and from savvy friends rather than from TV pitchmen or jingles.) At the same time, no one who wants to participate is excluded, since the secret items are accessible to all. And because the many secret variations let people customize burgers to their preferences, it transforms the usual impersonal fast-food experience into an opportunity to express their personal taste.

This comes close to the heart of the In-N-Out experience. Whereas McDonald's is a *Fortune* 500 corporation, In-N-Out is the local place where they make my burger fresh and just the way I like it. No wonder its customers are so loyal.

Other unique twists make In-N-Out Burger special. There are the discreet Bible references printed on paper goods like the cups and burger wrappers. Look closely at the inside rim on the bottom of a shake cup, and you might spot the characters "JOHN 3:16" printed in tiny red type. The complete Bible verse does not appear; if you're curious, you have to look it up in your own copy of the scriptures, where you'll read, "For God so loved the world that He gave His only Son, that whoever believes in Him should not perish but have eternal life." Different chapter-and-verse citations appear on other cups and wrappers.

Now, in a world where religion can be controversial, what effect does this gentle proselytizing by In-N-Out have on its relationship with customers? On the whole, it seems to be positive. The fact that the Bible verses themselves do not appear on the cups and wrappers softens the message; most customers agree that if a quotation from the Bible were blazoned across the front of a soda cup, it would be too "in-your-face" and would probably turn them off. As it is, the almost-hidden lettering appears to add to the mystique of In-N-Out, prompting more rumors and questions: Is the chain owned by a religious sect? Do the Bible verses convey some secret message?

(The answers are No and No. For the record, the Snyders, who founded the chain, consider themselves a religious family, but not unusually so. A company spokesperson has said that the Bible references are a tribute to Rich Snyder, son of the founders and president of the company, who was killed in a plane crash on December 15, 1993. But aficionados report that the citations began appearing on cups and wrappers as early as 1987, which casts some doubt on this official explanation. Perhaps In-N-Out is deliberately cultivating a sense of mystery about the Bible verses to generate even more word-of-mouth among their fans.)

Then there's the broader corporate culture, which is unusually friendly. In-N-Out is one of the few fast-food chains to pay workers (including part-timers) significantly more than the minimum wage, as well as providing unusually generous fringe benefits. The company's store managers earn close to $100,000 annually and participate in profit sharing. No wonder the chain has far lower employer turnover than is usual for their industry.

And this in turn further enhances the customer experience. Doesn't seeing a friendly, familiar face at the service counter (as opposed to the fifth sullen teenager to be hired this month) make a store feel warmer and more welcoming? And if you happen to read a newspaper story about the generous labor policies of a store you like to patronize, doesn't it make you appreciate the store even more?

In-N-Out's devotion to its unique customer experience carries with it some downsides. Because the food is always made fresh, customers may wait up to 10 minutes for their burgers, which is slow by fast-food standards. More significant, the company's insistence on all-fresh ingredients limits growth. Because In-N-Out prepares its meat in a single company-owned plant and ships it to stores in refrigerated trucks, the chain's operations are restricted to three states—California, Nevada, and Arizona, with Utah currently on the drawing board. Expansion to other regions would require creation of new supply and logistics chains, something the family-owned firm doesn't now plan on doing.

Even with these restrictions, it's hard to argue with the business results that In-N-Out has achieved. (The privately held firm doesn't release exact figures; the following impressive figures are informed estimates.) A 2005 survey found that each store pulled in $1.75 million in revenue, double the industry average and fourth highest among American fast-food chains (and that's without serving breakfast, unlike such competitors as McDonald's).[5] Profit margins are said to run around 20 percent, unusually high for the industry.[6] And when *Restaurants and Institutions* magazine surveyed patrons of 15 top fast-food chains on a range of satisfaction issues, from food quality and service to atmosphere, cleanliness, and convenience, In-N-Out scored at the top of the list, with a cumulative rating of 66.6—way ahead of competitors like Wendy's (49.8), McDonald's (37.3), and Burger King (37.2).[7]

How will In-N-Out maintain its unique customer appeal in the years to come? What will happen to the company when the founding generation passes from the scene? (Already there have been legal rumblings, including at least one lawsuit, that suggest the transition to new management may not go smoothly.[8]) If the company decides to expand more aggressively, will it water down the chain's old-fashioned attitude, its reputation for product quality, and its made-from-scratch, satisfy-the-customer philosophy?

Only time can tell. But millions of In-N-Out fans are hoping and praying the company will keep on doing what it's doing because they love it just the way it is. That's an attitude every organization would like to instill in its patrons.

In-N-Out isn't the only fast-food chain that is proving you can compete with the industry giants through a unique customer experience. Head a couple of states north, and you'll encounter Burgerville territory. Burgerville is a 39-store chain of restaurants located in Oregon and southern Washington where the emphasis is on high-quality food, fresh local ingredients, and environmentally-friendly policies. Seasonal items based on regional favorites, like hazelnut or fresh pumpkin milkshakes, sweet potato fries, and Walla Walla onion rings, have won praise for the chain from Public Radio's prestigious gourmet review, *The Splendid Table.* And Burgerville's forward-thinking ecological programs—including a new initiative to convert its used cooking oil into biodiesel fuel—have won praise from "green business" advocates. No wonder burger fans in the great Northwest have taken Burgerville to their hearts.[9]

YOUR BIG AHA'S

In-N-Out Burger operates in one of the world's most competitive industries—fast food. Somehow it manages not only to survive in that crowded marketplace but to stand out from the competition, transforming casual customers into loyal patrons for life. What lessons can leaders of other organizations learn from In-N-Out? Here are some.

(continued)

Look for ways to give your customers both simplicity and flexibility. In a world of ever-burgeoning complexity, where many people avoid essential tasks (like investing for retirement) because they feel overwhelmed by the sheer number of choices to consider, your customers don't want to deal with a confusing array of product or service options. Yet at the same time, they want their favorite offerings to reflect their own needs and preferences. Balancing these conflicting demands is a tightrope act that calls for creativity, imagination, and insight into what customers really want. In-N-Out's solution is an ultrasimple public menu supplemented by a whimsical, seemingly infinite secret menu. What unique and clever solution to the choice dilemma can your organization devise?

When quality and ease of operation conflict, pick quality every time. Life would be easier for the managers at In-N-Out if they used frozen meat and precut french fries, as other fast-food chains do. If meals were cooked in advance and kept warm under heat lamps, more customers could be rushed through the stores, boosting sales and profits. But quality would suffer, and In-N-Out would become "just another hamburger joint" in the minds of customers. Quality takes a commitment of time, energy, and resources that makes it a tough differentiating attribute for rivals to copy, and the heart of a simple yet highly effective competitive strategy.

Don't be afraid to stand for something. Some of In-N-Out's choices are idiosyncratic, even quirky. Undoubtedly, there have been customers, employees, and managers over the years who have questioned and challenged them: "Why not expand the menu to cater to people who like chicken or salads or pizzas?" "Why not post the secret menu on the walls of our stores?" "Why not eliminate the Bible verses and reduce the risk of offending someone?" There would be logical justifications for any of these changes. Yet each one would make In-N-Out *less* unique, less memorable, and less different, thereby reducing the special bond between customers and company. Be yourself! You'll be surprised how many people appreciate it.

When you find a formula that works, stick with it. In-N-Out developed a winning approach to the hamburger business within a few years of its founding. Today, over half a century later, very little has been changed. Not only the menu but even the styling of the restaurants has remained virtually the same, giving In-N-Out a retro look that was never planned but has become part of its charm. Too many organizations introduce change for the sake of change, perhaps because CEOs and marketing managers get bored promoting "the same old thing." When customers or changing circumstances *demand* change, go for it. But if your customers love what you do, why monkey with it?

The Dell Experience—Let Us Build One for You

The idea of engineering a great customer experience may seem obvious for a restaurant like In-N-Out (though the details of how In-N-Out does it are very special). After all, eating out, even in a fast-food place, is inherently an experience from which people expect to get fun and enjoyment. But what if you work for an organization that sells products—especially mundane products that many people take for granted? How can you offer customers a unique experience that will create a powerful bond between them and your company?

For an answer, we need look no further than the leader in the personal computer industry—Dell Computer, which has built today's leading computer and personal electronics business based on its uniquely user-friendly, we-build-it-to-your-specs computer purchasing system.

In one sense, computers are an out-of-the-ordinary product for most customers. They're relatively expensive; not everyone owns a computer; those that do own just one or two; and the average user shops for a computer rarely, once every three to five years. Therefore, buying a personal computer (PC) is a special event, unlike such routine purchases as a bottle of shampoo or a pair of shoes.

But, in another sense, few people would consider computer shopping fun or enjoyable. In the two decades since PCs have ensconced themselves in the home, they have rapidly become commoditized, developing features, attributes, and even styling that are largely interchangeable. For most people, there's very little difference between a PC from Hewlett-Packard (HP) or IBM and one from Sony, Acer, or most other brands. They all run Windows, they all sport CD and DVD drives and ports for various plug-ins, they all offer large amounts of RAM and hard-drive memory, they all offer simple wireless links to the Internet, and they all handle audio, video, and other media files with ease.

In most ways, this is a good thing for consumers. If you've been using one brand of PC, it's fairly easy to switch to a different brand when you buy a new machine. And commoditization exerts powerful downward pressure on prices—which is why you can get a great desktop computer today for less than $700, a fraction of what you would have had to pay just five years ago.

But it poses a vexing dilemma for computer makers. How can you make a decent profit when customers literally don't care about any product specifications except price? How can you capture customer loyalty when they see no difference between your products and any others? Is there even any point to being in the computer business in the first place?

Two companies have come up with meaningful answers to these questions. One is Apple, which has differentiated itself from the PC pack with its unique, less-buggy, less-crash-prone, and more user-friendly operating system. As you know, many Apple fans are fanatics; they wouldn't *think* of buying any other computer, and will even pay a premium price for the newest Apple machine.

However, Apple lovers are few in number. The sheer number of Windows users, the familiarity of the Windows operating system (OS), and the huge number of applications programs available for Windows, all offer advantages that most computer users don't want to pass up. (Apple recently developed new technology that allows Windows to be used on Apple computers, but some users report that performance is slowed as a result, which removes one of the advantages Apples usually enjoy.) As a result, Apple today controls just 4 percent of the home computer market. The Apple experience is a great one, but for most people the advantages of using the same software as "everyone else" are just too great to make Apple the computer of choice.

The other computer maker with an outside-the-box strategy is Dell. They have managed to create a unique customer experience while remaining firmly grounded in the familiar Windows universe. How? By rethinking the process of buying a computer, from the ground up.

Through the early 1990s, PCs were manufactured and sold like most other products. Companies tried to design computers that consumers would like; they forecast demand for various models and manufactured them in quantities they guessed would sell; they shipped them (at a steep wholesale discount) to outlets like department stores, office supply stores, and electronics specialists like Circuit City; and then they absorbed losses from unsold inventory, product returns, and obsolete merchandise. It was an inefficient way to do business, but it was the way that was familiar to everyone.

Dell had always been a little different. Since the company's founding by Michael Dell in 1984, it had practiced what it called the "direct model," selling computers direct to consumers (individuals and companies) via telephone sales. Eliminating the middleman saved Dell lots of money, and the direct connection to customers gave the company a depth of knowledge of the marketplace its competitors couldn't equal. (News of shifting consumer preferences reached Dell's managers a lot faster through the company's own phone banks than they reached managers at other companies, filtered via store managers and sales reps.) For a decade, Dell grew steadily, capitalizing on its low costs and its intimate link to customers.

The big breakthrough came in 1996, when Dell shifted the bulk of its sales to the Internet. The interactive power of the World Wide Web made it possible for Dell to dramatically improve the experience of buying a computer (see Table 2.1).

Table 2.1 Traditional Sales versus Internet Sales

	Traditional Retail	**Dell's Direct Model**
Choice	Customer visits retail store looking for a computer. The choice of models is limited to what the store has on hand.	Customer logs on to Dell.com. The choice of models is virtually unlimited, since Dell will manufacture a computer to the customer's specifications.
Specifications	Customer selects a computer that comes as close as possible to meeting his or her needs. Compromises on particular specifications are inevitable.	Customer designs his or her own computer—selecting the operating system, memory size, external drives, software package, and other specifications—to fit particular needs.
Price	Customer pays whatever price is charged for the particular computer he or she chooses, often paying for unnecessary features.	Customer only pays for those features and components he or she wants.

A tremendous ancillary benefit of the Dell direct model was the improvement in the company's financial and supply chain management. Building computers only after customers had ordered them virtually eliminated the problem of unsold inventory. It dramatically cut warehousing costs, since only those parts that were needed immediately were ordered from suppliers. And it improved cash flow, because customers paid for their machines as part of the ordering process, instead of Dell having to build and ship computers in hopes of receiving payment for them weeks or months down the road.

But for our purposes, the crucial element in the Dell revolution was the empowerment of consumers. People loved buying from Dell. No more dealing with pushy salesclerks who might be ignorant about computers (but all-too-eager to sell the most expensive model) or armed with confusing jargon that customers were probably too shy to question. No more settling for whatever model happened to be available at the store. No more wondering about whether the store in the next shopping mall or the next town might have a cheaper model or one more suited to your needs. You could shop from home, at any time of the day or night, and click, browse, and redesign machines to your heart's content, until you were satisfied that you had created exactly the computer you wanted.

Dell's reinvention of the computer-buying experience led to an enormous spurt in the company's growth and profitability. Dell was the single best performer on the Nasdaq stock market for the decade of the 1990s, as it overtook competitors like IBM and Hewlett-Packard to become the world's largest maker of PCs. Even when the technology market took a tumble with the dot-com bust and stock market decline of 2001, Dell continued to grow: from 2001 to 2005, its consumer PC sales increased by 449 percent while the rest of the industry shrank by 8 percent.

Today, Dell still enjoys a huge lead over its competitors in the PC business. In the fourth quarter of 2005, it sold 10 million PCs, a first for any company.[10] However, Dell has been hitting some speed bumps that represent the first major adversity the company has had to deal with.

The most publicly visible problem has been the discovery that some of the batteries used by Dell to power laptop computers (and provided by supplier Sony) pose a safety hazard. In mid-August 2006, the company had to recall 4.1 million batteries after several Dell computers caught fire or exploded. It was an embarrassing episode that immediately made Dell the butt of jokes on late-night TV and caused its stock to nosedive. (The fact that several other computer companies, including Apple, Matsushita, and Toshiba, had to recall models of their own for the same reason soon thereafter was small consolation for Dell.)

The safety issue should soon be resolved. A more long-term competitive concern for Dell is that the advantages of its direct model aren't as great as they once were. Other companies have imitated Dell's web site and are allowing customers to design and buy their own computers online (though most observers say that Dell's web site is still the easiest to use). As the consumer PC market becomes saturated, sales growth has slowed, and Dell's stock is down a bit from its high. (After all, once you're the biggest company in the business, it's hard to keep capturing still more market share.)

To solidify its leadership position and recharge its growth, Dell is working to take the customer experience to a new and even higher level. With more and more PC users setting up wireless networks in their homes and using their machines for all kinds of information and entertainment, Dell is finding that customers have increasingly complicated service questions related not just to their Dell hardware but to software and Internet connectivity. And as computer use gets more complex, demands for high-quality service grow—hence recent decreases in customer service satisfaction scores throughout the PC industry, including at Dell.[11]

In response, Dell is doubling its staff of on-call service agents to 2,500 and testing a new Web-based tool called TechConnect. This will allow Dell service staff to remotely connect to a customer's computer to diagnose and fix problems, remove spyware and viruses, and demonstrate routine maintenance tasks.[12] It will be like having a tech expert sitting at your elbow—only better, since the work can be done from a distance.

The goal is to make the experience of using a Dell computer as painless and efficient as the experience of buying a Dell computer. If Dell can pull off this next step in its evolution, it has a good chance of regaining its position as the most-admired company in the PC business—all because it has found ways to turn its commodity product into the basis for a unique and positive customer experience.

YOUR BIG AHA'S

Dell's transformation of the computer buying experience made it the company of choice among PC buyers the world over. What can leaders at other organizations learn from Dell's success?

Your business isn't about product features, it's about the customer experience. Leaders in product-based companies—especially managers who come out of specialties such as research and development (R&D), design, engineering, manufacturing, and operations—often view strategy through a product-centric lens, reducing the quest for customers to a features war against the competition. But product features are meaningful only if they improve the customer experience in a specific way. Dell didn't become the world's biggest computer company by attaching new and better bells and whistles to its PCs. Instead, it rethought the experience of buying a computer, making it easier and more efficient for customers.

Think about all the touchpoints where you connect with customers and work to make each one better. Product-based companies sometimes lose track of their many connections to customers, from initial contact, sales, shipping, delivery, and installation to service, repair, upgrade, use, return, recycling, and second purchase. Each represents an opportunity to serve and please the customer and thereby build a strong, enduring connection. Look at every touchpoint, and think about how you can improve and enhance each one. Dell built its success around an improvement of the sales touchpoint. For you, some other touchpoint may become the critical factor.

Create opportunities to link with customers directly. Even if you don't sell your products directly to consumers as Dell does, you should look for opportunities to provide service, information, advice, support, and product enhancements directly to customers. This gives you a chance to create and enhance customer loyalty, and to increase the sales and profitability of your business. New technology (the Internet, cellular telephony, podcasting) provides opportunities for such direct links, but so do such longstanding technologies as the telephone, direct mail, and face-to-face contact.

Customers and their needs are often a moving target. Within a few years, Dell's innovative Internet selling model had been imitated by competitors, eroding the company's advantage and threatening its unique lode of customer loyalty. Today, Dell is moving to rebuild its customer relationships through enhanced service programs. Leaders always need to be thinking two steps ahead—considering what their organizations can do next to further enhance their connections to customers and create even greater loyalty.

Engineering a great customer experience isn't only for service companies (like In-N-Out Burger) or product makers (like Dell Computer). It is for any kind of organization that wants to attract and retain loyal clients, supporters, or members—generically referred to here as customers.

It is for government agencies that want to help more citizens and encourage more positive attitudes toward the law—as some forward-looking managers are doing by reshaping the state motor vehicles bureaus and creating customer-service programs like the 311 telephone systems. These improvements are turning some of the most dreaded government bureaucracies into models of efficient, friendly service that clients no longer hate.

It is for nonprofit groups and cultural institutions that want to attract and uplift a broader array of patrons than ever before—as museums are doing by providing wonderful ancillary services, such as one-of-a-kind stores and gourmet restaurants that broaden the appeal of museum-going beyond its traditional core audience.

It is for health care organizations that want to meet the emotional, psychological, and spiritual needs of their patients and their families as well as their physical needs—as hospitals are doing through innovative building plans and outreach programs that ease the anxiety of sickness and speed total recovery.

And it is for educational institutions, like my own alma mater— Tufts University near Boston. Over the last several years, Tufts has developed an unusually powerful system for creating lifelong connections with its students. Its graduates are becoming some of the most loyal, committed, and involved alumni in the world, and the school's program for making the most out of every opportunity to connect with students is a big reason why.

It begins on the very day when freshmen arrive on campus for the first time. The students gather for a grand assembly on the university quad, joined by their families and by faculty members in full academic regalia. (The scene is very much the same as the one they'll experience four years later, at commencement.) University president Lawrence S. Bacow greets and welcomes the students, and among other themes his speech always focuses on the lifelong Tufts community. "Here at Tufts," he explains:

> [W]e have a tradition in which each generation of students helps the ones that come after. Although today is your first day here, you've already experienced this tradition. During the admission process, each of you was interviewed by a Tufts alumnus. Many of you have received scholarship support provided with generous help from past Tufts graduates. And as you've discovered, many of our upperclassmen have returned to school early this year just so they could be here to help you move into your dorm rooms and answer your questions about campus life. So, in a very real sense, this isn't simply your first day as a Tufts student. It's your first day as a Tufts alumnus-in-training.

Later that night, at a welcoming dinner, the freshmen receive a gift provided by the alumni—usually a Tufts hat and shirt, as well as a book specially chosen for group reading and discussion among that year's class. In 2006, the book was *Mountains Beyond Mountains,* the inspirational biography of Dr. Paul Farmer by the Pulitzer-Prize-winning author Tracy Kidder (New York: Random House, 2004).

Having planted the idea of a lifetime connection on the very first day of school, the university lovingly nurtures the concept in a dozen ways throughout each student's career. Alumni visit the campus periodically to give lectures and seminars about their work and life, providing an invaluable glimpse of the future for students pondering what to do after college. Alumni groups organized around specific vocations—the Tufts Lawyers Association, Tufts on Wall Street, Tufts Alumni in Communications and Media, and others—offer advice on job opportunities and interviewing skills to interested students. And thousands of alumni participate in the online Tufts Career Network, providing guidance and personal contacts to students seeking an entry into the work world.

During their senior year, students attend special dinners at the university president's house, each hosted by alumni who use the opportunity to explain why they've remained engaged with Tufts throughout their lives and to invite this new generation of students to do the same.

As the years pass, Tufts stays in contact with its graduates, building further on the connection they've already established. As at most colleges and universities, Tufts alumni have established local clubs around the United States and the world, and they hold periodic reunions and other get-togethers. These often involve opportunities for community service; during our New York City gathering in October, 2005, just a few weeks after Hurricane Katrina devastated the Gulf Coast, we collected school supplies for kids and packaged them for delivery to children who'd lost everything in the disaster. And the university also works hard to give something extra to its alumni. Unlike most schools, Tufts maintains a full-time career services counselor dedicated to providing job search help to alumni throughout their working lives—a program that's especially valuable nowadays, when most people will change careers more than once.

This isn't a complete description of all that Tufts does to nurture its connections with students. But just as you can enhance your connections with your customers, Tufts does an exceptional job of consciously examining all the potential touchpoints between the university and its students and making sure that each one is designed to be as positive, rewarding, and inspiring as possible. In fact, Tufts actually records and counts every time it "touches" one of its alumni, and it keeps track of the touches to make sure that no one loses contact with the university. The result: an unusually close-knit college community, with benefits that span the generations. And President Bacow reports that the last four years have been the university's best fundraising years ever—no small consideration in a time when most educational institutions are increasingly strapped for cash.[13]

The chapters to come illustrate how any organization can attract and retain loyal followers by reimagining the many touchpoints that make up the customer experience.

PART TWO

Reimagining the Customer Experience

CHAPTER 3

Reimagining the Sale

Creating Customers Who Are Happy to Buy

For many customers, the first time they touch or are touched by a company is the moment of the sale. And that fact generates one of the big challenges every organization faces. The sale is, at its most basic, about money changing hands. Yet, the start of a customer connection should be much more than merely a financial transaction. How can you make the sale a positive experience for the customer and the beginning of a mutually rewarding, long-term relationship?

In business today, "selling" has almost become a dirty word. College and university groups often invite me to speak to students, and I always enjoy the opportunity to exchange ideas with some of the bright, idealistic young people who will be tomorrow's business leaders. Many have strong ideas about the kind of work they hope to do, whether in the for-profit sector, government, or the worlds of charity, philanthropy, and social activism. But very few of them express any interest in selling, and the number who say they plan on becoming salespeople is practically nil.

Selling is a perfectly respectable occupation and, in the business world, an absolutely vital one. But it's understandable that young people regard selling with disdain. They associate it with what some call the "hard sell"—high-pressure tactics to lure, bully, or trick customers into buying goods or services they don't really need and perhaps can't afford. In periodic surveys to determine which occupations are most respected by the general public, it is no wonder that salespeople, like stock brokers and real estate brokers, tend to rank at the bottom—even lower than members of Congress.[1]

Maybe the word *sale* is the problem. It puts the sole emphasis on a single moment in the relationship between customer and company when money changes hands (or, more often nowadays, a computer blip indicates an entry on someone's credit card account). It is an important moment, to be sure. But it is only one moment in a complexly interwoven ballet of connections. And companies or individuals who put too much emphasis on the moment when the cash register goes *ching* may lose sight of those other connections. Once that happens, the chance of future sales starts to shrink.

In the hospitality business, the sale is much more than a financial transaction. This fact is brought home to hoteliers and hotel employees each and every day, since once people purchase our services (by checking in), they don't walk away with their goods like customers of other businesses: instead, they literally *move in* with us. The link between the hotel and its clientele is one of the most intimate connections between any organization and those it serves. Thus, serving hotel customers effectively and keeping them coming back for more requires getting inside their psychology and emotions in a way that is pleasurable, relaxing, and stimulating. And that means creating "a supremely comfortable, vibrant, and uniquely local experience." (The words come from the Loews Hotel brand promise, and I quote them not to boost our business but because they are such an appropriate description of the magic of hospitality.)

In our industry, the key to attracting lifelong patrons is transforming customers into guests. This means that the hotel and all who work for it must behave not like salespeople but like hosts, with all the human qualities that implies—warmth, openness, generosity, welcome. And any organization that can capture this spirit, no matter what the industry, will create a growing body of loyal and appreciative patrons.

When it comes to turning one-time visitors into lifelong guests—and customers—the first requirement is making entry into the organization easy, pleasant, and fun. This may sound straightforward, but in truth it's complicated and a real challenge that the majority of organizations never quite master.

The first challenge is defining the entry point. How and where do customers first encounter your organization? The answers will differ for different kinds of organizations, and often the same organization will have multiple portals that vary by customer.

Consider a retailer like Sephora, the global purveyor of cosmetics, fragrances, and beauty aids owned by LVMH. This luxury brands company also owns Louis Vuitton, Donna Karan, Moet & Chandon, Givenchy, Tag Heuer, and many other prestigious names. Sephora's customer portals include:

- The 515 Sephora stores and retail outlets, located in 14 countries in a variety of settings, from downtown shopping streets to suburban malls to airport shopping concourses.
- The Sephora web site, Sephora.com, where over 14,000 products bearing 265 brand names can be purchased online, and where Sephora fans can also access articles about beauty trends, tips from cosmetics experts, information about Sephora stores, and services from gift cards to a personal registry of wished-for items.
- Other online links to Sephora, many on beauty-related sites that participate in the Sephora.com affiliate program. When customers travel to Sephora.com through a link on an affiliated web site, the individual or organization that hosts the affiliate receives a commission on every product sold.
- Sephora's telephone service lines, which connect customers to service reps or "Beauty Advisors" who are trained to answer questions and recommend products.
- Sephora's direct mail catalog, which reaches many thousands of additional customers.

Each of these represents the face of Sephora to a potential customer. Each has the potential to attract the interest of a shopper or to alienate or annoy her. Depending on how well each portal is designed and maintained, it may convert a high percentage of passive bystanders into active participants in the Sephora experience or lead them to conclude that "Sephora isn't for me," perhaps eliminating the company from their radar permanently.

One of the basic challenges to keeping the Sephora business growing is making each portal as attractive and welcoming as possible. It is particularly true in today's hypercompetitive world, where every Sephora portal faces an uphill battle for customer share-of-mind. In the retail environment, department stores (which derive an outsized share of their income from the highly profitable fragrance and cosmetic business) remain a key competitor with Sephora, but there are many other challengers for the same dollars, including chain and local drugstores, specialty stores like Elizabeth Arden, and the dozens of fashion stores that now market their own branded fragrances, from Calvin Klein to Diane von Furstenberg. On the Internet, there are countless sites available where products like those sold at Sephora can be purchased (a Google search keyed to the words "fragrance and cosmetics" yields over 15 million hits). And on the direct selling front, there are dozens of catalog companies and direct marketers offering beauty products, from the cable TV shopping outlets like QVC to venerable firms like Avon, which boasts five million individual sales reps in countries around the world.

There's a science to designing each type of portal to be user-friendly. There are experts who specialize in designing retail stores so that visitors feel welcome, excited, and ready to shop. And this is one area where Sephora has excelled, rethinking the look and feel of the retail beauty store in ways designed to attract and retain customers. For starters, Sephora eliminated some of the pet peeves reported by its mainly female clientele, such as aggressive perfume spritzers stationed at the ends of aisles to spray samples of fragrances onto passing customers. Rather than displaying products in sealed plastic packages or enclosed glass cases, Sephora provides open shelving where goods are arrayed by brand and available to be touched, examined, and sampled. There's a "lipstick bar" with 365 colors to be tested. Plenty of mirrors and ample supplies of cotton swabs, tissues, and bottles of makeup remover are scattered around the store, encouraging customers to try the goodies on display. And salespeople are trained not to pester browsers but to provide information and help only when requested, which makes Sephora a comfortable place for shoppers to linger (usually with a gradually filling shopping basket in one hand).[2]

Equally important is the art of crafting an Internet presence that is powerful, comprehensive, fast, intuitive, and fun to use. Sephora fans report that the company's web site is one of the best shopping sites on the Internet—clearly laid out by product category, easily searchable by brand or product name, and quickly customizable so that you can buy a fresh supply of your favorite items in just seconds. It also offers such direct-purchase perks as free shipping (on orders over $75), free gift wrap, a selection of free samples for the asking, and easy product returns.

Sephora's powerfully attractive portals are the key ingredients in the company's success story, which includes rapid expansion in the lucrative U.S. market since the firm's entry into North America in 1998, and double-digit growth every year since 2000, making Sephora one of the fastest-growing retailers in the world.

The art of welcoming customers may also include streamlining the processes whereby customers gain entry to an organization. It's not always as easy as strolling into a Sephora store at the local mall. Other customer entry points may be time-consuming, complex, or even intimidating. Examples include the check-in experience at a hotel or car-rental counter, the first 30 seconds of a telephone conversation with a customer service representative for a computer or electronic company, or the process of applying for a credit card or a home mortgage. Organizations providing services like these need to start rethinking their customer welcome with some basic questions: How easy is it to find us? How long does it take a customer to get her foot in the door? How tricky and confusing are the stages in the process? How many customers drop out at each step due to frustration, confusion, or annoyance?

Furthermore, it's not enough to create individual entry points that are attractive and effective. Another consideration is the number, type, and accessibility of your customer portals. Many major businesses have been built around the simple strategy of multiplying customer access points and thereby making a desirable good more widely available than ever before. Starbucks was based on the notion that Americans would respond to having gourmet coffee available on every third street corner.

Other businesses are finding that adding a new kind of portal to their array can enable them to dramatically energize and deepen their customer connections. Founded in 1932, Lego, the Danish maker of colorful plastic building bricks for kids, survived and thrived for decades relying solely on retail sales through toy stores, department stores, and other outlets. In recent years, however, Lego has found powerful new ways of reaching customers, including not just the usual Internet site but also the four wildly popular Legoland theme parks and 34 concept stores where kids (and some adults) can experiment with Lego constructions to their hearts' content, using pieces from up to 240 different bins.[3] Of course, many families walk out of the Lego stores with new sets of Lego products. But the greatest value to the company lies in the stores' power to turn casual fans into Lego fanatics. The ultrastylish Apple stores, where technology fans can try out the latest computers, iPod music players, and other gadgets, play a similar role for that company.

Following still another strategy, Charles Schwab has outstripped other financial services firms in part by making investment advice and basic transactions (purchase and sale of securities, fund transfers, and the like) available through storefront offices, the Internet, the telephone, and mail, while linking the database of customer information to its service reps at all these locations. Thus—unlike at some other brokerage firms—Schwab customers know that details about their account can be easily accessed and discussed with a Schwab rep whether the contact is in person, on the phone, or on the computer.

Organizational leaders also need to think about how they want to channel customers toward particular portals where the richest value and the most rewarding experience can be enjoyed by the customer while also generating financial benefits for the organization. Keith Reinhard, chairman emeritus of DDB Worldwide, has been urging advertisers to use traditional 30-second television spots as invitations to their web sites, in effect transforming the TV commercial into a foyer where customers are ushered into the organization's online entry point, where the real teaching, service, and selling experience begins.

All these challenges have one thing in common: Meeting them requires organizational leaders to step outside their usual point of view. In many cases, identifying with customers can be very difficult, especially when demographic differences like gender, race, age, education, or income loom large.

In the world of high-tech consumer products, the companies that make and market goods like computers, cell phones, DVD players, and plasma TVs are generally dominated by male technophiles for whom high-tech jargon is second nature and who instantly understand the purpose and significance of new product features. Yet they must design, package, and market their wares for a broad, general audience that is increasingly female, harried, and unwilling to devote hours to learning technobabble to unravel the meaning of arcane product descriptions. Making customers like these feel truly welcome when they shop for the latest gadgets takes skills akin to those used by translators at the United Nations.

Best Buy, a retailer of electronics is stepping up to this challenge with its so-called Jill Initiative, a program to redesign the customer experience to make buying high-tech products easier and more fun for female shoppers. Personal shopping advisors have been trained to talk about product features in down-to-earth terms, asking questions like, "What kinds of pictures do you usually take?" and "Do you think you'll be printing them out at home?" rather than, "How many megapixels of memory will you need?" or "Will you want auto exposure bracketing with that?" The company's "Geek Squad" service sends experts in a custom white-and-orange Volkswagen Beetle to visit customer homes to install hardware and software. Even the stores are being redesigned to extend a more friendly welcome: Sixty Best Buy locations have been relaunched with pastel colors replacing the traditional, more aggressive blue-and-yellow format.[4]

The challenge of reading customers accurately isn't just about demographic differences. There are barriers to customer understanding that simply go with being an organizational leader. As an insider, you are invariably part of the organization looking out. You automatically feel at home whenever you walk through the doors of your company. This makes it extremely difficult for you to objectively gauge the warmth of the welcome your customers receive. Newcomers may perceive your organization as cold, unfriendly, complicated, intimidating, or difficult to enter; and if so, it is unlikely that you will ever notice it.

To overcome this blindness, leaders must adopt the outsider's view of their company. Pass through the portal as if you were an outsider:

- Visit your organization's retail outlets, sales offices, or service departments in an unfamiliar town without identifying yourself.
- Call the customer hotline with a complaint, concern, or question.
- Visit the public web site and try ordering a product or asking a question.

You may be surprised—perhaps dismayed—by the reception you get. If so, take it as a wake-up call. Maybe your organization, like so many others, needs to rethink the welcome it extends to customers.

In the business I know best—hospitality—every kind of portal is important, from the company web site to the colorful brochure that highlights a hotel's special amenities. But at Loews Hotels, people will always be the key to a strong sales connection. That's the thinking behind a new training program called "Living Loews," which some 400 of our best coworkers will have experienced by the time you read these words.

Living Loews is designed to help successful salespeople and other hotel executives raise their people skills an extra notch. Unlike most such training programs, which last an hour or two, ours runs two full days and covers a wide range of topics, such as how to work a room full of strangers without feeling shy, awkward, or embarrassed.

The program upgrades people's basic knowledge and practices in such areas as business etiquette, public speaking, and attire. Even the vocabulary used to describe Loews Hotels is being spruced up by replacing overused words like "beautiful," "spacious," and "upscale" with fresher terms like "effortless," "authentic," and "supremely comfortable."

Most important, we're urging our people to encourage hands-on experiences as a way of selling Loews. Rather than simply describing the softness of our beds, the quality of our bath products, or the fluffiness of our towels, we want prospective customers to touch, feel, smell, and savor those qualities for themselves. Once that happens, there is a great chance they'll become guests of Loews—not just once or twice, but for a lifetime.

A New Kind of Welcome: Teaching Bankers to Think Retail

For as long as anyone can remember, banks have been considered one of the world's *least* welcoming organizations. Most banks are difficult, even painful to deal with. Their hours are short, their lines are long, their fees are large and apparently arbitrary, and their attitude is all too often an insufferable blend of arrogance and incompetence. Many consumers think of banks the way they think of the state motor vehicles bureau or an airport security screening line—as a black hole that sucks up an hour of their valuable time in the middle of the day for no good reason.

Today, at long last, that is beginning to change. Even bankers, long famed for being tradition-bound and slow to change, are learning that being customer-friendly pays off. More impressive, some banks (though not all) are starting to make the difficult, costly changes in systems, procedures, and corporate culture that are necessary to transform banking from being institution centered to being customer centered.

There are several reasons for these overdue changes. One is increased competition. A generation ago, government regulations and practical restrictions meant that your local bank or savings and loan was basically the only source for the services it provided: savings and checking accounts, home mortgages, business loans, and so on. No more. As state restrictions on banking operations have been lifted, banks are becoming national institutions, expanding and competing in communities across the country rather than merely locally or regionally. And organizations other than banks are providing more and more services in competition with banks. The General Motors Acceptance Corporation has become one of the largest financial institutions in the United States. Brokerage firms like Charles Schwab offer products that operate very much like savings and checking accounts. Mortgage specialists are taking over the home lending business from banks and savings and loan associations (S&Ls). And the giant retailer Wal-Mart cashes checks, offers wire transfers, and provides other banklike services. In fact, Wal-Mart is rattling the cages of traditional banks by applying for a limited banking license. In classic fashion, the specter of increased competition is having a wonderfully focusing effect on once-complacent bankers.

Another reason for the change is technology. In a wired world, it's easier and cheaper than ever to provide instantaneous, round-the-clock financial services—and more and more people are coming to take such convenience for granted. With labor costs for in-person transactions rising steadily, banks are happy to take advantage of technology by encouraging customers to perform more transactions via the Internet and automatic teller machine (ATM), saving big money in the process. But the availability of 24-hour service produces a rising spiral of expectations. Banking customers wonder, "If I can transfer funds from one account to another at 9:00 P.M. on Thursday or in the middle of Sunday afternoon, why can't I also apply for a loan?" Customers who think nothing of shopping for shoes or CDs on the weekend or evenings can't understand why the bank that sits next to the shoe store or the record shop isn't also open for business.

Technology is increasing pressure on banks in another way. Electronic information management is reducing the cost to banks of opening and maintaining a bank account. This means that smaller accounts once considered marginal or even money-losing by most bankers (e.g., checking accounts with an average balance lower than $1,500) have now become profitable. This makes the "unbanked"—households with no bank account at all, estimated at some 12 million in the United States alone—a suddenly desirable market, and the target of growing competition among banks.

For all these reasons, bankers can't go on operating by the old 3-6-3 Rule: "Pay depositors 3 percent, lend money at 6 percent, and be out on the golf course by 3 o'clock." Instead, they have to battle to attract and keep customers, and that means behaving less like bankers and more like retailers. *Service* and *convenience* are the new watchwords.

The leader in this trend is Commerce Bank, based in Cherry Hill, New Jersey, and now opening branches in states throughout the Northeast.

Commerce is winning new customers using both old and new tactics. A popular oldie is providing thank-you gifts such as toasters, irons, waffle-makers, golf umbrellas, and George Foreman grills to customers who open a new account. But new is the emphasis on customer convenience. It starts with extended hours. The bank's 11 Manhattan locations are open from 7:30 A.M. to 8:00 P.M. during the week, 7:30 A.M. to 4:00 P.M. on Saturdays, and 11:00 A.M. to 4:00 P.M. on Sundays. Plus, Commerce branches practice what they call the "10-minute rule," opening 10 minutes ahead of schedule and closing 10 minutes late—just to make customers feel that much more welcome.[5]

Even more surprising, Commerce is open every day except Easter, Thanksgiving Day, Christmas, and New Year's Day. After all, the bank reasons, "Many of these holidays are often major shopping days. While customers are out there shopping on their days off, they should be able to do their banking—like they visit any other retailer that day. And since not everyone is comfortable with online banking, we need to provide them with physical locations where they can bank at *their* convenience."

Feeling the same competitive pressures as Commerce, other banks are extending their hours on a test or branch-by-branch basis, depending on what they perceive as local preferences and needs. Others are relying on ATMs to provide after-hours service, and frankly hoping that the aggressive customercentric style of Commerce won't become the new standard. An executive of a regional Southeast bank who insisted on anonymity commented, "There's nobody in our market who has taken on convenient hours as a central initiative or core strategy, unlike in the Northeast, where there are banks like Commerce Bank open every day. We're glad we're not in those markets and not having to meet those types of demands."[6]

The bad news for that banker: It's only a matter of time before Commerce, or another in the new breed of aggressive, customer-centric bankers, will come knocking on his door, no matter where in the country he may be. Of course, that's the *good* news for banking customers.

Commerce is also devising brand-new forms of service to prove they're different from other banks and to demonstrate that customers' patronage is welcome, even when it generates no direct revenues for the bank. An example is free coin-counting machines, which are available in Commerce Bank lobbies for customers and noncustomers. This generates extra traffic at Commerce locations and even attracts curious passersby, who enjoy watching kids and grown-ups empty jingling jars or piggy banks full of change into the mechanical gadget and get the full value in bills at the end. Commerce is also one of the few banks that don't charge customers an ATM fee—even when they use machines at competitors' banks.

Knowing that customers hate wasting time on banking, Commerce is also using technology to speed transactions. For example, customers' signatures are scanned into the computer system, so that the signature appears on screen instantly when a teller enters the account number. This makes comparing signatures for a routine check-cashing faster than ever—around 20 seconds at last count.[7] Even Commerce's automated voice response system is getting updated; new software is being developed to track and analyze the options customers select before asking for help from a live customer service rep. This enables the call-center staff to identify the customer's needs without making him or her repeat a lot of basic information—something few phone answering systems currently do.[8]

All this innovation reflects a culture shift at Commerce that the bank's management is deliberately driving. Chief retail officer Dennis DiFlorio puts it this way: "The greatest insult you can give someone here is to say, 'You're thinking like a banker.'" To translate this out-of-the-box thinking into customer benefits, Commerce has a "Kill a Stupid Rule" program that rewards employees with a $50 bonus every time they identify a rule that prevents them from wowing customers.[9] And the bank conducts 100,000 "mystery shops" per annum. They evaluate the overall condition of the branch, and look for a handshake and other key elements of the prescribed greeting including a genuine, not canned, welcome.[10]

Perhaps you're wondering how Commerce can afford its new, higher level of customer service. It costs extra to keep bank branches open longer and to staff them on weekends and holidays. (Employees who volunteer for holiday service get extra pay.) But the bank has kept its revenues and profits growing even faster than expenses by building cross-selling opportunities off its reputation for customer service. Commerce's investment services business, launched in 1995, has been growing faster than others in the industry, with Commerce reps selling a broad array of mutual funds, pension plans, fixed-income products, and insurance. Tellers who notice that a particular customer could use a bit of advice or help with such products are eligible for a $25 bonus, a system that generates between 1,800 and 2,000 referrals every month.[11]

The phenomenon isn't mysterious: When your customers like you—and when you're open for business at times they find easy and convenient—they're more likely to buy more stuff from you.

In the newly competitive banking arena, it's not surprising that competitors are beginning to follow Commerce's lead. Some, such as Citibank, are now offering membership reward programs modeled on those pioneered by the airlines. Others are redesigning their storefronts to be more user-friendly and attractive. Wainwright Bank & Trust in Boston offers a lounge featuring a plasma TV and free coffee and donuts, while El Banco de Nuestra Comunidad, a Georgia-based bank that serves Latino immigrants, has piles of toys, free Internet service, and (of course) customer reps who are equally fluent in English and Spanish.[12]

All these changes reflect an important shift in mind-set on the part of bank managers and marketers. It remains true that, for almost all customers, banking is something they *have* to do rather than something they *want* to do. But bank customers today have more choices than ever, which means they don't have to patronize Hometown Bank any longer. So just as Hometown Hardware and Hometown Grocery learned long ago, Hometown Bank is now learning to compete for customers by making them truly welcome. It is a change that benefits customers in the short run and, for those banks that do it best, it will produce greater loyalty and profitability in the long run.

YOUR BIG AHA'S

Yes, your organization can learn a thing or two from the wave of change that is sweeping over the once-staid banking industry. Here are a few lessons to consider.

Benchmark your organization against those you don't compete with. It's important to compare your standards of customer welcome and follow-up services with those of others in your industry. But that's just the price of admission. If you hope to excel, look for comparisons with other organizations in different arenas, including those known for much higher standards of excellence. It's not enough for Commerce to be the most customer-friendly bank; it aspires for a level of service comparable to fine retailers like Nordstrom or Neiman Marcus.

Use technology to trim costs, but give customers a choice. Like other banks, Commerce saves money when customers use ATMs and the Internet for routine transactions. But Commerce also knows that some 92 percent of bank customers need face-to-face assistance at least once a month. By extending their in-person service hours, Commerce lets customers choose the form of interaction that's best for them, rather than trying to save pennies by pushing customers in a direction they may not like.

Your welcoming face is also a selling face. Friendly, convenient service is essential to attracting and retaining customers in today's ultracompetitive world. But it also creates opportunities to cross-sell and up-sell, introducing customers to new products or higher-end products they might not otherwise consider buying from you. Don't pressure customers into buying more, but make it easy for them by recommending extra purchases that are truly appropriate for them.

Rules should serve the business, not vice versa. Any sizable organization needs policies and procedures; otherwise, your people would have to improvise constantly, creating chaos. But always remind your staffers that the purpose of the rules is to enhance customer service, not to make business more convenient for you. When a rule conflicts with a legitimate customer need, break the rule rather than disappoint the customer.

Better than the Mall: Welcome to the Lifestyle Center

As bankers struggle to learn some of the customer-welcoming techniques that retail store owners mastered decades ago, retailers are facing new challenges. New places to shop keep popping up all over. More kinds of stores offering greater varieties of goods keep being invented. (Nowadays you may buy your next television at a traditional electronics store or department store, but you could also buy it at a big-box retailer, a discount merchant like Sam's Club, or an outlet store.) And entirely new channels for buying and selling, from web-based "department stores" like Amazon to auctioneers like eBay to cable TV shopping networks pose additional competitive threats.

In response, retailers and real estate developers are creating new shopping venues designed to attract customers who've been drifting away to other sources of goods and services. Among the most promising: the new "lifestyle centers" which are starting to replace traditional shopping centers and malls. These attractive outdoor areas include gardens and landscaped paths, high-end restaurants, theaters, and other entertainment opportunities along with stores that feature highly trained clerks, live products demonstrations, and computer kiosks for online shopping. By combining many attractions into a single, highly welcoming experience, the lifestyle centers are driving the next generation of retail growth in hundreds of locations around the country.

The lifestyle center movement traces its origins to 1987, when The Shops of Saddle Creek opened in Germantown, Tennessee. It was created by pioneering developer Poag & McEwen, which now opens an average of two new lifestyle centers each year—two among the 50 or so that are estimated to be opening annually. (By contrast, ground is broken on just 6 to 10 traditional malls each year.) The trend accelerated in 1999, when the term "lifestyle center" was coined by the International Council of Shopping Centers (ICSC), a New York-based industry group that tracks changing retailing styles. Now lifestyle centers are spreading from the warm-weather areas of the South to midwestern and northern locations, where shoppers are showing a willingness to leave their cars and the climate-controlled spaces of the familiar indoor mall, even in chilly weather.

What makes a lifestyle center different from other retail developments? Actually, there are no hard-and-fast rules. And the lifestyle center moniker has become so fashionable that some say developers are starting to apply the term to almost any retail project. ("It's like putting lipstick on a pig," says a Pennsylvania town manager who has been besieged by developers eager to win local approvals for more such projects.[13]) However, here are the parameters of a lifestyle center as laid out by the experts at ICSC:

• Upscale specialty stores (instead of the general merchandise and fashion outlets found in a typical regional mall). Typical lifestyle center tenants include such national chains as Banana Republic, Coach, Williams-Sonoma, Restoration Hardware, Talbots, Chico's, and Barnes & Noble, as well as smaller retailers unique to a locality,
• Dining and entertainment in an outdoor setting (as opposed to the windowless indoor space of the classic enclosed mall).
• No anchor tenants (unlike community, regional, or "power" malls, which have department stores, home-improvement stores, or large warehouse stores as anchors).
• May include a large-format bookstore, a multiplex cinema, and a small department store.[14]

The average size of the lifestyle center depends on whom you ask. The ICSC guidelines suggest that the lifestyle center may range from 150,000 to 500,000 square feet. At the upper end, that makes for a pretty large mall, comparable in size to the typical department store-anchored regional mall. However, some developers and consultants say that lifestyle centers tend to be smaller, around 50,000 square feet—"like a cute little village," according to one commentator.[15]

"Cute" is a key word here. What all observers agree on is the ambience of the lifestyle center, which is designed to evoke other, older urban settings: if not a quaint, old-fashioned village, then perhaps a bustling and prosperous main street from a Middle American town or even the faintly bohemian atmosphere of a (cleaned-up) Greenwich

Village, with plenty of coffee shops and snack bars intermingled with boutiques, furniture stores, cosmetics emporiums, book and CD shops, and other specialty stores. The precise style varies by location. Aspen Grove in Littleton, Colorado, resembles a mining town in the old West; The Shops at Saddle Creek evokes a gracious vision of the South with a mixture of fountains, curved archways, and abundant floral plantings; a center built on the site of a former naval air base retained its historic control tower, while another in a Las Vegas suburb has a casino.

Designers of lifestyle centers borrow a page from the so-called New Urbanism movement, trying to mimic the visual variety, human scale, and continual change that once made great city centers powerful magnets for people from surrounding communities—along with their money. Many lifestyle centers also incorporate office and residential space within easy walking distance of stores, striving for the "mixed-use" ideal that New Urbanist thinkers like the late Jane Jacobs championed.

Perhaps most fascinating of all is the link between the rise of lifestyle centers and the growing popularity of nontraditional forms of shopping, including the Internet, cable TV, and direct-mail catalogs. In an age when ordering a product and having it shipped to your doorstep is as easy as a few clicks of a mouse, bricks-and-mortar retailers can't take their connection with customers for granted. The lifestyle center is one response.

First, it's designed to attract customers who've been turned off by traditional malls. Gone are the vast expanses of concrete that make up the usual outdoor parking lots, as well as the polluted and claustrophobic spaces of the usual indoor multilevel garage. In their place are small clusters of parking spaces located for easy access to individual shops, so that customers who want to dash in for an item or two can do so quickly. But if customers have the time and inclination to linger, the typical lifestyle center includes winding paths among trees and shrubbery, restaurants and cafes with a mix of indoor and outdoor seating, and play areas for children. Natural sunlight replaces fluorescent fixtures; comfortable lounge chairs take the place of plastic benches. The more ambitious centers have the amenities of a great urban space: Crocker Park outside Cleveland, Ohio, boasts a village green, a skating rink, a community fire pit, and a heated garden area with marble tables for picnicking or playing chess.

Second, many of the retailers in lifestyle centers are deliberately designing their stores to take advantage of links to other forms of shopping. In many new lifestyle centers, catalog retailer Coldwater Creek is opening stores that include Internet kiosks where shoppers can browse and buy from the company's web site—free shipping included. This virtually extends the store's inventory to include the entire online merchandise selection, saving on physical space without limiting customer choice.[16]

Lifestyle centers are offering other payoffs to retailers and developers. Studies by the ICSC show that patrons of the lifestyle centers enter more stores and spend more per shopping trip than visitors to other kinds of malls. They also tend to return to the center more often. As a result, sales average $298 per square foot, almost 25 percent more than at traditional malls.[17] Yet, lifestyle centers are actually *cheaper* to build and operate than enclosed malls, largely because they forgo the enormous expense of giant heating and air conditioning systems. And because they consist of smaller individual retail units instead of a single vast complex, they can be built up in stages, gradually expanding from an initial nucleus as warranted by customer traffic and demand for retail space. As a result, they are easier to launch and build.

It's always tempting to follow the path of least resistance—to keep following the business model that worked a decade or a generation ago. Older styles of shopping centers drove the expansion of retailing in the United States from the 1950s through the 1990s. But smart companies are recognizing that today's shoppers—busier, more frazzled, and more demanding than ever—want a retail experience that is qualitatively different from the one they found satisfying in the past. The lifestyle center represents a successful attempt to create a new kind of welcome that works in a changing economic and cultural environment. And savvy companies are riding it to success, at least until the next wave of customer change comes along.

YOUR BIG AHA'S

Even if you are not in retailing, your organization can glean useful insights about the nature of customer welcome from the success of the lifestyle center movement. Here are a few of them.

Think about how to welcome your customers in the context of the total shopping experience. A friendly façade is a crucial component in designing your organization's interface with customers, but it's not enough. You need to take several steps back and think about how customers find and reach you in the first place. Do they encounter you online, via direct mail, through advertising, or while moving through urban or suburban space? Are the surroundings in which your organization appears amenable to frequent, comfortable, prolonged visits? Can you move to or create a new home base, either in the real world or in the virtual space of the Internet, to enhance the welcome your visitors receive?

Mix it up. One of the insights of New Urbanism is that people prefer mixed-use communities that blend residential, retail, recreational, and commercial spaces over those in which different functions are rigidly separated. Hence the appeal of traditional city centers, as well as the new lifestyle centers that seek to emulate them. Look at how your own organization greets and welcomes visitors, live and on online. Are you offering a variety of activities, interfaces, and potential connections to customers? Think about how your organization can provide visitors with many opportunities to shop, learn, play, explore, relax, experiment, and just hang out.

Make your various interfaces work together. Maybe your organization has an attractive office, service center, or storefront where customers can visit you; a well-designed and useful presence on the Internet; and a staff of well-trained telephone and mail-order service personnel. The next challenge is to find ways to integrate these customer interfaces so that they work seamlessly together. Can an online customer get ordering information quickly and easily by phone? Can a catalog shopper return an item to one of your retail branches? Will a discount coupon from a local newspaper be honored on the Internet?

As people's lives change, so should the face of your business. The lifestyle center is just the latest evolutionary stage in the history of shopping centers. Each new form—the regional mall, the super-regional, the specialty mall, the power mall, the festival mall, and the outlet mall—was created in response to a specific demographic, environmental, or economic shift. In the same way, your organization needs to modify the face it presents to customers as the interests, needs, problems, and desires of your customers evolve. Has price become a major issue for your customers? Are they more concerned about speed and convenience? What about simplicity of use, variety of applications, safety and security, or round-the-clock availability? As specific factors rise and fall in importance, be prepared to adjust the form of your offerings accordingly.

CHAPTER 4

The Hospitable Organization

Turning Customers into Guests

THINK OF THE MOST ENJOYABLE HOTEL STAY YOU'VE EVER EXPERIENCED. Maybe it was a business trip where a hotel manager went out of her way to provide exceptional service, impress your clients, and thereby help make a big deal come to fruition. Maybe it was a family vacation where you, your spouse, and your kids were all provided with treats and activities that made each day especially fun and memorable. Maybe it was a honeymoon or a romantic getaway where you and your special someone were provided with pampering, privacy, and the perfect setting in which to renew your love. Whatever it was, think back to the way you felt during that wonderful time. Creating that same sensation is the goal of everyone in the hospitality business—not just because we like making people feel good (which is a big reason we choose our line of work) but because that's the best possible way of ensuring return business and continued growth in our company's profitability.

Probably every hotelier has a collection of favorite stories that illustrate the personal rewards our industry offers as well as the management style that tends to produce those rewards. Here's one of my favorites, as recounted in a gracious e-mail by a guest of Loews Hotels named Ellisa J. Cassuto:

My fiancé Danny left New York for a rafting trip along the Colorado River. (Danny is a New York City firefighter. I am a nice Jewish girl from Long Island . . . not bred for activities that involve risking my life.)

During his trip, Danny had a near-fatal accident. The raft flipped, he fell out, hit his head, and was found floating face-down in the Colorado River.

Luckily, he was traveling with an experienced rafting guide and tour organization. He was given CPR and rescue breathing until he was airlifted by life-flight helicopter to a trauma center in Denver.

Originally, our plan had been for me to meet Danny in Colorado for a romantic weekend getaway. That's why I had booked that weekend at the Loews in Denver. (A good friend recommended the hotel because he frequents the Loews Regency in New York.)

When I heard of the accident, I left for Colorado the very next day. I called the hotel and explained the situation to Lauren [Constable], the manager. She was very understanding and offered me a room at the hospital rate.

When I arrived, I was pleasantly surprised to find that shuttle service to the hospital was offered. I left the hotel each morning at 8:15, then returned from the hospital at 10:45 P.M. via return shuttle. Being alone in an unfamiliar town without family or friends, the shuttle service was a huge relief.

This routine went on for five days. And every bellman and driver was so courteous, gracious, accommodating and kind that I just can't say enough about them.

When Danny was released from the hospital, I still needed some assistance, because I didn't want to leave him alone in our hotel room. Dan [McNamee], the concierge, came to the rescue. He picked up and delivered Danny's prescriptions. He was extremely compassionate and genuine.

Loews staff made an emotionally draining experience tolerable. We just wanted to extend our thanks. We hope to be part of the Loews family in our future travels.

As you can imagine, a story like this makes me proud to be part of the Loews Hotel family. (By the way, manager Lauren Constable has since moved on to our Madison Hotel in Washington, DC, but Dan McNamee still manages the concierge desk in Denver—drop in and say hello next time you're in the Mile-High City.) But as I've said, most other hoteliers can share similar stories. It represents the wonderful tradition of hospitality that Loews shares with our entire industry. We are used to taking responsibility for the total well-being of our customers, going beyond any printed list of "services provided" to consider the human needs of guests as individuals including, on occasion, individuals experiencing an extraordinarily difficult time, as Ms. Cassuto was.

Her story has a nice sequel. She and her fiancé, Danny, were married on August 13, 2006. They wanted to stay overnight in one of New York's finest hotels before flying off on their honeymoon. "Out of all the hotels that we could have stayed at," Ms. Cassuto says, "we insisted on the Loews Regency." And she adds, "Who cares that it's only nine blocks from our apartment? It felt like miles away."

As you can see, this customer-centered approach to business pays real dividends, both for us and for our customers. It's an approach that underlies the success of every great hotel or hotel chain as well as that of other great hospitality venues, including restaurants run by chefs like Emeril Lagasse and Wolfgang Puck; out-of-the-ordinary airlines like JetBlue; and top-notch tour operators, travel agencies, and cruise lines.

What makes for a truly inviting and satisfying hospitality experience is also continually changing. Visit an early-American inn, the eighteenth-century Ferry House located on the grounds of historic Van Cortlandt Manor (near the Hudson River in New York's Westchester County), and you may be shocked by the primitive accommodations guests were provided. For travelers along the Albany Post Road, this dark, tiny building, with its two guest rooms, its crowded tavern, and its array of clay pipes hanging by the fireplace—for rent— was, by current standards, a four-star hotel. Today, high-speed Internet access, a luxurious extra-thick mattress, a multispeed shower-head, and a well-stocked minibar are all taken for granted. And as a modern hotelier, I'm constantly looking for opportunities to add even more amenities and additional ways of delighting our guests. Sometimes it costs millions, as when we expand a property to include a spa with pools, massage rooms, and all the latest exercise equipment. It's all part of keeping up with the current definition of hospitality.

Sometimes the newest trends in hospitality are difficult to anticipate. The boutique hotel movement is a case in point. In reaction to the spread of large, standardized, chain-run hotels around the world during the 1950s, 1960s, and 1970s, boutique hotels, sometimes called "design hotels" or "lifestyle hotels," replace predictability and reliability with creativity and freshness, focusing on design, style, personality, and individualized service. They are generally small and intimate (with 3 to 100 guest rooms) rather than large and anonymous, casual rather than formal, and designed to appeal especially to younger travelers such as businesspeople who are more likely to wear khakis and polo shirts to meetings than pin-striped suits and wingtip shoes.

Boutique hotels have transformed what many guests expect from hotels, and they have fueled an exciting explosion of creativity and imagination on the part of hoteliers and designers. Many boutique hotels have been run as one-off properties or as parts of small collections owned by entrepreneurs. An example is Ian Schrager's Morgan Hotel in New York's Murray Hill neighborhood, which opened in 1984 and was one of the first boutique hotels. But major hotel chains are also active in the trend, led by Kimpton Hotels & Restaurants, which owns boutique properties in 17 cities (including 10 in San Francisco alone) and has aggressive expansion plans, as well as the W Hotels, owned by Starwood Hotels & Resorts Worldwide Inc.[1] Now Intercontinental has the new Indigo chain of boutiques, and the Marriott chain is considering whether to launch its own chain of boutique hotels.

Other hoteliers are already planning for the *next* new trend. Such companies as Europe's EasyJet, restaurant chain Yo! Sushi, and Cambria Suites are launching boutique chains designed in a style that might be called "minimalist chic": tiny, low-priced rooms equipped with high-tech amenities and ultramodern decor.[2] Starwood has announced plans for *aloft,* a new string of hotels that rechannel the boutique style into casual rooms with loftlike, nine-foot-high ceilings, oversized windows letting in plenty of natural light, and landscaped backyards that even have barbecue grills for customers to use. One year after unveiling the concept—and a year before any of the hotels are actually open for business—Starwood is claiming over 100 deals in works for aloft locations in cities around the United States and overseas.[3]

Meanwhile, Ian Schrager, godfather of the boutique movement, is creating a new portfolio of properties (including both hotels and apartment buildings) with a very different esthetic sensibility. The first property to be opened (August, 2006) is the renovated Gramercy Park Hotel in New York, a grand Renaissance Revival building dating back to 1925, that Schrager and his team have designed in a defiantly retro style: opulent, regal, extravagant, gothic, with touches of bohemian artistry reminiscent of *fin de siècle* Europe. "There is no more hip," Schrager now declares, even as he positions himself to redefine hip for another generation of travelers.[4]

Like other businesses, the hotel industry, or what I like to call *the business of hotels,* is constantly evolving. But the common thread—the underlying hotel business on which the entire industry is based—remains the same. It is a variation on legendary business guru Peter Drucker's famous dictum, "The goal of a company is to create a customer." *The goal of a hospitality company is to create a guest.* That means providing people not just with rooms and meals but with wonderful, memorable experiences.

More and more companies in a range of industries as well as nonprofit organizations are beginning to learn and apply some of the secrets we in hospitality have long practiced. The goal is to turn mere customers into guests who view your organization as a home-away-from-home to which they eagerly return again and again.

Reimagining Health Care—Turning Patients into Guests

Health care has long been one of the most troubled American industries. Now absorbing fully 15 percent of our gross domestic product, it's an enormously costly drain on business (through employee health insurance costs), government, and individual families. Yet, the results are unsatisfactory. Citizens of the United States lag those in most other developed countries in such crucial health care statistics as life expectancy and infant mortality. Tens of millions of Americans have no health insurance, which leads many families to skip routine checkups and other important services. And spiraling health care costs are a leading cause of personal bankruptcy. Obviously, it's an industry in drastic need of reform.

Can health care organizations learn anything from us hoteliers? The answer is yes. Of course, there are huge differences between the health care and hospitality businesses. Hotels don't depend on the services of licensed caregivers like physicians, nurses, and therapists; they don't work closely with business and government agencies to provide essential services for the poor or for the uninsured; and hotels aren't subject to same kinds of regulation or public scrutiny that affect hospitals, clinics, and other health care providers.

But there are also interesting similarities between health care and hospitality. Both businesses must find ways to care for individuals as total entities, nurturing people's hearts, minds, and spirits as well as their bodies. Like health care companies, hotels must serve customers of every age, gender, ethnic background, and physical condition, a level of diversity that often creates significant business challenges. Hotels must provide round-the-clock care for guests who entrust us with their physical and psychological security, just as hospitals do. And some of the business metrics we use are shared with hospitals—in both industries, occupancy rate is a key indicator of the well-being of an institution.

I would never claim the expertise needed to reform the health care system in the United States. Wiser heads than mine are tackling the problem. But it's fascinating to note that, as winds of change begin to blow, elements I find familiar from the hospitality business are finding their way into health care. The common thread is the transforming of patients into active guests—participants in their own care.

Some of the changes are driven by successful businesspeople diving into health care and applying concepts derived from the hospitality business. The programs they are launching vary greatly. But all rethink the traditional attitude toward the patient by transforming a passive recipient of health care into an active participant in the healing process, a welcome guest in the house of healing.

Gerry Levin, former CEO of AOL Time Warner, now serves as presiding director of Moonview Sanctuary. It is a Santa Monica clinic designed to help high-profile clients, from movie stars and executives to pro athletes and agents, deal with physical and psychological problems like depression, anxiety, insomnia, and stress. (It so happens that Levin is also the husband of the clinic's cofounder, psychologist Laurie Perlman.)

Patients at the 30-room facility can take advantage of psychotherapy, acupuncture, neurofeedback, reflexology, and massage. It all takes place in a luxurious setting that resembles a five-star hotel, staffed by a concierge and decorated with art and antiques from Bali, including a white marble Buddha that has been converted into a gently splashing fountain. (When the clinic opened, one visitor was heard to joke, "Forget going to a spa, I want to come here for my next vacation."[5])

Moonview's approach offers no broad solutions to the social problems of U.S. health care—the fees are steep and insurance is not accepted, which ensures that the clinic will cater solely to the well-heeled. But it's an example of the kind of experimentation that is now taking place in a field that is sorely in need of innovation. By treating patients as guests, Moonview makes the therapeutic experience inviting rather than forbidding, which should encourage those in need of health care to seek it out rather than avoid it.

One of the world's hippest and most innovative companies is the Virgin Group, whose founder, British billionaire Richard Branson, has built a global brand around his own colorful, fun-loving persona. It is a style that might not seem a natural fit with the health care industry. But now Virgin is launching an effort to make getting and staying healthy hip and fun. Launched in partnership with the Louisville, Kentucky-based insurance provider Humana, the new business has been dubbed Virgin Life Care, and it focuses on rewarding individuals for taking steps to prevent illness rather than simply coping with disease after it strikes.

Here's how it works: An individual signs up for Virgin Life Care online and fills out a Health Snapshot questionnaire. He or she immediately receives a reward of 1,000 points, redeemable for gifts and prizes that range from CDs to travel. When you visit a participating health club to take a comprehensive fitness assessment, you earn more points. Then you can begin to participate in what Virgin calls the *Gozone, Healthzone,* and *Lifezone*—three forms of activity, online and offline, that help you set fitness goals, log in your activities, learn more about health-related news, and monitor your results. Each stage in the process yields more rewards. The entire program is linked either to employer-provided health insurance or to individual coverage available directly from Humana through Virgin.

Virgin Life Care is only a first step toward "marketing fitness" the way other companies market fast foods or video games. But if Branson applies the same tenacity and flair to this business as he has toward his other enterprises, it may spur meaningful changes in the health care industry. Again, the central concept is key: Give people an experience they enjoy, and they will be more likely to return, thereby receiving the long-term benefits that fitness can provide.

A third example is the (somewhat immodestly named) Revolution. It's a private holding company funded by Stephen M. Case, founder of America Online, to invest in health care, wellness, and resorts—three closely intertwined arenas that Case believes are due for massive economic growth as baby boomers age.

Up to half of Case's $500 million nest egg will be invested in companies designed to help patients take a more active role in managing their own health care, from online data services to health coaching services to local clinics. Revolution also owns 70 percent of Miraval spas (Case hopes to help the company build wellness centers in 100 communities around the United States) as well as 50 percent of Exclusive Resorts LLC, a posh time-share-style vacation operation that allows members access to fancy homes in glamorous locations around the world. Case appears to have dreams of linking all three businesses in a single brand that will provide consumers with many ways of nurturing their own health through better nutrition, exercise, and psychological and physical therapies.[6]

Case has enlisted an impressive collection of investors and board members for Revolution Health Group (RHG), which represents just one part of the overall company's holdings. They include former secretary of state Colin Powell, former Fannie Mae CEO Franklin Raines, former Netscape CEO Jim Barksdale, and former Hewlett-Packard CEO Carly Fiorina. RHG has already made a series of strategic acquisitions, including MyDNA Media, a health news company; Simo Software, which manages health care spending and financial records for individuals; and Extend Benefits LLC, which manages individual health care benefits for corporations.[7]

Case has attributed his interest in health care to two factors—his belief in the enormous business opportunity it represents, and his desire to bring dramatic change to an industry badly in need of reform.

(Case's brother, Dan, died of brain cancer at age 44, and Steve says he was appalled to find how difficult it was to make well-informed decisions about care.) The next few years will reveal whether Case's program is a major step toward helping American health care customers feel more like guests—cared-for, nurtured, and secure.

It's not only outside business leaders who are driving change in the world of health care. In other cases, health-care organizations are deliberately borrowing ideas from other businesses, including the hospitality industry. Take hospital food service, long notorious for its inedibility. (Studies suggest that up to one-third of hospital food goes uneaten, which can pose health risks for patients who need sound nutrition to get well.) In response, a growing number of hospitals are adapting hotel-style room service techniques. As of 2005, according to a survey conducted by the National Society for Healthcare Foodservice Management, one hospital in six had already switched to a room-service food program, in which patients can order meals of their choice (within medical restrictions) and be served within an hour, day or night. Another survey puts the number of hospitals planning such a switch as high as 40 percent.

Running a hospital kitchen is no easy job. There are as many as 80 diet variations that may be required due to patients' health conditions. And with average hospital stays growing shorter in recent years due to increasingly strict health insurance rules, patients who do stay overnight tend to be sicker than in the past, posing more complicated dietary challenges.

This makes solving the hospital food service puzzle all the more important. Use of the hotel room-service model appears very promising. At New York's Memorial Sloan-Kettering Cancer Center, poor patient appetites had long been a problem, as chemotherapy and radiation therapy tend to produce nausea. In 2002, Sloan-Kettering became the first hospital on the East Coast to provide room-service-style meals. Twenty-one attractive menus were designed, along with special plate-warming systems to keep food appetizingly hot on its trip from kitchen to bedside. Other small touches were carefully planned, such as real china plates, a personal greeting from the server, and removal of tray covers before the food is brought into the room (so that the strong aroma from a suddenly exposed dish won't induce a rush of nausea). Today, the hospital reports that over 80 percent of its patients eat most of their meals.[8]

Hospitals are finding other opportunities to become more customer-friendly. One example is the growing use of humor as a therapeutic technique. (As a hotelier, I've long known that people get cranky if you don't provide them with entertainment.) New York's Memorial Sloan-Kettering has a "Clown Care United," staffed by professional funnybones from the Big Apple Circus who visit hospitalized youngsters several times a week. At Baptist Medical Center in Oklahoma City, a mostly geriatric wing goes by the name of the Medical Institute for Recovery Through Humor (MIRTH), where water fights and corny jokes (delivered by staffers with each meal) are part of the daily regimen.

Humor is also part of the healing regimen at Duke University Medical Center in Durham, North Carolina. In August 2004, when my father Bob Tisch was diagnosed with a brain tumor, Duke was one of the excellent medical facilities that handled his treatment. Our entire family was so impressed with the humane and caring treatment Dad received there that we're now proudly affiliated with the center, through its Preston Robert Tisch Brain Tumor Center. Duke's Laugh Mobile travels the hospital floors, providing patients with audiotapes of stand-up comedians like Bill Cosby as well as comic props (squirt guns, clown noses, Groucho glasses) for do-it-yourself fun.

Humor can make the serious battle against disease more endurable for patients and staff alike. More important, it appears to have measurable medical benefits. One expert in neuroimmunology calls laughter "internal jogging" and says that it decreases stress hormones while increasing the immunoglobulins that help to fight infection.[9]

Duke's Laugh Mobile isn't that hospital's only program designed to provide patients and their families with the therapeutic benefits of a happy, positive experience. Duke also provides cancer patients with a series of other hospitality-style amenities, including:

- A genealogy program that helps them research their family trees during a hospital stay.
- Music therapy, including sing-alongs, jam sessions, drum circles, and musical games like "Singo" (Bingo with song titles).

- Pets at Duke, in which specially trained dogs provide patients with furry companionship, affection, and fun.
- Look Good . . . Feel Better, which helps female patients adjust to the changes in their appearance that cancer and related treatments sometimes produce.
- Hoop Dreams, which lets kids who are patients at Duke or nearby University of North Carolina Hospital hone their basketball skills under the auspices of "Coach Z," Michael Zeillmann, a former coach at Durham Academy.

Feel-good programs like these can have their maximum benefit only when allied with a comprehensive array of the latest medical technologies, deployed by leading professionals—and on this score the Duke Cancer Center is a world-class institution. (I mentioned Steve Case's brother Dan, who suffered from brain cancer. Dan came to Duke for some of his treatments.) But Duke (and hospitals like it) are learning how to care for the entire patient—including soul, mind, and spirit—not just a collection of disconnected biological systems.

Even the physical design of hospital facilities is being revolutionized, transforming the traditional dreary, antiseptic wards into vibrant settings that give patients and their families a psychological boost toward faster healing. (The power of well-designed public spaces is another secret that we in the hotel business have known for a long time.)

A brilliant example is the new Children's Hospital at Montefiore Medical Center in the Bronx. It was designed by the famed architect David Rockwell, whom I first met some 18 years ago when we were both staying at the Canyon Ranch in Arizona. Later we got the chance to work together on a couple of projects for Loews Hotels, including The Library bar and restaurant at New York's Loews Regency Hotel and a restaurant and marketplace at the Loews Coronado Bay Hotel in San Diego—so I've seen David's genius at work, firsthand.

The Children's Hospital at Montefiore opened in 2001 to rave reviews from patients, families, and physicians alike, and is helping to inspire new thinking about hospital design around the country. If being hospitalized is traumatic for adults, think about how tough it is on children, who often don't fully understand their illnesses, may have trouble expressing their needs clearly, and are more psychologically and physically vulnerable than grown-ups. To help them cope, and to make it easier for their families to provide the support they need, the Children's Hospital at Montefiore includes features like those in no traditional hospital.

They start with universal Internet access via 42-inch plasma screens at the foot of every bed. Two thousand web sites specially selected for their fun and educational qualities are available, along with a mini-library to answer kids' questions about their health. "Smart cards" programmed with data about the patients are used to turn the computers on and off, so older kids automatically receive more complex explanations than younger ones. The monitors also double as conventional TV sets.

Every floor of the hospital includes science displays, each keyed to a different age-appropriate theme. The lobby sports a Foucault pendulum that tracks the rotation of the earth, and there is a giant mural of the Milky Way, with a tiny dot representing the earth labeled, "You Are Here." (The hospital's president, Dr. Irwin Redlener, was a long-time friend of astronomer Carl Sagan.) On the eighth floor, where babies are treated, clay models illustrate how a seed grows into a plant; on the sixth floor, where teenagers stay, lunar rocks and space shuttle parts donated by NASA are displayed.[10]

As other new health care facilities for children are being developed, they are incorporating similarly imaginative, customer-friendly elements. The Maria Fareri Children's Hospital at Westchester Medical Center in Valhalla, New York, features a sports arcade, a fire truck, and a 15,000-gallon saltwater aquarium that handicapped kids can actually ride through in their wheelchairs. At the Morgan Stanley Children's Hospital of New York Presbyterian, patients (and their siblings) who enter the building are greeted not by an admitting desk or an emergency room but by a playroom filled with toys. And the Blythedale Children's Hospital, also in Valhalla, was recently redesigned to include nine colorful, low-ceilinged playhouses where kids receive various forms of therapy.[11]

All these innovations in health care—from Gerald Levin's new-age spa to the Duke Cancer Center's wonderful array of patient-friendly activities—illustrate the kind of radical reimagining that needs to take place in many businesses and nonprofit institutions around the world today.

Your Big Aha's

We often associate health care with sad things like illness, disability, even death. Yet the health care industry, at its best, also brings us good things, from the joy of childbirth and the happiness of healing to the solace of a peaceful end to life. Today, health care organizations are learning to accentuate the positive, redesigning their operations to transform patients and their families into guests who are cared for and nurtured. Here are some of the lessons leaders in every organization can learn from them.

Don't be afraid to learn from seemingly unrelated businesses. Like many industries, health care has long been tradition-bound, led by physicians who tend to follow the customary practices handed down by their mentors of past generations. With health care under enormous social and economic stress, companies in the field are finally drawing on the experiences of businesses in such seemingly unrelated arenas as hospitality and are finding some surprisingly powerful new insights along the way.

Never underestimate the power of information. Most current efforts to reform U.S. health care include providing more, and more accurate, information to patients, as illustrated by Richard Branson's online fitness database, Steve Case's investment in patient-information programs, and the Internet-enabled educational systems installed at the Montefiore Children's Hospital. When customers must cope with complex problems they don't normally confront, which is certainly the case when serious illnesses strike, providing them with plenty of the information they need is one of the most important benefits you can offer.

Sometimes, an idea that looks wasteful can be amazingly efficient. Standardized hospital-style food service, in which hundreds of thousands of patients are served almost-identical dishes simultaneously, may seem more efficient than customized room service. But when trays must be distributed throughout the hospital all at once, many meals are bound to get cold or spoil, which increases waste. Furthermore, patients who have the chance to choose their own meals have been shown to eat more, improving their nutritional status and speeding recovery. In the end, the "extravagant" practice of room-service meals proves to be more efficient than mass feeding.

Your customer is a whole person, not just a collection of specific needs. Most physicians are trained to think of health care customers as biological systems in need of treatment: a digestive tract, a circulatory system, a neurological system. Yet, patients are people, whose social, psychological, and spiritual needs interact with biological states in complex ways. Health care providers who recognize this truth find that rates of healing (as well as the satisfaction reported by patients and their families) improve dramatically.

CHAPTER 5

Home Away from Home

The Art of
Welcoming Customers

As a hotelier, I've always been fascinated by the challenge of *welcoming* guests. It's a unique and in some ways paradoxical challenge—to combine the friendliness of home with the freshness, excitement, and stimulation of travel. It means finding ways to attract customers into your world, making them feel comfortable there, providing great experiences that make them want to stay, and leaving them with positive memories so they'll want to return soon.

Over the years, I've learned a lot about the art of welcome. It's something all successful hoteliers must master, each in their own way. (The welcome you'll enjoy at a Four Seasons Hotel, a Universal Studios theme resort, and the Loews Regency Hotel on Park Avenue in Manhattan will all feel very different, though all can be equally rewarding.) It's also a skill that virtually *every* organizational leader must learn since nowadays we're all in the business of attracting and keeping customers.

In this chapter, I offer a primer on the art of welcome, illustrated with examples from some people who do it especially well.

Masters of Welcome: Morris Lapidus and Paco Underhill

When I think about the art of welcome, I think about certain master practitioners—people who are the equivalent of Picasso or Leonard Bernstein when it comes to creating environments that welcome and delight guests.

Morris Lapidus was one such master. Born in Odessa in the Ukraine in 1902, he came to the United States as an infant when his Orthodox Jewish parents fled the repeated pogroms in their homeland. One of his earliest memories was of visiting Coney Island's Luna Park, a gleaming fantasy of oriental spires, colonnades, and minarets lit by a million electric lights. It changed his life forever and gave Lapidus a mission—he would create magical spaces like Luna Park, to which people would be powerfully drawn.

When Lapidus graduated from the Columbia University School of Architecture in 1927, he landed a job as a draftsman at one of the city's top firms. To make a little extra money, he started to moonlight as a designer of retail interiors. Pretty soon his night job outpaid his day job. Lapidus was fascinated by the challenge of capturing the interest of passersby and luring them into a store. Decades later, he recalled the experience:

> There were three things—took me years to develop—that created an effect which actually stopped people on the street. The stores depend on brilliant light, the use of color, and one other thing I noticed: people do not make a beeline for the thing they want to buy. They meander. So I shaped the walls in unusual forms.[1]

Designing oddly shaped storefronts isn't the most typical basic training for an architect. But it proved to be the perfect jumping-off point for Morris Lapidus. It taught him certain truths that most other architects either never learned or chose to ignore. First, design is all about human emotion. People crave visual stimulation, and they are drawn to places that fascinate, engage, and stir their souls (the way the amazing Luna Park affected Morris as a child). Second, rules of design are made to be broken. If straight lines, harmonious colors, and logical forms don't draw the attention you want, then go for curves, garish hues, and fantastic shapes—the more outlandish the better. At the very least, no one who sees your work will ever forget it.

Lapidus's real architectural career began when he was commissioned to design the Fontainebleau Hotel in Miami Beach. It was built in 1954, the heyday of the austere, boxy style associated with the Bauhaus and the International School of Mies van der Rohe. Lapidus despised van der Rohe and his famous dictum, "Less is more." For Lapidus, *more* was more, and the Fontainebleau was his showcase. The hotel was a Busby Berkeley-esque Hollywood fantasy painted in 27 different colors, its 500 rooms arranged in a sweeping quarter-circle curve, its lobby adorned with a terrarium housing live alligators and a vast "stairway to nowhere" designed solely for fur-draped guests to parade down in starlike splendor.

The critics had a field day panning the Fontainebleau. "Superschlock," said the *New York Times.* "Pornography of architecture," wrote *Art in America.* "It's probably not too disturbing to people who have lost their eyesight," joked the *Miami Herald.* The only ones who liked Lapidus's work were the *people,* who flocked to the Fontainebleau to rent rooms, enjoy meals, and live out their own fantasies of glamour, flamboyance, and excess. Americans going on vacation—especially during that era of gray-flannel-suited conformity—wanted a touch of fantasy, and Lapidus's hotel provided the movie set for their grand escape.

Lapidus started getting more and more commissions, especially for hotels. He designed the Eden Rock, next door to the Fontainebleau; Grossinger's and the Concord in New York's Catskill Mountains; and the Americana Hotel (now the Sheraton Center) in New York City, which has been aptly described as "a beaux art building doing the twist."[2]

As they developed the family hotel chain, Bob and Larry Tisch—my father and my uncle—built several of Morris's creations, including the Americana Hotel of Bal Harbor (1956—now called the Sheraton Bal Harbor) and the Summit Hotel in Manhattan (1961—now the Doubletree Metropolitan). My dad knew all along that Lapidus's critics were missing the boat. "I don't think they ever understood him," Dad once said. "He was a showman in addition to being an architect, and if you are building a resort hotel, you need a showman!"[3]

Years later, my own first jobs, paid and unpaid, took place in hotels designed by Lapidus. At the age of eight, when I was bored with playing or reading, I would sometimes help out by answering phones at the Americana in Bal Harbor (don't ask me what the guests must have thought when an eight-year-old boy took their calls). When I was fourteen, I actually earned a paycheck working behind the front desk at the Americana on Seventh Avenue in New York (it's now known as the Sheraton Center). So I got to know those buildings pretty intimately, and believe me, they are amazing.

Lapidus eventually codified his architectural principles into a series of rules. They included:

- Get rid of corners.
- Use sweeping lines.
- Use light to create unusual effects.
- Use plenty of color.
- Try to get drama.
- Keep changing the floor levels.
- Keep people moving.
- People are attracted to light (the Moth Complex).[4]

These rules are a pretty good description of Lapidus's own work, but in reality no rules can capture what he was after—a kind of space that people are instinctively drawn to. His amazing success at creating such spaces—while violating every norm of his profession—is what makes Morris Lapidus a master at the art of creating welcome.

Later in his life, Lapidus received the critical recognition he deserved, including a 1976 retrospective at the Cooper-Hewitt National Design Museum; several respectful scholarly studies of his work; and in 2000, an American Original award bestowed by the Smithsonian Institution. But I think he would be most pleased by the fact that a generation later, his great hotels and other buildings are still provoking attention—and occasionally controversy—and drawing gawking visitors by the million.

Another master of welcome is Paco Underhill. He's not an artist or architect but rather a business consultant, researcher, and psychologist. What he shares with Morris Lapidus is a fascination with the challenge of creating great public spaces and an intense curiosity about people, their emotions and behavior. Underhill has put those traits to work as one of the world's foremost experts in teaching retailers how to design stores that customers never want to leave.

Underhill likes to describe himself as a "retail anthropologist," and the phrase effectively captures his methodology. His first career was in urban planning and design, where he developed a technique of using time-lapse cameras and discreetly placed observers with notebooks to study traffic patterns and the ways in which people interact with city spaces. On one project in 1977, he found himself tracking pedestrian behavior in an underground concourse in Lincoln Center and he noticed two shoppers competing for the attention of a salesperson at a temporary souvenir kiosk in the concourse. "It made me realize," Underhill later commented, "that the same tools I had been using to look at how people move in a transportation mode or interact with signs, I could take inside a store."[5]

Underhill started a firm called Envirosell to apply scientific techniques of observation and analysis to the design of retail spaces. "We've calculated about 900 different measurements over the past 20 years," he reports, "From how much time somebody spends in a section, to grab-and-go ratios, to the degree to which somebody handles the impact of a sales associate, whether they're being greeted before or after they have merchandise in their hands—our list of deliverables changes with each job."

Many of Underhill's observations result in small, simple adjustments in store design and layout that produce remarkable changes in customer behavior. Back in the days when single records (45s) were the staple of music stores, he recommended that a client lower the height at which the Billboard 100 chart was posted on the wall—closer to the eye level of an 11-year-old than that of an 18-year-old. Sales of singles immediately shot up.

Another time, when working with a home center chain, Underhill's team realized that the weekly shopping circulars would get more attention if they were displayed deeper inside the store (beyond what he calls "the decompression zone" where shoppers are shifting gears into browsing mode) and elevated onto a fixture where people didn't have to bend over to pick them up. "By Sunday night I had the store manager apoplectic with rage because he had used up a week's worth of circulars in one day."

Some of Underhill's observations may seem mundane, even commonsensical (though few business managers are likely to think of them on their own). But others are derived from deep insight into the psychology of customers and an understanding of what makes them feel welcome, comfortable, and relaxed. Take his famous "butt brush" theory, which simply states that when people shop, they dislike being brushed or touched from behind. Here's how Underhill applies the theory to one of the major revenue sources of many retailers—the jewelry counter:

> Here you have something that is often displayed at a height where someone has to lean over to look at it. Part of the purchase of jewelry is the fantasy life of seeing it on your hand or around your neck. There's a certain amount of reverie that's required to getting to the purchase decision. Making that reverie possible is an important part of getting it to move.
>
> [So] putting a jewelry counter right smack in the middle of an active aisle or on a major transit aisle may not be a great idea. . . . Jewelry counters do better on cul-de-sacs. Or if you're going to put one adjacent to a busy aisle, there has to be something else around it to create catchment basins.[6]

The comparison with architect Morris Lapidus is striking. Paco Underhill initially was fascinated with human psychology and an array of social science techniques for observing, analyzing, and quantifying behavior, while Morris Lapidus started with his childhood sense of awe at the glamour and mystery of a brilliantly lighted amusement park. But they ended up in similar places: devising physical, esthetic, and behavioral guidelines for creating public spaces where people feel welcome. And each in his own unique way is a major contributor to making the environments in which people live and move more fun, interesting, and pleasant.

Today, organizations of every sort need to learn and apply some of the same techniques of welcome, whether they are applied to physical spaces like stores, offices, hotels, restaurants, theaters, or sports arenas, or to virtual spaces where clients interact with you—the Internet, a telephone line, a television screen.

Join the Treasure Hunt: Urban Outfitters, Fashion's Hip New Home

Ever visited an Urban Outfitters store? Don't rack your brain—if you've ever been in one, you'll definitely remember it. An Urban Outfitters clothing store is like no other. Some apparel chains sport identical racks of bland, color-coordinated khakis and look-alike polo shirts. Instead, picture a café-cum-thrift shop run by a couple of globe-trotting ex-hippies who haul back clothes, accessories, and other stuff from their treks to places like Chile, Vanuatu, and Sri Lanka and toss it at random onto the floor of their store. That's Urban Outfitters.

It's an illusion, of course; Urban Outfitters is really part of a rapidly growing apparel corporation that is traded on the Nasdaq exchange. It also owns two other superhip clothing businesses, Anthropologie and Free People. But it's a remarkably powerful illusion that draws a cadre of dedicated customers for long, frequent visits to their favorite shopping hangout and is helping to fuel one of retailing's biggest success stories.

Urban Outfitters was born in 1970, when 23-year-old Richard Hayne opened a boutique selling new and used clothing, furniture, and psychedelic gear like scented candles and posters to a student crowd in Philadelphia.[7] By 1993, the store had grown into a chain, based largely in college towns, and had gone public. Today, the company operates 140 stores under two brand names, each aimed at a slightly different demographic: Urban Outfitters appeals to Gen Xers, while Anthropologie aims at sophisticated yet free-spirited women in their late 30s and 40s. Both store chains have similar design and marketing philosophies. The company's wholesale division, Free People, creates casual wear for young women that it markets through department stores and 1,500 specialty shops across the country. But the shrewd strategizing is deftly disguised by an image of spontaneity that echoes the company's funky origins, only expanded on a nationwide and now an international basis (Urban Outfitters recently opened stores in Canada, Ireland, and the United Kingdom).

One of Urban Outfitters' secret weapons in capturing the attention of its restless, short-attention-span Gen-X clientele is an atmosphere of deliberate semi-chaos, in which displays of clothes, housewares, bedding, costume jewelry, and decorative items jostle hand-painted signs, recycled architectural elements salvaged from neighborhood junkyards, and beat-up pieces of retro furniture from Salvation Army outlets on which customers feel free to lounge. "Shopping here should be like a treasure hunt," comments Laura O'Connor, the company's 34-year-old general merchandising manager—and if that means making it hard (as well as fun) for customers to unearth the goodies they want to buy, so be it.[8]

Another key to the Urban Outfitters look is rapid change. Merchandise is delivered to the stores in small batches every day, guaranteeing that returning customers will always have new goods to check out. The fact that items are purchased in small quantities also reduces the company's financial risk. Other apparel chains sometimes bet the business on a particular style, color, or hem length, flooding stores with hundreds of thousands of units and praying the anointed look will take off. The Urban Outfitters style is about diversity, not standardization.

The merchandise pipeline is kept filled by 20 designers and buyers who travel up to three months per year, visiting clubs, bazaars, bars, and other hangouts in some of the globe's hippest neighborhoods—New York's Soho, Covent Garden in London, Le Marais in Paris—where they look for new trends in clothing and home decor. When they notice a hot new item, they decide on the spot whether to import a batch or arrange manufacturing for a knockoff version. As a result, stylish new goods get into Urban Outfitters' stores before they turn up in other retail venues.

Unlike competitors such as the Gap, Urban Outfitters doesn't advertise. Instead, it invests 2 to 3 percent of revenues in the unique look of the stores. A team that typically includes four artists per store is constantly developing fresh themes for twice-monthly redecorating forays.[9] The effect is the same as the steady flow of new goods—regular customers never feel as though they're visiting the same store twice, which makes a weekly visit almost a necessity.

The treasure-hunt atmosphere, combined with the store's steady turnover in merchandise encourages customer visits that average 45 minutes, about twice the industry average. To encourage such lingering, the stores add video game consoles and vintage arcade games to the general clutter, hoping to keep impatient males occupied while their girlfriends browse.

New experiments to further enhance the customer welcome are constantly in the works. The Urban Outfitters store located on London's Kensington High Street has launched a series of "open-mike Sundays" for aspiring local musicians, a collaboration with indie record label Carbon Music.[10] The best performances will be broadcast, and some will find their way onto a mix CD to be sold (naturally) in Urban Outfitters stores.

What all the details add up to is a retail environment that is less about selling to customers than about welcoming them and enveloping them in a world that is relaxing, engrossing, surprising, and rich. Here's how the philosophy is described by Kristin Norris, the young visual director of Anthropologie, Urban Outfitters' sister chain:

> I think of everything [in our stores] as a story. . . . A bedding story isn't just about linens and comforters. It's about the feeling of nighttime and a sense of place. It's about the pictures on the wall, the soft glow of a lamp, a closet with robes and soft clothing peeking out. . . . We try to create little environments that tell a story. The idea is to capture a customer's attention so that she'll explore every corner and let her imagination go. We mix up the stock in a way that gives the customer ideas—ideas about how to mix colors and textiles that she'd never think of combining or ideas about how materials like turquoise and leather can cross categories from clothing to accessories.[11]

There's no arguing with the financial results. Urban Outfitters' sales have grown an average of 30 percent each of the past five years, passing a billion dollars in 2006.[12] Revenues average $596 per square foot, which is 80 percent higher than at The Limited or Express. Profit margins run a healthy 18 percent, and in just the past two years the stock has soared by 91 percent.[13] Over the next seven years, the company plans to expand its store lineup by 20 percent annually, up to a total presence of some 400 locations.[14]

The competition has taken notice. In October 2005, Gap Inc. announced a new retailing concept, Forth & Towne, based on the notion that a great shopping space could attract customers who might not be caught dead in a traditional Gap outlet. The new stores are designed by David Rockwell's New York architecture firm (which, you'll recall, was also responsible for the Children's Hospital at Montefiore Medical Center—Chapter 4). They feature a round salon of fitting rooms that is decorated like the lobby of a luxury hotel with plush seating, an array of fashion magazines, displays of fresh flowers, and chocolates and bottled water for sampling. Early results have been promising: Forth & Towne stores have been opened in Chicago and New York, with seven more cities scheduled to come online by 2007. While the new chain is no Urban Outfitters' knock-off, it borrows the notion that an alluring, intriguing place for shopping can help to create a great customer experience that leads to longer store visits, more sales, and greater company profits.

Urban Outfitters' stores are definitely not for everyone. But those who get it, get it big time—and they've made Urban Outfitters their store of choice while helping to launch a powerful new trend in fashion retailing.

YOUR BIG AHA'S

"Funky," "hip," and "cool" may not be the words most people use to describe your organization, and they may be far from the atmosphere you desire to create. But you can still derive some powerful lessons from the way that Urban Outfitters has harnessed the power of welcome to attract customers. Here they are.

Start with your customers, not with goods or services. Both Urban Outfitters and sister chain Anthropologie are apparel stores—but they don't limit their offerings to clothes. Rather than think in terms of product categories, the managers start with what interests their customers and try to assemble a collection of items that will intrigue and delight them. If mixing in furniture, jewelry, housewares, and even music with tunic tops and Indian-print skirts will send a more welcoming message to the target audience, go for it.

To keep people interested, tweak your look. It isn't only Gen X-ers who have short attention spans these days. In a headline-news world, you need to give people excellent reasons to stay curious and keep returning to your place of operations. At Urban Outfitters, that means daily shipments of new merchandise and twice-monthly store redesigns. For your organization, it may mean fresh web site content every week; a regularly updated newsletter, catalog, or brochure describing your latest offerings; a redesign of your outdated logo; or cycling back-room employees through customer-facing jobs, so that no one goes stale.

Big organizations can think small. Urban Outfitters combines the broad reach of a big chain with the customized, local look and quirky, personal feel of a small, one-off store. If you help to run a large organization, look for ways to incorporate the most appealing aspects of a small organization. Give local managers some autonomy to customize products, services, and style to fit local needs and tastes; vary your uniform look by injecting elements of regional color; and where possible, decentralize service functions so that customers experience face-to-face contact with people from the neighborhood who represent your organization.

Your style is your best form of advertising. There's no way Urban Outfitters can match the vast TV budgets of competing clothing chains like the Gap or Old Navy. Instead, they invest (smaller) sums of money in creating a one-of-a-kind style. The result is stores that are like three-dimensional billboards—visually striking and memorable. They generate word-of-mouth whose financial value can't even be calculated.

The Electronic Welcome: Cable News Wars and the Battle for Viewers

The art of welcoming customers doesn't apply only to physical spaces like hotels and stores. It also applies in such virtual spaces as web sites and TV screens, where the competition is for that valuable commodity known as "eyeballs."

As it happens, I've had quite a bit of experience both behind and in front of the TV cameras, so I've thought a lot about the broadcast business through the years. My first job after graduating from Tufts University was as a cinematographer and producer at WBZ-TV in Boston, where I spent about four years working on news programs and documentaries. That background, I'm sure, made it easier for me when I was given the opportunity, in 2005, to become the host of my own interview program. It's a show called *Open Exchange: Beyond the Boardroom* that appears on Plum TV and provides CEOs with the opportunity to talk about their lives and work in a relaxed, casual setting—often in their own homes or in a familiar location such as a favorite restaurant.

Open Exchange has featured interviews with such interesting and significant business figures as Kenneth Chenault (American Express), Barry Diller (IAC Interactive), Bob Johnson (BET), Sir Clive Davis (Arista Records), Alan "Ace" Greenberg (Bear Stearns), Susan Lyne (Martha Stewart Living OmniMedia), and even "the Donald"—Donald Trump himself. As you can imagine, the opportunity to engage leaders of this quality in serious conversations about business is fascinating for me, and the shows have been well received by both the public and the critics. The secrets we've tried to apply in creating memorable TV interviews are few and simple:

- Surround the host with a great team—excellent producers, camera crews, editors, and other professionals.
- Do your homework—try to know everything there is to know about your guests before the cameras roll.
- Be respectful but challenging—ask tough, probing questions without crossing the line into rudeness or "gotcha" game-playing.

- Above all, listen—make the show into a real conversation between two human beings rather than an artificial volleying of questions and answers.

If people enjoy *Open Exchange* (and the comments I've gotten suggest they do) it's probably because we strive to make it an inviting, comfortable, and stimulating television experience . . . a bit of my hospitality philosophy applied to the world of cablecasting.

Working in television has made me especially interested in following the evolution of the TV news business, which is one of the most important, competitive, and challenging industries in today's world of media.

At one time, television news was strictly a matter of public service and corporate prestige. In the 1950s and 1960s, the major networks spent millions maintaining news bureaus around the world and prided themselves on hiring the world's most trusted anchors and reporters, from Edward R. Murrow and Walter Cronkite to Chet Huntley and David Brinkley. Ratings and income were secondary considerations.

Today, as the economics of the media business has evolved over the past four decades, the stakes have risen dramatically. TV news has become a hotly contested business, with hundreds of millions of dollars in advertising revenues at stake. And now that news broadcasters are expected to support themselves and their networks with revenues rather than operating as prestigious loss leaders, they are battling to develop powerful ways of attracting and retaining viewers, the more the better. So CNN, Fox, MSNBC, and other news networks are competing to find the visual formula that will convince viewers to extend their average visit by just a few minutes each day. If they can find it, that recipe will be worth hundreds of millions in advertising revenue. Think of it as a kind of arms race, in which the most effective form of electronic welcome will be victorious.

Of course, the esthetics of welcome that apply to TV news are different from those that work when designing a retail environment. They're based on a host of factors that involve how viewers connect with news—the kinds of stories they want, the depth of information they prefer, the personalities they like and dislike, and the density and speed of presentation. All these elements are in a constant state of flux as audiences evolve, competition escalates, and the nature of news changes.

The terrorist attacks of 9/11 and the subsequent wars in Afghanistan and Iraq drove millions of viewers to their TV sets, looking for 24-hour-a-day sources of information that might have literal life-and-death importance. One immediate result was the birth of the "news crawl," the bannerlike ticker along the bottom of the cable TV screen that carries up-to-the-minute news in brief headline form. Fox News Channel launched its ticker just an hour after the second plane crashed into the World Trade Center. MSNBC followed suit, and CNN produced its own version by mid-afternoon. For several weeks thereafter, the crawls were dedicated to terror-related news and information, but since then, they have become a fixture of televised news, carrying everything from sports scores and traffic alerts to quotations from newsmakers and weather reports.

Why do viewers like the crawl? There are several theories. When big news is breaking, the crawl helps viewers stay in touch while their attention is diverted. Just three weeks after 9/11, one commentator wrote:

> In a news environment where television has not only been a source of information but a security blanket, the crawls are strangely reassuring. "We know people watch cable TV with the sound down while they run around at work or at home," says [MSNBC executive producer Ramon] Escobar. "That's why it has value."[15]

Related to this are generational changes in people's ability to absorb data. The baby boomers grew up with the electronic media, and in the process became some of the first "multitaskers," comfortable with tackling several jobs at once—scanning the newspaper, chatting on the phone, peeking at their BlackBerries, and watching TV news. For them, seeing an anchor discuss one story while the crawl provides headlines about a couple of dozen other stories isn't confusing but rather comforting, giving a sense that they are on top of everything that is happening in a complex world.

The same desire for speedy access to many stories also underlies the steady shortening of individual news items and the year-by-year abbreviation of sound bites to illustrate and clarify stories. (During the 1968 presidential campaign, the average sound bite was 43 seconds; by 2000, it had shrunk to nine seconds.[16]) Underscoring the trend, CNN's Headline News affiliate—designed to purvey bite-size versions of the day's news—recently passed MSNBC for the number three slot in the cable news ratings, after Fox and CNN.

As viewers from Generation X and beyond—heavy multitaskers accustomed to juggling devices such as iPods, cell phones, and PDAs—become more dominant in TV news ratings, the flow of information across screens seems likely to accelerate even more. In other words, the definition of what makes a comfortable TV news environment is undergoing a steady evolution as viewers' expectations, desires, and needs continue to change.

Changes are occurring on the content front as well. A generation ago, it was highly unusual for a broadcaster to inject personal or political opinions into the news. The rare exceptions tended to occur at moments of national trauma, as when Murrow editorialized against Joseph McCarthy's red-baiting tactics in 1954, or when Cronkite expressed doubts about the Vietnam War in 1968—both events that were startling enough to be talked about decades later. Now, the conservative-leaning Fox News has shown that viewers are ready to absorb a dose of commentary or analysis with the facts: Beginning in 2001, Fox has regularly drawn higher viewer ratings than rivals CNN and MSNBC, and the most-watched news show on cable TV is Fox's heavily opinion-laden *O'Reilly Factor*. In response, Fox's rivals have launched their own opinion-and-commentary shows, some equally conservative (such as MSNBC's *Scarborough Country*), some liberal (the same network's *Countdown* with Keith Olbermann).

Media experts and political pundits have been debating whether these trends—the speeding-up of news and the injection of opinion—have been good or bad for the national discourse. There are arguments on both sides. But with hundreds of millions in ad revenues at stake, there's no doubt that the experimentation will continue, with viewers using their remote controls to vote for the electronic welcome they find most appealing. Recent developments include:

- ABC News naming the youthful male-and-female co-anchor team of Bob Woodruff and Elizabeth Vargas (44 and 43 years old, respectively) to fill the shoes of long-time anchor Peter Jennings after his death from lung cancer. ABC simultaneously launched the first live (rather than taped) broadcasts of its *World News* program on the West Coast, as well as the first live daily Internet webcast by network anchors.[17] The Woodruff-Vargas teaming was short-lived. (Soon thereafter, Woodruff was seriously injured in Iraq; Vargas announced that she would be taking maternity leave; and Charles Gibson eventually took over the network's anchor chair.)

- A CNN Headline News producer circulating a controversial e-mail to his writing staff, urging them to consult a slang dictionary as a source of vocabulary for on-screen graphics: "[U]se this guide to help all you homeys and honeys add a new flava to your tickers and dekos."[18] CNN was widely derided for the memo, which seemed to illustrate the network's desperation to reach a younger and broader audience.

- CBS News breaking precedent by wooing and winning NBC's Katie Couric, the long-time cohost of *The Today Show,* to become the first solo female anchor of a network evening news program, sitting in the seat once occupied by the revered Cronkite. Even as CBS launched its recruitment campaign for Couric, it was also developing and testing prototypes for a radical new evening news format that includes only a brief selection of news items, followed by two to three longer segments modeled on stories from the network's venerable newsmagazine *60 Minutes*—investigative reports, celebrity profiles, and tear-jerking human-interest tales.[19]

- Fox News fine-tuning such details as the content and pacing of the tease that precedes a commercial break. Senior vice president of programming Bill Shine remarks, "If you want to annoy your ad sales guys, tease out with 'We'll be right back,' because that doesn't say anything and you're not showing anything." Fox claims the difference helps explain why viewers stay tuned to Fox for 25.4 minutes on average, compared with CNN's 19.1 minutes.[20]

Obsessive? Nit-picking? Even a little desperate? Maybe. But TV executives know that their only source of revenue—the only thing they have to sell—is their ability to welcome and keep viewers. That's why they're willing to invest millions in fine-tuning their broadcasts to boost those ratings and those viewer-retention figures even by tenths of a point. The art of the electronic welcome is their livelihood.

YOUR BIG AHA'S

Even if you are not in the media business, the art of the electronic welcome may be important to you—think about your organization's Internet presence, or its TV or radio advertising. Here are some insights suggested by the cable news wars that may apply to your challenges.

Any place you vie for the attention of customers is a place where the art of welcome is crucial. It's important that your physical spaces be welcoming to customers. But it's equally important that you send the same message of welcome through every medium that touches customers, especially when you are competing for their attention with other organizations.

Do your research. You may assume that you know how customers react to your messages and outreach. But far more valuable than assumptions are facts based on hard research. The broadcasters spend millions on research, from the Nielsen and Arbitron ratings to custom-designed surveys that measure every detail of audience reactions to programming, formats, and commercials. Back up your own understanding of customers with research, which may be as simple as handing out a printed questionnaire, conducting in-depth interviews with a cross-section of customers, or arranging to watch customers navigate your web site and talk about the features they like and don't like.

Think outside the box. Some of the most powerful recent innovations in news broadcasting, including the 24-hour news crawl and the advent of opinion-laden news programming, violated long-standing industry norms when they were first introduced.

Now, having proven enormously popular with viewers, they are staples of the business. Are there similar unquestioned norms in your business that are worth testing in pursuit of a more customer-friendly style?

Little things can mean a lot. Agonizing over the number of seconds it takes to enter and exit a commercial break may seem extreme, but it takes only an instant for a valuable viewer to click away from one station to another. Nowadays, your customers may also find it all too easy to abandon your organization for another, just by clicking on a different web site, phoning a different number, or walking a few yards to the next storefront in the mall. This means that details you once might have felt safe ignoring may be increasingly important and worth agonizing over.

CHAPTER 6

Haven Wanted

Providing Security in an Unsafe World

CUSTOMERS WANT A SENSE OF SECURITY AND SAFETY WHEN THEY VISIT or interact with your company or organization. That goes without saying, perhaps—but the nature of the challenge has changed and intensified in recent years.

Think of the major news stories of the past half-decade: The terrorist attacks of September 11, 2001. The financial collapse of a series of big companies—Enron, WorldCom, Global Crossing. The mysterious, still-unsolved anthrax mailings that killed several people in Washington, DC. The wars in Afghanistan and Iraq. The ongoing, slow-motion breakdown of the social safety net, as millions of Americans lose their health insurance coverage and once-secure pensions. The devastation caused by Hurricane Katrina and the disappointing response by government agencies like FEMA. Spikes in home heating bills and soaring prices at the gas pump.

What do these feel-bad stories have in common? All have contributed to unprecedented levels of insecurity and anxiety in Americans. Sometimes the fear is targeted and specific: the fear of flying or of visiting a national landmark due to worries about terrorism, or the fear of losing a job and the precious health care benefits that go with it. In other cases, it's vague and free-floating, contributing to a general sense of malaise and stress that makes millions of people go through life saying, "I just can't cope any more."

What this means for managers of organizations is that security has moved up the agenda from being a secondary or tertiary issue and is becoming a primary one. On the negative side, people want to know that patronizing your business or using your services won't add to their stress and anxiety. On the positive side, they are hoping that, somehow, you can offer some respite from the tension that permeates daily life. Many are desperately seeking a break from their worries, whether those worries are physical, financial, or simply psychological. Any organization that can provide it will be deeply appreciated, maybe even loved.

It's a new challenge for most businesses, but a familiar one to hoteliers. As I note whenever I speak to audiences in the hospitality industry, any time people leave the comforts of home to travel, they are trusting the proprietors of a variety of establishments to provide a homelike setting in a strange environment. This includes *physical* comfort in hotels, stores, restaurants, airlines, cars, and other locations that a traveler might visit. It also includes *psychological* comfort by making it easy for travelers to request special help or amenities (from an aspirin at midnight for a sudden headache to an infant seat in a hotel dining room) without hassle, embarrassment, or undue expense.

Occasionally, our responsibility to care for the security of our guests requires us to take actions above and beyond the norm. When Hurricane Katrina struck the U.S. Gulf Coast in August 2005, Steve Ferran, the general manager of the Loews New Orleans hotel, found himself coping with challenges no manual or training course could have prepared him for.

Most of the Loews employees and guests had managed to evacuate safely from the city during the days prior to Katrina's landfall. But when the storm surge hit, some 40 employees and about 20 guests were still at the hotel. With no other choice, they rode out the devastation together, subsisting on food from the hotel kitchen and even raiding the minibars in the guest rooms when water supplies ran out.

On August 29, as frightened New Orleanians sought refuge at the Superdome stadium and the city Convention Center (just two blocks from our hotel), a contingent of National Guards arrived and spoke to

Steve. "Everyone here must leave the city—right now," they declared. "There's a single bridge open, and we can provide you with safe passage for the next hour. After that, you'll be on your own."

Steve and his team set to work organizing a caravan to shuttle the hotel's employees and guests to safety—somewhere, anywhere north of the city where the lights were still working and travel facilities like airports and bus depots were still in operation. After filling up all the available employee cars, Steve found that he and another manager were left with eight additional stranded guests. What to do?

Suddenly, someone remembered that the syndicated television game show *Wheel of Fortune* had been in New Orleans taping a series of programs—and that two brand-new SUVs, prizes for contestants, had been stored in the Loews garage. The keys were available in the hotel front office. "Let's get them!" Steve decided. They siphoned gas from some other abandoned cars in the garage and used the prize vehicles to drive the last few guests to safety. (Of course, the cars were later refueled and returned to the production company that owned them.)

All in a day's work for the dedicated hotelier.

Today's era of terror threats poses new security challenges for hotels. Frankly, it's not an issue that hoteliers like to discuss much in public. Not only do we want to avoid arousing excessive anxiety on the part of our customers, but we also prefer to keep the exact nature of our security programs under wraps, so as not to tip off any would-be troublemakers about how we plan to thwart them. But since 9/11, we've taken serious steps to improve hotel security, including more careful monitoring of entrances and exits, installing cameras to track people's comings and goings, and training our employees about the danger signs to look for—all while striving to balance the need for security with everyone's desire for open doors and an atmosphere of welcome.

Today, all kinds of organizations face similar challenges. Stressed-out consumers demand physical comfort from the companies they deal with, from shorter waiting lines in government offices and more spacious, well-lit dressing rooms in clothing stores to e-commerce web sites that are designed with clarity and easy readability in mind. They also demand psychological comfort, which smart organizations are providing through a variety of techniques, from helping patrons of a web site feel safe in revealing their credit card data and other personal information to walking clients through complex, intimidating processes (such as filing income tax forms, planning retirement investments, or buying a new car) so that they feel confident and in control. And when customers don't receive the sense of physical and psychological comfort they require, they walk away, offering comments like, "Who needs more hassle?" "Life is too short," and "Give me a break!"

Today's tough security issues have serious implications. Your organization may be legally responsible for the safety of your patrons in ways you never anticipated. A few families of 9/11 victims are still pursuing lawsuits against the airlines and government agencies they claimed were negligent in guarding against terrorist attacks. And paranoia over legal liabilities has led some organizations to develop defensive strategies, from elaborate disclaimer statements to complex and intimidating consumer warnings that only heighten the atmosphere of anxiety.

When it comes to security issues, you need to take the advice of your organization's attorneys seriously. But the challenge of making customers truly secure—physically and psychologically—can't be left to lawyers or even security experts. Sales, marketing, design, and service experts who are close to the customer must be intimately involved to help find the right balance between safety and comfort, making the customer feel at ease and secure without creating the feeling of a fortress.

Airport Design: Balancing Security and Comfort in a Post 9/11 World

Air travel has long been one of the most uncomfortable experiences for many people. Every frequent traveler can easily recount the hassles: the expense and time spent getting to airports that are often distant from city centers; the long waits for departures in lounges that are usually dreary, noisy, and crowded; the discomforts of the flight itself, with its increasingly narrow seats, declining quality of food and service; the battles for space in the overhead baggage compartments—the list goes on and on.

It's easy to pity the poor airline passenger who must put up with this. But spare a thought for the executives who run the airlines as well. Ever since the industry was deregulated in the late 1970s, competition among airlines has been driven by price. Most air travel customers can't or won't pay more for greater comfort and service—although that doesn't stop them from wanting it. So the downward spiraling of ticket prices has forced the jettisoning of more and more amenities by most airlines—even as low prices attract more and more flyers, making planes more crowded than ever. Most airlines are having a terrible time trying to figure out how to escape this destructive cycle.

Into this already painful business situation, throw the horrific events of 9/11. Talk about bad publicity: Imagine having the proudest symbol of your industry, a jumbo jet, used as a weapon in history's worst terrorist attack, featured in frightening video images that have been repeated thousands of times on television networks around the world. The entire travel industry was thrown into recession in the wake of the attacks.

One of the hardest-hit components of the air travel industry has been the airports themselves. Usually operated by municipal, county, or state governments as quasi-private enterprises, airports play a vital role in local and national economies, providing a portal to the region for business travel and tourism, a shipping point for mail and cargo, and directly or indirectly creating thousands of jobs and generating billions of dollars in commerce.

The airports are also a target of much of the resentment and hostility that air travelers feel. And since 9/11, the hostility has grown. Onerous new safety regulations mandated by the Aviation and Transportation Security Act (November, 2001) have made passage through airports more time-consuming than ever. (According to a study by *Airport Interviewing and Research,* passengers now spend an average of 109 minutes at the airport before boarding their flights.[1]) Lines at security checkpoints have grown, methods for inspecting baggage and examining passengers have become more intrusive, recommended check-in times have gotten earlier, and overworked airport personnel have become more stressed, leading to confrontations with angry passengers.

Perhaps most distressing of all, many Americans don't believe that the new security measures are making air travel safer. Polls show that travelers are skeptical about the value of such seemingly petty yet annoying routines as shoe doffing, body pat-downs, and the confiscation of personal items like nail files and bottles of hair gel. Many say they think future terrorist attacks are inevitable and aren't being deterred by the new procedures. And there's evidence they may be right: Tests have shown that an alarming percentage of contraband items (such as knives and other weapons) pass undetected through airport gates.[2]

For the airport manager, then, it seems as if today's travel dilemma is a no-win situation. How can they possibly make the airport experience pleasant or even bearable?

Some airports are rising to the challenge.

Harrisburg, Pennsylvania, is not a major metropolitan hub. But thanks to a happy accident of timing and the foresight of local officials, Harrisburg now has one of the world's most up-to-date airports. In fact, since August 2004, Harrisburg International Airport (HIA) has boasted the first terminal in the United States to be designed and built specifically to comply with post-9/11 security standards. Furthermore, it has combined its safety systems with amenities that make travel time more pleasant for customers and increase the revenues enjoyed by businesses and local government agencies alike.

The strict new rules for baggage inspection played a major role in dictating the design of the new facility in Harrisburg. The old van-sized baggage screening machines sat in the lobby of the terminal. They were unsightly, blocked traffic, and created potential security breaches as bags were pushed on carts across the lobby from one checkpoint to the next. The new terminal has a unique, underground in-line baggage screening system almost three quarters of a mile in length that is equipped with three electronic scanners capable of handling 1,200 bags per hour.

There are also 130 surveillance cameras, some equipped with night-vision capabilities and integrated with the alarm system, so that any breach in a secure door will immediately prompt the nearest camera to zoom in on that door. In the passenger screening area, cameras are linked to flat-panel monitors that allow travelers to see exactly what security officers are seeing, which both eases fears of Big-Brother intrusion and enlists civilian help in spotting potential troublemakers.

Obviously, there have been no compromises with safety in the design of HIA. But the airport was also built with new standards for passenger comfort in mind. The airport's paging and announcements

system is a far cry from the traditional systems in most airport terminals, which seem to alternate between ear-splitting volume and inaudi-
ble mumbling. The new sound system was designed and built by
Morefield Communications, a Camp Hill, Pennsylvania, company,
using a three-dimensional computer-aided design model that allowed
acoustical testing of the components *before* they were installed. Ambi-
ent sensors throughout the facility measure background noises and automatically adjust the volume on the 650 JBL loudspeakers accordingly.
(When the baggage belts are running, the sound level swells; when the
belts stop and the crowds thin, it fades.) Between announcements, customized background music is selected from among 8,000 titles to suit
the mood that airport officials want to induce at any given time.

It all sounds very high-tech and costly. But Morefield actually un-
derbid competing contractors by some $30,000, which means the new
sound system was fiscally responsible as well. (Great design is about
smart, creative thinking—not throwing money at problems.)

HIA offers many other amenities as well. Free wi-fi Internet access
is available to travelers throughout the terminal. A powerful centralized data network is open to every tenant, from airline ticket counters
to restaurants, shops, and newsstands, eliminating the "spaghetti mess
of wires" from multiple information technology (IT) systems that de-
faced the old terminal. Most important, HIA has been designed as a
"multimodal, intermodal transportation facility" linking many forms
of travel—not just planes, busses, and cars, but also an Amtrak train
station linked to the airport via pedestrian walkway—still another
first. Thus, many of the hassles of getting to the airport have been reduced at Harrisburg.

Other airports are also being designed to combine post-9/11 security systems with improved amenities for travelers. The new Terminal
A at Boston's busy Logan International Airport has a column-free
main ticketing hall that provides long views in every direction, creating an open, airy feel that passengers enjoy while making it easier for
security personnel to survey the action. Outside, auto traffic has been
patterned to prevent vehicles from getting too close to the terminal
(thereby thwarting would-be car bombers) while providing a sheltered
area under a cantilevered canopy for dropping off passengers. A glass

curtain wall broken up with aluminum panels and capped with sky-lights is both efficient and environmentally friendly, using recycled materials and drawing light and warmth from the sun. (Perhaps it's no surprise that the new Terminal A has such a smartly innovative design: It was planned by HOK Inc., the St. Louis architectural firm that fa-mously launched the 1990s-era renaissance in sports stadium design with Baltimore's beautiful Oriole Park at Camden Yards.)

What's more, the nature of the special services offered at airports has been intelligently evolving in the security-intensive years since 9/11. During the 1990s, the emphasis was on upscale shops—Brooks Broth-ers, Brookstone, The Sharper Image. Now airports are opening venues with comfort in mind, deliberately designed to offset the stress and anx-iety associated with travel. McCarran International Airport in Las Vegas offers a 24-hour gym with locker rooms, workout gear, steam room, and sauna. Michigan-Metro Airport in Detroit features the Ora Oxygen spa, providing aromatherapy and oxygen treatments that refresh and revital-ize weary travelers. And airports from Chicago to San Francisco have opened medical clinics that can provide relief for anything from air sick-ness to a broken toe from dropping a heavy suitcase on your foot.[3]

Services like these not only reduce the discomfort of spending time in the airport but also generate revenues for the businesses that oper-ate them, fees for airport authorities, and taxes for local government—a winning proposition all the way around.

YOUR BIG AHA'S

You probably will never be called on to design a new airport ter-minal. But the lessons to be learned from the new wave of air-port designs are applicable to many organizations. Here are a few of them.

Security and comfort are not *incompatible.* If you run an orga-nization with significant security concerns—which nowadays in-cludes almost any organization that is open to the general public—don't assume that security automatically equates to has-sles, annoyance, and inconvenience. Creative design that starts with rethinking basic assumptions can usually find ways to combine security with comfort and even fun.

Design from the ground up to meet both institutional and individual needs. Part of what makes the new Harrisburg Airport terminal so attractive and comfortable is its sophisticated IT design, planned from day one to accommodate the needs of airport security, airlines, retail tenants, and travelers. When creating any new organizational system or structure, bring representatives of all the affected groups into the room, and insist on crafting a plan that will satisfy everyone's needs.

When you can't avoid inconveniencing your customers, transparency softens the hurt. In the post 9/11 era, travelers understand the need for intrusive security measures—but they still dislike them. By providing video terminals that let passengers watch themselves being screened, the Harrisburg system eases the discomfort and reassures travelers about the experience.

Look for ways to turn customer negatives into win/win positives. Having to spend two hours or more in the airport for security reasons causes inconvenience and resentment for many travelers. Smart airport authorities are taking steps first to neutralize the negatives (by making security systems less ugly and unpleasant), then to transform them into positives (by offering amenities that reduce stress and even make time in the airport enjoyable).

Designed for Safety: Target Reinvents the Prescription Drug Package

Prescription drugs offer incredible health benefits, saving, prolonging, and improving countless lives. But they also create significant dangers. Every year, hundreds of thousands of people suffer from misuse of medications, either by overdose, taking the wrong drug, misreading the directions, or some other kind of error. Many die from the mistakes; many more get ill. According to one poll, 60 percent of prescription-drug users have taken medication incorrectly.[4] Another study attributes at least 7,000 deaths a year to medication errors.[5]

Now imagine that you are the CEO of Target, the innovative discount retailer known for stylish, affordable home products, kicky fashions, and visually striking TV commercials. You're engaged in an ongoing battle against the colossus of discount stores, Wal-Mart, continually seeking new ways of stealing market share and profitability from the world's largest retailer. It isn't easy. Wal-Mart has far more locations, a much larger revenue base, and a big competitive head start, especially in such categories as groceries, cosmetics, and health and beauty aids— important categories because they drive daily visits to the store.

In this context, what does the national problem of misused prescription drugs mean for you as the CEO of Target?

If you are risk-averse, it might make you want to shy away from the prescription drug business altogether. Why take a chance on a multi-million-dollar lawsuit if a Target customer dies after mistakenly overdosing on a medication one of your pharmacists dispensed?

Or it might drive you to take defensive measures: Insist that pharmacy customers sign waivers eliminating their right to sue you. Post big signs warning customers about the dangers of medication errors. Simply stop carrying some of the most risky drugs. Hey, you'll probably lose some customers as a result, but isn't that better than taking a chance?

Target chose neither approach. Instead, it recognized that the safety issues surrounding prescription drugs offered a fabulous opportunity for creative problem solving. And they tackled the issue using Target's characteristic weapon—innovative design. Specifically, a brilliant new approach to prescription drug packaging designed to improve readability, enhance ease-of-use, and reduce errors—preventing illnesses and saving lives in the process.

Actually, the new packaging didn't start with a Target initiative. It was the brainchild of a 29-year-old independent designer named Deborah Adler. After Adler's grandmother Helen accidentally swallowed pills prescribed for her husband, Herman, Adler realized that the weaknesses of traditional pill bottles made errors all too likely. She decided to create a new design as a thesis project for a Master of Fine Arts degree at New York's School of Visual Arts. A creative director at Target saw the design, understood its value, and purchased the patent.

Adler's new design improves on traditional drug packaging in a host of ways:

- The broader, flatter bottle shape provides a larger surface area, making the label easier to read and allowing the use of larger type.
- The name of the medicine is printed on the top of the bottle, so it's easy to read even if kept in a drawer.
- A color-coded rubber ring fits around the neck of the bottle, each color assigned to a different family member. This makes it harder to mistakenly grab someone else's medicine, even if several people share a cabinet.
- The label and directions—traditionally inconsistent and often confusing—have been redesigned with a clear hierarchy of importance. Drug name, dosage, and instructions for use appear on top; less-important data like the doctor's name appear below a horizontal line.
- New, simpler warning symbols were designed by Adler in partnership with famed graphic artist Milton Glaser (known, among other things, for creating the world-famous "I♥NY" tourism logo). And subtle but important changes in wording have been specified. For example, the word *daily* is used rather than *once*, since the latter means "eleven" to Spanish-speaking customers.
- More detailed information (such as side effects) appears on a card tucked behind the label rather than on a separate, easy-to-lose sheet.
- The new, easier-to-grip bottle is bright red, which is not only Target's distinctive color but also the universal symbol for "caution."

By mid-2005, the new design was being rolled out at more than a thousand Target pharmacies across the nation. Under the name of ClearRx, the redesign program also included a new, easier-to-use dispenser for children's liquid medicines.

ClearRx provides obvious safety benefits to Target's customers. What does it do for the company?

First, it offers big reputational benefits. Target has long been admired as the chic, smart place to find bargains. When ClearRx was trumpeted with glowing stories in national publications, the company's image as one of the most creative and consumer-friendly businesses was further enhanced.

Second, it provides a huge competitive edge to Target in its battle for market share. Pharmacy is the fastest-growing retailing sector, and Target's research shows that its pharmacy customers spend three to five times as much as the average Target shopper.[6] With Target pharmacies multiplying at the rate of 100 to 150 per year, anything that lures customers away from other retailers is important and valuable.

Third, it identifies Target in the minds of customers as a leader in providing safe, user-friendly health aids. Over the long term, the effect on the Target brand name may extend well beyond pharmacy sales. Fourteen Target stores (in Minnesota and Maryland) already include emergency health clinics, operated by a firm called MinuteClinics and staffed by nurse practitioners. The clinics provide quick diagnoses and treatments for simple ailments like sore throats and stomachaches while attracting extra foot traffic to Target. And of course, the vast majority of prescriptions written by the clinic's nurse practitioners are filled at the Target pharmacy. Eventually, Target may be positioned as the favorite provider of fast, low-cost health care in the United States.

For the average business, a problem like misused prescription drugs might appear to be simply a headache and a liability. Target recognized the problem as an opportunity to provide its customers with an extra measure of security in a dangerous world—and to profit handsomely in the process.

YOUR BIG AHA'S

Here are some of the broadly applicable lessons to be learned from the success of Target's innovative ClearRx program.

Look at the security issues your customers face, and try to come up with innovative solutions. Stop thinking about your customers' security challenges simply as negatives—fodder for complaints or lawsuits. Instead, think about how you can address them in creative ways and thereby seize a competitive advantage.

Rethink your business—especially those aspects that most people take for granted. The traditional amber-colored prescription pill bottle had remained virtually unchanged for the past 50 years. Its look was so familiar that for most customers—and certainly for most pharmacists—it was practically invisible, the last thing one would consider changing. That's precisely the kind of business element you most want to reexamine in search of the hidden opportunity for innovation.

Scour the world for new ideas. ClearRx came to pass when a Target manager, aware that his company was in search of a competitive edge for its pharmacy business, encountered Deborah Adler's design innovation in a roundup of student work. Smart organization leaders spend some of their time looking everywhere for fresh ideas, even in some of the most unlikely places. Most of the wells you'll drill this way may come up dry, but you'll come up with one or two gushers that may be worth millions.

Remember that special customer groups may have special security needs. Don't examine your organizational practices only from the point of view of the average customer. Also consider those who are distinctly different. Part of what makes ClearRx such an effective program is that it provides benefits to such subgroups of Target customers as children (the liquid medicine dispenser), the nearsighted (larger label fonts), and Latinos (simple English labeling that can't be confused with Spanish).

The Worm That Ate My Brain: Microsoft Gets Serious about Security

Personal computers are miracle machines, making all kinds of activities easier, faster, and more fun, from playing games, filing your income taxes, and catching up on the news to swapping photos, collecting pop songs, and editing movies. They can also be incredibly mystifying, frustrating, and even frightening. No other gadget—not even that window into the world's cultures known as television—brings more weird, unnerving, and sometimes dangerous stuff into our homes . . . especially since the advent of the Internet, the information superhighway on which worms, viruses, spam, and spyware make up half the traffic.

Using computers isn't physically risky. But it poses huge threats to our psychological security. Among the more benign dangers are adware; these stealth programs create pop-up ads that are annoying and almost impossible to eliminate once they infiltrate your machine. More devilish are fraudulent e-mails and phishing messages that seek to separate you from your money, stealth programs designed by hackers that hijack your computer for ulterior purposes or slow its workings to a crawl, and (worst of all) worms that can destroy your computer's memory and with it thousands of hours' worth of work or irreplaceable data.

You might assume that Microsoft—the world's largest and richest company in the computer business, and the one with the most at stake—would have always been at the forefront in the quest for computer security. Until fairly recently, however, you would have been wrong.

For years, Microsoft resisted calls to focus on computer security. The company had been built on the promise of cheap, fast, easy-to-use software. In the days before broadband, when most PCs worked on a stand-alone basis, the risk from hackers was small, and designing software with built-in safeguards was unnecessary. Even as Internet use spread and with it the danger of infection, Microsoft was loath to invest the time and money needed to retool its major programs. Would anyone really pay a premium for a hackerproof version of Windows? Bill Gates and company doubted it.

That began to change in 2001, a year when people's sense of their personal safety dramatically shifted for the worse, and not just because of 9/11. That was the year when worms and viruses with names like Slammer, Blaster, Sobig, and Mydoom began to wreak havoc on Windows-based computers around the world, causing an angry revolt among millions of Microsoft customers. Newspapers blasted the company for its lax approach to safety: "MICROSOFT WINDOWS: INSECURE BY DESIGN," declared the *Washington Post*.[7] Rival operating system Linux—less widely used than Windows and therefore less frequently targeted by hackers—began to make serious inroads in the corporate marketplace, and the chief information officer of General

Motors threatened to replace his company's 125,000 PCs with Apple or Linux machines.

Belatedly, Microsoft responded. The giant company actually suspended its entire vast programming development effort for two months in 2002 so that its 20,000 programmers could attend remedial classes on security.[8] It was the start of a cultural revolution inside Microsoft. The deeper the company and its army of brilliant nerds plunged into the world of hackery, the more they realized that fixing the security problem would require more than a one-time investment.

Like most important initiatives at Microsoft, the evolution in attitudes can be traced through the shifting messages delivered by the company's founder and CEO. At first, Gates appeared to underestimate the difficulty of the problem. As late as January 2004, he was brashly promising to rid the world of spam within two years. (If you've looked at your e-mail inbox lately, you know that promise shows no sign of being kept.)

By March 2004, Gates was backing away from the "no more spam" promise and adopting a more realistic approach. In a 3,200-word e-mail to his colleagues, he acknowledged that "security is as big and important a challenge as our industry has ever tackled," and declared that a massive rethinking of the company's processes was needed to solve the problem.

In August 2004, Microsoft launched a major salvo into the security wars—a new software package called Service Pack 2. The cryptic name obscures the importance of the product—a free download that fixes thousands of flaws in Windows XP that had rendered the software vulnerable to attack by hackers. Creating Service Pack 2 cost Microsoft a reported one billion dollars. It's a huge sum, but an essential investment in the long-term health of the company, whose viability is totally dependent on consumer trust.

Now Microsoft is retooling the entire software development process to put security at its center. Today, programmers at the company are required to document the security aspects of every feature as they create it, listing ways a hacker might attack it and the protective devices they intend to install. After a section of program is written, hackers are hired to do their worst, uncovering weaknesses that made it through the development process so they can be corrected before the program is released. It's expensive and time-consuming; security issues have delayed the release of Vista, the new version of Windows, from mid-2006 until at least January, 2007, costing Microsoft billions more.[9]

Today, Microsoft has dedicated a thousand engineers and about one billion dollars per year to fixing security problems. That's almost one-sixth of the company's huge research and development budget. But this may be a significant underestimate of the resources Microsoft is devoting to security. In a recent interview, Bill Gates described the portion of Vista development monies going to security issues at between 30 and 40 percent of the total, depending on definitions.[10]

If any company can battle the hackers to a standstill, it is Microsoft. But every move Bill Gates makes is matched by several moves on the attackers' side. New viruses are being invented all the time, and some of the world's most dangerous people are said to be looking for ways to employ them as weapons. Richard Forno, a former senior security analyst for the House of Representatives, calls Microsoft "a threat to national security." As Forno explains, most of the U.S. government, including the White House, Congress, and the Department of Defense runs Windows, offering a "target-rich environment for malicious code" that hackers can easily access through e-mail.[11]

No wonder one commentator on high-tech business has remarked, "The more you look at the world of Windows the more you wonder how Microsoft coders sleep at night."[12] And no wonder Bill Gates insists, "Security is our top priority. I can't see that changing any time soon."[13]

Will online dangers spell an end to the world of personal computing? No more than the terror attacks of 9/11 have destroyed travel and tourism, or medication errors have shuttered the prescription drug business. But it's clear that lack of security can severely damage entire sectors of our economy. Just as travel fell measurably in the aftermath of 9/11, it seems likely that the spread of computing, the Internet, and e-commerce have been slowed by fears of spam, worms, and viruses. And if Microsoft and other computer companies don't find solutions soon, their efforts to take over the living rooms of America by providing hardware and software for managing music, video, and other forms of entertainment are likely to be slowed as well.

What all the stories in this chapter bring home is that the quest for customer security creates definite winners and losers. Organizations that understand our needs for physical and psychological safety, and that develop innovative ways of meeting those needs, will outcompete others—particularly in today's stressed-out, post-9/11, post-Katrina world.

Without a sense of security, nothing gets done. It's just that simple.

Your Big Aha's

What can you learn from the struggles of Microsoft to make computing safe and secure? Here are some of the most important lessons that apply to any organization.

Security isn't optional—it's the price of admission. Microsoft fell behind in the battle for computer security because it initially considered antihacking technology a luxury that few users would pay for. Today it is playing an expensive and risky game of catch-up as it desperately tries to retool its vast, complicated operating system to retrofit security features that could have been integrated from the beginning.

Customer security should be on the agenda of every *department.* Giving your customers a sense of safety and freedom when they use your products or services can't be outsourced to a security department or applied like a fresh coat of paint. Think about security issues from the very start of the process of designing your offerings, just as Microsoft's programmers are now striving to build safety into software from the very first line of code.

Your customers' security needs represent a moving target. Whether the enemy is terrorism, crime, or computer hackers, or impersonal forces like natural disasters or human errors, the threats to your customers' sense of safety are constantly changing. This means that security can't be addressed by a one-time-only program. Instead, you need to constantly monitor the mind-set of your customers, strive to understand what they fear or worry about, and continually seek new ways of allaying those concerns and making them feel comfortable with you.

Growth depends on your customers' trust. Your customers' sense of vulnerability will vary greatly. Some will be like power users of computers, relatively unconcerned about risks and happy to ignore minor dangers. Others will be insecure and fearful, and will shy away from your products or services if you don't take special care to make them feel safe. To attract new customers or expand your business into new arenas (as computer companies are hoping to expand into the world of entertainment), you need to win the confidence of an ever-growing universe of users. Which means that yesterday's security solutions—even if they were effective—will not be good enough for tomorrow.

CHAPTER 7

Open-Door Policy

The Challenge of Transparency

IT IS A BIT IRONIC: EVEN AS TODAY'S STRESS-FILLED, DANGEROUS WORLD creates new customer demands for security, safety, and peace of mind, customers are also demanding unprecedented levels of openness. One of the major trends defining world-class customer service today is finding ways to let people access enough information about their accounts, your products and services, and your organization's processes and policies. They want to feel truly at home when they patronize your organization, can communicate with you interactively about their needs and problems, and can even handle many transactions on their own, without the help of a company intermediary. It's called *transparency*.

Why is this ironic? Because in many ways, the demand for security and the demand for transparency cut in opposite directions. On the one hand, security is, at least in part, about restrictions that limit free access to your organization's spaces (whether virtual or real) and to information about your customers, so that no one with bad intent can harm or take advantage of them. This kind of security is exemplified by the new trends in airport design and the battle against computer hackers and viruses described in Chapter 6.

Security is also about artfully controlling and designing the flow of information to make it easy for your customers to find, choose, and use your products or services without being distracted or confused by irrelevant, false, or misleading information. This is the kind of security that Target is pioneering with its new pharmaceutical package designs.

On the other hand, transparency, is about removing restrictions and controls—eliminating barriers to the flow of ideas and data, so that anyone can move freely into and around your organization, glimpse its inner workings, and use them for their personal benefit. A completely transparent organization would let anyone inside, giving them access to all information at all times.

Thus, perfect security and perfect transparency can't logically coexist. Yet, in these troubled times, customers often seem to be demanding and expecting both—or at least a close approximation of both.

The challenge for organizational leaders lies in balancing the value of transparency with the realistic need for confidentiality about certain data; expectations of privacy regarding customer information; and the need to avoid overwhelming the client with too much information and too many choices.

This chapter describes how organizations in some of the world's most complex and data-laden industries are tackling these challenges; how they are developing user-friendly ways to share information that allows clients to manage their own transactions and find answers to their questions without needing expensive human assistance, thereby saving everyone time, money, and energy; and how they are using ever-more-ingenious technological and managerial systems to provide the right kinds of openness while controlling the flow of sensitive data. There is also a discussion of the continuing challenges involved in balancing transparency with customer security and the organization's internal needs. In the case of business organizations, it includes the all-important demand for profitability.

Letting in the Sunshine: Bringing Transparency to Big Government

When you think about positive customer experiences, government bureaucracy is probably one of the last things to come to mind. After all, government agencies have all the characteristics of organizations that we would expect to be the opposite of customercentric, responsive, open, and flexible. Consider:

- Governments by definition do not face direct competition from other organizations, which eliminates the pressure that forces many organizations to improve their customer service.
- Government employees are often shielded from firing and other disciplinary measures by civil service rules and union contracts. (Over the past 30 years, government employees have become this country's major remaining bastion of union power.) So the fear of losing job security that helps to motivate most private-sector employees is less intense among government workers.
- Government agencies are driven by mandates embodied in legislation or executive orders, both of which in turn are shaped by electoral strategies, interest-group pressures, and horse-trading among politicians. So agency leaders can't develop programs and policies based purely on what's best for their customers.
- Government budgets are derived primarily from taxes and divvied up among agencies by executive and legislative action once a year. This means that agencies don't have any profit-based incentive to provide better service, since they won't have any more money to spend no matter how great the service they provide. And government workers earn salaries based on statutory mandates, civil service rules, or union contracts, so incentives to provide great service are lacking on an individual basis as well.
- The selection of top leaders of government agencies is sometimes based on political favoritism, cronyism, personal loyalty, party affiliation, or interest-group demands rather than on experience, competence, and intelligence.

Considering these structural characteristics of government work, most of which are difficult or impossible to change, it's not surprising that government agencies find customer service an ongoing challenge. In fact, just the opposite is true: The degree to which government departments—including such generally well-regarded agencies as the Social Security Administration, the National Parks, and the Veterans

Administration—succeed in providing good service is fairly amazing and a tribute to the staffs and leaders of those agencies.

Today, some government agencies—spurred by pressures from politicians and interest groups demanding smaller and leaner government, as well as increasing demands from constituents for service comparable to that received in the private sector—have begun reinventing themselves, shaking off their traditional lethargy and adopting some of the customercentric policies that the private sector has developed.

In particular, some notoriously hidebound government bureaucracies are starting to learn the benefits of transparency, using new electronic technologies to make it easier for their citizen-clients to help themselves to information and services instead of relying on help from overworked government employees.

The popular E-ZPass electronic toll-collection system is an example of the way in which new technologies are streamlining government processes and making life easier for customers. Traditionally, the process of collecting tolls was a black box that customers experienced purely passively, from the outside: Their only role was to ante up the (ever-increasing) fees charged by local authorities at toll-collection stations for driving on bridges, tunnels, and highways around the country. Drivers had to remember to bring cash on car trips, had to fumble with exact change and paper receipts, and faced delays as traffic backed up behind toll booths, especially during rush hours. And the need to employ human toll collectors ate up a sizable fraction of the tolls collected, diverting the funds from their intended purpose of highway and bridge maintenance.

The advent of E-ZPass in the mid-1990s changed all that. Now a part of the toll-collection system has actually been transferred into the hands of the driver, in the form of an electronic scanner affixed to the windshield of the car and an E-ZPass account accessible via mail, phone, or the Internet. Drivers using E-ZPass no longer have to wait in line; instead, they breeze through special lanes where it takes just a second or two to read the scanner signal. Fewer cars idling in congested toll plazas means lower fuel consumption and air pollution. There's no more handling of cash, change-making, or fussing with paper receipts for tax or expense-account purposes; an E-ZPass statement delivered electronically or by mail conveniently details all toll expenses. And because E-ZPass costs less to administer than traditional toll-taking, users of the system get a welcome discount on their tolls.

Bridge, highway, and transportation departments from a dozen northeastern states and parts of Canada now participate in E-ZPass. Customers love it: When 15,000 randomly selected E-ZPass users were surveyed recently, 92.7 percent praised the service.[1] Similar systems are up and running around the country, from FasTrak in California to SunPass in Florida and I-Pass in Illinois.[2]

E-ZPass is a simple example of how government agencies are finding more customer-friendly, user-accessible ways of providing services. Now even the dreaded state departments of motor vehicles (DMVs), where generations of drivers have spent countless millions of hours waiting in line to renew their car registrations or drivers' licenses, are beginning to pursue the virtues of transparency in their programming.

Around the country, DMVs are adopting a wide range of transparency strategies, with varying degrees of effectiveness. In Massachusetts, the DMV has begun opening drive-through windows that allow motorists to handle routine paperwork without having to park their cars and wait in line, perhaps with small children in tow.[3]

In California, an Internet-based information systems lets drivers learn with a few mouse clicks how long the current wait for a drivers license or car registration will be at any DMV office, so they can pick the location where the lines are shortest. Once they arrive, a computerized line-management system, modeled on the FASTPASS system used at Disney theme parks, assigns them a numbered ticket so they don't need to physically wait in line for service.[4]

Best of all, in many states, a wide range of DMV services can now be accessed entirely online, eliminating many in-person visits altogether. In Virginia, drivers now have to show up at a DMV office just once every 10 years for a vision test.[5]

E-ZPass and improved DMV service are effective examples of making government operations more transparent and easier to use, but they are limited in scope. The most ambitious attempts to introduce transparency to a broad range of government services are the 311 nonemergency telephone information services now in operation in some 20 cities around the United States. The success of 311, as well as the problems it continues to grapple with, illustrates the power of transparency programs as well as the challenges involved in designing and implementing them.

The 311 concept dates back to 1996, when the U.S. Department of Justice proposed using the number as a general-information alternative to the nationwide 911 emergency system. The following year, the Federal Communications Commission directed phone companies to set aside 311 for nonemergency calls for government information, and within a few years cities such as Chicago, Dallas, Detroit, Baltimore, and San Jose had set up 311 programs.

The nation's biggest and most complex 311 system was launched in New York City on March 9, 2003. The reasons for the complexity are apparent. Not only is New York the most diverse and populous city in the United States, it also boasts the largest and most complicated city government. With its annual budget of $52.9 billion (larger than the budgets of all but four states), its five county-sized boroughs (just one of which, Brooklyn, would be the nation's fourth-largest city all by itself), and its maze of agencies, departments, commissions, bureaus, and divisions, each with its historically determined fiefdoms and power centers, New York's government is overwhelmingly complex. No wonder many say that being mayor of New York City is the second-toughest job in the United States.

The 311 telephone system helps citizens make sense of this complexity by providing a measure of transparency about city government. Callers can get information about government services, register complaints, ask about volunteer activities or small business programs, get schedules for city events, or offer an opinion to be passed along to the mayor's office. A citizen who calls to complain about a specific problem—missing swings in a city playground, excessive noise from a party or car alarm, or a blocked sewer on a neighborhood street—receives a tracking number to use when seeking a progress report.

Mayor Michael Bloomberg began planning for the implementation of 311 soon after his election in 2001, thanks in part to the urging of one of his daughters. Today, he is the program's most enthusiastic booster. In fact, he has called the number personally dozens of times, usually to report potholes, broken schoolroom windows, or streets in need of sweeping.[6] Perhaps it's not surprising that Bloomberg is a fan of the system; before entering public service, he made a fortune by founding and building Bloomberg, Inc., the highly successful financial and general-interest data company, so he knows a thing or two about the value of electronic information systems.

Since New York's 311 service was launched, 300 full-time and 200 part-time operators ensconced in a 45,000-square-foot call center in Lower Manhattan have fielded over 32 million calls, an average of some 40,000 calls per day. The city claims that the average call is answered by a live operator within 14 seconds. Each operator undergoes four weeks of training in the complexities of city government as well as the niceties of phone etiquette—an important and difficult challenge when fielding problems from distraught, sometimes confused or belligerent citizens. As befits the world's most polyglot city, New York 311 is equipped to handle some 170 languages. (English and Spanish are used in the vast majority of the calls, but translators for the other 168 languages are always on call and can be patched in to the phone line as needed.[7])

Backing up the human operators is a complicated and impressive set of computer programs and databases that can provide needed data on a mind-boggling array of problems, usually within seconds. The "geo-codes" system can take a caller's address and instantly divine his or her local community board, school district, voting location, and police precinct—essential data that few citizens know by heart. Another program can quickly identify the specific city agency charged with tackling even the most arcane problem. When a woman in the Bronx, embroiled in a rent dispute with her landlord, found a live, "rather menacing" chicken placed outside her front door, the operator who took her call typed "Chicken on stoop" into the computer terminal and was promptly informed that the Department of Health would tackle the case.[8]

The program has undergone significant modification and expansion since its inception. In July 2004, on the eve of the Republican National Convention in New York, 311 worked with NYC & Company, the city's nonprofit tourism agency, to add travel, entertainment, dining, and cultural information to the menu of services—concert schedules, museum exhibits, restaurant recommendations, and the like. Now citywide calendars of events and lists of activities are continually updated and organized by location, so a caller can learn whether a street fair has been canceled due to rain, find out which performers are slated to appear at a free concert in Central Park, or locate the municipal golf course or city pool that is closest to the caller's home.[9]

In November 2005, the city announced a plan to partner with the local United Way to use 311 to provide information on social services offered by over 2,500 private, nonprofit organizations in fields such as health care, housing, and job training.[10]

The direct benefits provided to New Yorkers by 311 are impressive. But the ancillary benefits produced by its existence are equally noteworthy.

The creation of 311 has improved the efficiency of preexisting emergency service programs. In the past, New Yorkers would often call the 911 emergency line when faced with a nonlife-threatening problem—an open water main, an unplowed street, a question about parking regulations. The police department had to employ dozens of extra operators to field such calls and transfer them (in a haphazard, sometimes inaccurate fashion) to various city agencies. The advent of 311 freed up 911 to serve its intended function, making police, fire, and ambulance services more responsive. Furthermore, the existence of a working hotline for nonemergency problems has actually helped save some lives, because conditions like blocked streets, apartments without heat, or electrical failures can become life-threatening if not addressed promptly.

The implementation of 311 has also driven the streamlining and simplification of city programs. When 311 operators began fielding calls and trying to figure out how to route them, problems such as overlapping jurisdictions, confusion, and inefficiency quickly became apparent. Street signs obscured by trees used to be dealt with by both the Parks Department and the Transportation Department depending on which *part* of the tree was to blame. (If it was the trunk, it was deemed a transportation issue; if branches needed pruning, the park workers would respond.) The creation of a centralized clearinghouse for citizen complaints exposed the bureaucratic tangles. In response, city policy was changed to designate one department as the lead agency for any single type of problem.[11]

The 311 program also feeds valuable performance and customer-service data to city agencies. The constant flow of messages received from ordinary citizens via 311 allows city officials to monitor their own performance in dozens of areas. City transportation commissioner Iris Weinshall says she spends several hours a month monitoring 311 call data. "It keeps you on your toes," Weinshall told a reporter. The stream of data leads directly to improved service: A flood of pothole calls to 311 after a harsh winter in 2003 prompted Weinshall to assign an extra 150 workers to street-repair duty, reducing the complaint backlog from 3,000 to 975. In a different department, complaints about illegal trash dumping received via 311 are being plotted on a city map to identify problem areas where improved enforcement of sanitation rules may be necessary.[12]

Best of all, 311 has provided these benefits at a surprisingly moderate cost. Obviously, it's not cheap to create a new call center, hire and train operators, provide 24-hour service, and publicize and promote the program. But 311 has absorbed some 40 other service centers and hotline programs operated by individual city agencies, producing efficiencies of scale and greatly reduced expenses.

New York 311 has been so successful and popular that more cities, including Philadelphia and San Francisco, are now planning to launch their own 311 programs. And even for-profit organizations are taking notice. The editor of a business magazine devoted to customer service praised 311 in a recent editorial and called it a challenge to businesses: "People will start to wonder, even if unconsciously, why they get better service from New York City than they do from their phone company. Or their airline."[13]

No system for providing customer service is perfect, and that applies to New York 311. The still-young system is struggling to achieve some of its goals, and the problems it faces teach us almost as much about the challenge of transparency as do its successes.

One problem is simply handling the vast number of calls that have flooded the highly popular program. Most calls to 311 get through quickly. But failed attempts, even if relatively few in number, may pose a real challenge for the city. Research has shown that people are far more likely to tell their acquaintances about bad experiences with customer service than good ones, which suggests that frustrated New Yorkers who can't get through to the help line are likely to spread their dissatisfaction to several friends and neighbors. If this happens often enough, it will put a real crimp in the city's well-intentioned and otherwise successful effort to put a friendly and open face on government.

Another problem is that many New Yorkers are still unaware of the existence of 311 or are hesitant to use it. Although fully 65 percent of New Yorkers are either immigrants or children of immigrants, just 2 percent of 311 calls are in a language other than English. It appears that large numbers of immigrant New Yorkers—many of whom are surely among the city residents most in need of vital government services—have shied away from using the service.[14]

City officials and advocates for immigrants' groups have been grappling with this problem. Some would-be callers may be afraid of giving their name to a government official, especially if their legal immigration status is in question. After all, government has a coercive law-enforcement role as well as a friendly service-provider role to play.

In response to such concerns, the city has established a strict privacy policy for 311 calls, under which client information may be used only for four specific purposes:

1. To efficiently address client needs.
2. To conduct and improve city business and/or services.
3. To help provide emergency assistance, if necessary.
4. As otherwise required by law.[15]

Not all residents of New York are aware of the privacy policy, and some are probably skeptical about the government's readiness to enforce its own rules. The difficulty of convincing all New Yorkers to feel comfortable using the 311 service illustrates one of the challenges for any transparency program: Customers must feel confident that they can trust your organization with any personal information they provide. Otherwise, they simply won't take advantage of any program you offer, no matter how impressive its benefits.

From the perspective of city leaders, another difficulty created by the 311 system is the flood of statistics it creates about citizen attitudes toward government service—the same flood of statistics described earlier as a great boon. Think about it this way: Data about customer satisfaction always represents a double-edged sword. When customers are happy, everyone in the organization is proud, pleased, and prepared to claim the credit. But when customers are unhappy, those responsible may wish the details weren't so readily available. For this reason, transparency programs often end up under internal siege, as organizational leaders are tempted to try to shut down the flow of information whenever it turns negative.

For New York City government, an annual report card of sorts is issued every September when the Mayor's Management Report is publicly released. The report includes data on government performance in dozens of areas, from street cleaning to infant mortality to bus and subway crime. Since 2003, these data have been greatly augmented by information gleaned from compilations of 311 phone call statistics. And when the data are negative, the 311 program itself becomes part of the predictable controversy.

In September 2004, the Mayor's Management Report showed an increase in the number of complaints about police misconduct directed to the Civilian Complaint Review Board. Some observers wondered whether the creation of 311 as an easy way of registering a complaint had actually fueled the increase. The answer wasn't obvious. Those who were eager to defend the police suspected that the telephone hotline made it all too easy for citizens to go on record with groundless complaints, but a city spokesperson was dubious: "It's very difficult to tell what makes them [complaints] go up or what makes them go down. But the increases started before 311 became available."

In any case, the availability of performance data facilitated by 311 puts city officials under even greater pressure than in the past to continually improve services. It is another lesson that any organizational leader considering a new transparency program needs to take seriously. Once the world has access to more information about your performance, you may hope to receive more credit for the things you do right—but you can be sure you'll receive more blame for the things you do wrong.

YOUR BIG AHA'S

Your organization may never create a transparency program with the scope of 311—or even of E-ZPass. But here are some important lessons any organization grappling with new demands for transparency can learn from government efforts to open informational doors to customers.

Transparency offers opportunities to learn—take advantage of them. Feedback from the 311 program is giving New York City administrators invaluable new insights into the workings of city government, from systemic glitches that formerly went unnoticed to detailed, week-to-week data on how well agencies are managing quality-of-life problems. If your organization creates a system that allows customers to communicate interactively with you, don't ignore the valuable data it generates; instead, use it to improve your policies and your performance.

Balancing security and transparency isn't easy. The two-way communication that is inherent in transparency requires genuine trust on both sides. If customers are to take advantage of the benefits your transparency program offers, they need to be assured that their personal information won't be used in ways they can't control or don't approve of.

Don't launch a transparency program until you're ready to live up to your customer promises. Transparency implies a willingness to expose your strengths and weaknesses publicly. It also implies a promise: "We will listen to the messages you send us and respond as effectively and promptly as possible." If your service program isn't up to snuff, or if you and your people are simply not ready to commit themselves to the kind of public scrutiny that transparency makes possible, start by revamping those weaknesses before opening yourself to the glare of the spotlight.

Transparency programs need to evolve continually. As customer demands and expectations change, your transparency efforts need

> to change in tandem. A level of service considered acceptable—even superlative—today is likely to appear inadequate just a year or two down the road. Just as New York City has added major new components to its 311 service within just three years of its creation, you need to consider improvements and enhancements for your own transparency program from the very day it is launched.

"A Peek into the Stockroom":
Customers Probe the Secrets of the Travel Business

The travel industry may not be as bureaucratic, complicated, or frustrating as big government; but don't tell that to the harried road warrior trying to navigate the maze of fares, ticket classes, restrictions, blackout dates, discounts, and upgrades that separates the customer from the best possible deal when buying an airline ticket or reserving a hotel room. You can understand why savvy travelers have begun taking matters into their own hands. Dissatisfied with the level of service and the clarity of information they get from travel agents or direct from the airlines and hotel chains, they are flocking to a host of web sites that specialize in unearthing, pooling, sharing, and interpreting travel information. Call it "do-it-yourself" transparency—if the industry won't readily provide the data, travelers will pry it out of them.

Travel information web sites take several forms. Some sites specialize in customer chat forums where travelers participate in uninhibited exchanges about the highs and lows of the travel experience. Along the way, they also share their insights into how the travel industry works, as well as the strategies they've found effective for getting the best deals and the most enjoyable travel experiences.

Two of the most popular such sites are FlyerTalk (at flyertalk.com) and TripAdvisor (at tripadvisor.com). Both are worth a visit when planning your next trip.

On FlyerTalk, there are dozens of specialized forums, open to anyone willing to spend a few seconds becoming a registered member. They are devoted to almost every imaginable aspect of the travel and hospitality experience. Every major frequent flyer program (and most of the minor ones, too) has its own forum where travelers swap stories, tips, and strategies for accumulating and using miles. Some write about their "mileage runs," flight sequences designed and flown specifically to earn the maximum number of miles in the shortest period of time.

FlyerTalk also features TravelBuzz! and DiningBuzz! Forums where members write about anything on their minds, from questions about airport security rules and luggage requirements to such offbeat travel-related topics as, "Have you ever seen Air Force One in real life?" to "Anyone have any good suggestions for killing five travel days between Clovis, New Mexico, and Cedar City, Utah?" There's a Travel Technology forum where members discuss the latest cell phones, laptop computers, MP3 players, and other road gear, as well as forums devoted to the needs of specialized traveler groups—women, gays and lesbians, the disabled, the religious, and travelers with children.

The TripAdvisor site has some overlap with FlyerTalk as well as some unique elements. It features members' accounts of travel adventures (and misadventures) that you can search by focusing on specific destinations (e.g., Barcelona, Spain), specific hotels or resorts (Hotel Montecarlo in Barcelona), favored attractions (Museu Picasso), and other travel elements. As on FlyerTalk, members can also create individual threads to launch dialogues on topics of interest to them: "Should I take euros or travelers checks when visiting Barcelona this summer?" "Are there any quaint villages within a day trip of Barcelona?" "What would it be like to spend Christmas in Barcelona? Will the restaurants be open on Christmas eve?"

TripAdvisor also has a Candid Photos section where members post their favorite snapshot from recent travels, and a goList section where members share personal recommendation lists ranging from a week's worth of restaurants in Provincetown, Massachusetts, to seven sights worth seeing during a weekend in Toronto. Other members can rate the lists for usefulness and accuracy, which provides an easy way to decide which lists to print out for your next vacation.

Both FlyerTalk and TripAdvisor are filled with interesting and potentially valuable information, which is why hundreds of thousands of people have discovered these sites and visit them frequently. These fans represent a huge audience of avid travelers that many businesses are eager to communicate with. It has buying clout even greater than their numbers would suggest. Randy Peterson, who runs FlyerTalk, quotes a 2002 McKinsey study that found users of Internet chat rooms represented just one-third of visitors to online retailing sites but generated two-thirds of their sales.[16]

So smart companies in the travel and tourism industry are piggybacking some of their own communications strategies onto these sites, trying to spin the transparency the sites provide to their own advantage. Top executives of Continental Airlines and SAS have met with FlyerTalk members to glean their insights into the needs, interests, likes, and dislikes of travelers.[17] Hilton Hotels and Starwood Hotels & Resorts provide live links on FlyerTalk to their corporate web sites. And Starwood has even assigned an employee to spend six to eight hours a week on the forums, reading items posted by members and, where appropriate, offering an official response on behalf of the company. His name is William Sanders, although he uses the name "Starwood Lurker" as his online tag. (In online parlance, a "lurker" is someone who reads dialogues on a web site without participating in them. It is actually an inaccurate moniker for Sanders, since he actively participates in the travel forums at FlyerTalk.[18])

Companies like Starwood that take part in the online chat rooms have found that responding to customer complaints and questions in these live, uncensored forums without coming across as a programmed suit is a lot harder than it looks. Online "spokesposting" requires a large dose of candor, including a willingness to confess to corporate screwups when they occur; readiness to do a bit of digging to uncover the real facts behind an irate guest's online horror story; an utter lack of defensiveness (since getting your back up and responding with sarcasm or hostility even to an unfair complaint is a sure way of making enemies); and, perhaps most important, a touch of self-deprecating humor.

Travel forum sites like FlyerTalk and TripAdvisor peel away one layer of opacity from the travel business by letting customers share and compare experiences. ("X airline told you they never provide a free upgrade if you get bumped from your original flight? Well, I had the same problem, and they told me something different.") Other web sites go even further, allowing travelers to actually dive into the once-secret inner workings of the airlines' online reservations systems.

At web sites like ExpertFlyer.com and itasoftware.com, tools for finding special fare offers and upgrades are provided for use by expert travelers who are willing to invest time and energy in mastering the arcane codes and systems used by travel agents and the airlines themselves. Armed with these tools, travelers can now actually pick and choose flights from among hundreds of fare and rule categories, often saving hundreds or even thousands of dollars in the process.

Here's one traveler's account of the experience:

> A few weeks ago, I was checking New York-London on American for the Fourth of July weekend and was offered a lowest price of $1,450, not including taxes and fees. Without restrictions, the lowest coach price was $2,910—full-fare in coach. But ExpertFlyer found a B-class round-trip of $1,644 without taxes, which was only $194 more than the cheapest coach ticket. [B-class is a special category of low-priced coach seats that upgrade for only 10,000 frequent flyer miles each way—half of what normal upgrades cost.] If you upgrade, you'd save more than $300 and 30,000 miles over buying the cheapest fare. And if you simply wanted the flexibility of a fully refundable ticket, you saved more than $1,200 by buying B-class instead of a full Y-class fare.[19]

In effect, these sites allow customers to browse the airline industry's trove of customized professional data, scanning lists of seats available at particular price points and other information once restricted to travel agents and the airlines. ("Basically, you're peeking into the airline's stockroom," as the traveler quoted above put it.) It's a degree of transparency that few industries are willing to permit; and it's especially valuable in the travel business, where arcane pricing rules and computerized "yield management" systems designed to maximize revenues from various classes of travelers lead to wildly varying fares on the exact same flight.

You might think that the airlines would fight tooth and nail to stop this trend toward customer-driven transparency. Some are. But a few airlines, recognizing that the instantaneous, incredibly easy transmission of information made possible by the Internet is making corporate secrecy increasingly difficult to maintain, have begun working with the web sites rather than against them. American, Air France, and Qantas provide visitors to ExpertFlyer with access to their frequent-flyer award inventory data, and American and Delta provide upgrade availability information.

Other airlines are still keeping this information private, forcing customers to visit their own sites or talk to a travel agent or airline rep to get the data. But it's probably only a matter of time before one of the existing travel web sites—or some new entrant—develops a program for translating airline frequent-flyer inventory and upgrade data into a format travelers can easily use, forcing a further degree of transparency on a reluctant industry.

The current state of play in the travel business might be called partial or hidden transparency; large swaths of information are publicly available, but only to customers who know which web sites to visit and are willing to invest some time in learning the codes and the rules of the game. The situation offers obvious benefits to a minority of fortunate customers. But it also raises questions that have no easy answers:

- Is it fair for more knowledgeable customers to enjoy markedly cheaper fares than others who don't know the secrets of ticket coding and upgrade strategies—especially since the computer-savvy travelers who access the insider web sites are likely to be individuals with greater resources than other, less well-connected flyers? Isn't this a case of "those who have, get more"?
- How will travelers feel about the fact that the amount they pay for a trip depends on their willingness and ability to play a complicated, time-consuming game of online bargain hunting? Will jealousy, envy, and suspicion be generated by the sense that an elite group of insiders are benefiting at the expense of everyone else?
- As more travelers become aware of the special deals available through the specialized web sites, will the only customers paying full fares be a minority who are too lazy or out-of-it to avail themselves of special money-saving offers? If that happens, will the industry

have simply added another layer of time-consuming effort to the task of booking a trip—a customer-unfriendly change that travelers will resent?

It would seem that there's a danger that today's partial transparency may create more negative feelings about the airlines and the travel experience than positive ones.

Joseph Turow is a professor of communication at the University of Pennsylvania who has studied the impact on marketing practices of electronic tools for gathering and managing data. Although he recognizes the power of the Internet to bring greater openness—transparency—to relationships between companies and customers, he is concerned about its potential for unfairness. Turow decries attempts by business to use variable pricing and yield management systems, augmented by new digital information-management techniques, to exploit consumer uncertainties and cherry-pick only the most profitable customers. In his book *Niche Envy: Marketing Discrimination in the Digital Age,* Turow writes:

> Much of the time, their [businesses'] recipe [for customer interaction] involves trying to take charge: attempting to inculcate a strong sense of brand trust while gathering information to decide whether or not the customer is worth engaging in customized digital relationships. But the decade-long attempts by marketers to exploit customer information in the digital world have led to an environment of mutual suspicion. Direct marketing to gain consumers' trust takes place alongside advertisers' deep fear of consumers' power and their attempts to use data on them in more ways than they want them to know (so they can profitably counteract their power). In that sense, trust and the undermining of trust often go hand in hand.[20]

In the long run, companies that try to use digital technologies to exploit or control customers rather than to inform and serve them are likely to be losers.

Consumers aren't dumb. They'll turn away from organizations that aren't honest and forthright with them. Therefore, it's dangerous for companies to think of transparency as a tool for manipulating their customers. Instead, they need to think of it as a way of entering into a new and more intimate form of partnership with customers. Otherwise, they may eventually end up with no customers at all.

Partial transparency in the travel business isn't likely to last. In the end, full-fledged transparency will prevail, and all customers will have access to complete information about how airline fares, frequent-flyer programs, hotel rates, special upgrades and discounts, and other industry systems work. Companies in the travel industry need to be preparing for that day now, making sure that their revenue-management systems will stand up to the public scrutiny they're likely to receive in the near future.

YOUR BIG AHA'S

Today's travel industry is a living experiment in how electronic tools can gradually force information into the open. Here are some of the lessons to be learned from the early stages of this transition.

Information known by one customer will eventually be known by every customer. As the Internet—the worldwide "network of networks"—evolves, millions of specialized online communities are developing whose sole purpose is to share ideas among all those who care about them. If there is not already an Internet chat room, blog, forum, or web site devoted entirely to information of interest to your customers, there soon will be. Under the circumstances, keeping secrets about your business will be increasingly difficult. Any fact known by any one of your customers is likely to become available, sooner rather than later, to all of them.

When your customers begin forcing transparency, don't fight them—join them. Smart organizations are already actively monitoring and participating in the online conversations that their customers are having about their needs and interests. When you find your organization's performance being publicly evaluated by groups of customers, don't try to squelch the discussion; instead, contribute to it in a positive way, offering information that will help ensure that you're rated fairly and that your perspective on industry problems is heard and understood.

Your most profitable customers are likely to be your best-informed customers. Those with the greatest incentive to participate in transparency programs (whether created by you or by others) are those who devote the most resources of time, energy, and money to their relationship with you. This makes participating in the conversation all the more crucial, since the people in the chat room may well include your most frequent and therefore your most important customers.

Openness is the price you pay for customer trust. Some leaders believe in the value of hoarding information, as if it were money locked in a vault. But in the digital age, that strategy doesn't work. Information gains value by being disseminated, especially when you are the one providing it. The reward your organization will receive for sharing information is the trust of your customers, along with an outsized share of their future business.

CHAPTER 8

One Size Does Not Fit All

The New Art of Customization

A KEY TO SUCCESS IN TODAY'S ULTRACOMPETITIVE BUSINESS WORLD IS offering patrons many choices of products or services, and making selection simple and pleasant rather than complicated and frustrating. It's a philosophy that was pioneered by the hospitality industry. After all, it was the innkeepers of the seventeenth century who first invented the concept of the "bill of fare," or menu, a simple list of goods on offer from which a patron might make a selection at leisure. (The idea of the printed menu is so simple and inherently convenient that it has become ubiquitous in the world of computing as a way of navigating quickly and easily among thousands of information and activity options.)

The availability of choice is especially important in today's world of vast and ever-growing global markets. Communities, cities, and nations are becoming more similar and increasingly share an international culture. Global corporations extend the reach of their brands, products, and services into every country. Worldwide media impose a growing uniformity even on the news, ideas, and entertainment that are enjoyed on every continent. As a result, consumers hunger for something different—for opportunities to enjoy experiences that are individualized and designed just for them. Perhaps it's ironic, but in a world where every TV carries CNN and MTV, every street corner has a Starbucks, and every town has a Wal-Mart, phrases like "cookie cutter" and "one size fits all" have become terms of derision.

The demand for choice, individualization, and uniqueness puts organizations that serve the public into quite a bind. If you're like most leaders, you want to reach out to as wide an audience as possible, always increasing the numbers of people whose lives you touch. But as the numbers grow, the difficulties of providing each patron with a unique experience grow even faster. How can mass offerings ever be truly customized? This is the conundrum that many organizations are now wrestling with.

Part of the answer lies in empowering your front-line employees to devise unique ad hoc solutions to your clientele's problems instead of merely following preordained policies. This means rewarding creativity and not punishing mistakes that are well intended and driven by the desire to meet a customer's need. This philosophy is built into the operations of today's best hospitality businesses, including Loews Hotels, where every housekeeper, bellman, engineer, and desk clerk knows that he or she is permitted—no, *expected*—to go outside the standard procedures when necessary to satisfy an unhappy guest or (better still) to provide that guest with a moment of unexpected satisfaction and delight.

Every experienced hotelier has a wealth of stories to share about the nonstandardized services he or she has provided when customer needs go beyond the expected. John Thacker, a regional vice president for Loews Hotels based in Santa Monica, has a couple of favorites that he likes to share. Some are simple but quirky, like the tale of the long-time customer who likes to keep a comb and hairspray stashed in the desk of John's administrative assistant, Marta. Periodically, he checks into the hotel, stops by to fix his hair, and returns the comb to Marta until his next visit.

Others are more dramatic. There's the case of the successful but overstressed businessman who checked into the Loews Ventana Canyon Resort near Tucson, Arizona, for a two-month revitalization stay. John worked with the experts at the resort's health club and the executive chef to tailor a fitness program just for this guest, and John even took him on hikes and runs in the mountains behind the hotel.

By the last week of his stay, the businessman had lost 30 pounds and was feeling great. To celebrate his new body, he designed a personal rite of passage that included a solo 18-mile run along a trail that climbs from the valley floor to a height of 6,000 feet and then back down.

He set out on his run, checking in with the hotel staff periodically to reassure them that he was safe. But by around 9 P.M., he hadn't returned. Worried, John donned his own hiking gear and started up the trail, armed with several flashlights, in search of his errant guest. Fortunately, before John had gotten far, a hotel manager called: The guest had turned up, exhausted but safe and very happy.

We in the hotel business love stories like these. They inspire us to provide even greater levels of customized service in the future.

Realistically, of course, a large organization can only go so far down the path of freeing employees to offer customers creative, unplanned services. In any big company, procedures and systems are necessary. Total spontaneity obviously doesn't work when thousands or millions of customers are seeking service; it's simply not efficient. So today's smartest companies are finding ways to provide customized experiences by building flexibility into the very structure of their operations.

Technology is a key to this new movement. One of the biggest buzzwords of the past decade has been "mass customization"—the notion that new technologies, especially the computer and the Internet, can empower organizations to provide individualized products and services to more people more cheaply, quickly, and efficiently than ever before. As discussed, companies like In-N-Out Burger and Dell Computer have built successful businesses on this very premise. In-N-Out Burger has its secret menu, which gives every customer the (somewhat illusory) sense of designing and ordering a specially prepared hamburger. Dell has its direct-selling, custom-building model that lets computer buyers get machines containing only the specific features they want to pay for. And online companies like Amazon and Netflix have pioneered programs for offering personalized product recommendations based on past selections and ratings by the same customer, harnessing technology to create "just-for-me" service that no large retailer could otherwise provide.

Pioneers of mass customization like these companies are showing the way. But finding ways to make the concept practical (and profitable) in other industries is no simple matter. Even discerning which aspects of their experience customers truly want to customize is a significant challenge—to say nothing of developing systems that provide them with the unique goods and services they want without overwhelming them with confusing choices.

The Perfect Fit: Returning Customization to the Clothing Business

Go back far enough in history, and you come to a time when all clothing was customized. Families or tailors made clothes on demand from locally produced cloth. But in the nineteenth century, with the advent of large-scale manufacturing, mass marketing, and high-speed transportation via train and steamship, inexpensive, ready-to-wear clothing produced in centralized factories became available in stores around the developed world. The new technology of mass production brought high-quality clothing into the lives of millions of people in the newly emerging middle class for the first time. But it also ended the era of custom clothing, except for the rich.

On balance, most people have benefited from the availability of mass-manufactured clothing. But like most benefits, this has come at a price. A significant minority of people find that standardized clothing patterns and sizes don't fit them well. People with body shapes that are outside the so-called normal range have been forced to find specialized clothing sources (like the euphemistically labeled "big and tall" men's shops), to buy clothing of inappropriate style (as when unusually small adults are forced to shop in children's departments), or to patronize expensive tailors who produce custom clothing from scratch. And millions more people with bodies that are less extreme are nonetheless required to compromise when buying ready-to-wear garments, settling for sleeves or hems that are a little too long or too short, shoulders that don't quite fit, or waists that hang a little too high or too low on the torso.

A wave of technological change may make possible a new era of custom clothing that can eliminate these minor but genuine irritants.

But transforming this promise into a practical business reality is proving to be tricky. The difficulties and the potential are illustrated by the contrasting stories of several organizations in the forefront of applying mass customization to the apparel business.

Hoping to spearhead the new era of mass customization of clothing is the Textile/Clothing Technology Corporation, or TC2, a nonprofit research organization. Sponsored by many leading companies in the clothing and textile industry and supported by a grant from the U.S. Commerce Department, TC2 has been working to apply advanced technology to the traditional art of tailoring. But although several of TC2's initiatives have garnered widespread media attention and some public interest, none has yet produced the kind of market breakthrough that clothing industry leaders are hoping for.

One flurry of coverage occurred in 1999 when TC2 unveiled an impressive but dauntingly complex system for automatically scanning a human body and using the resulting data to create a customized clothing pattern. Journalists traveled to TC2's headquarters in Cary, North Carolina, to serve as guinea pigs, shedding their clothes (except for underwear) and stepping into the giant eight-foot-tall scanner with its control panel and a vast array of projectors and cameras. In just a few seconds, the system generated 300,000 separate measurements to be used in creating a three-dimensional portrait of the subject's body from which perfectly fitting shirts, pants, dresses, or suits could be fashioned in the customer's choice of colors, styles, and fabrics.

It was a remarkable technological feat reminiscent of something from the old *Jetsons* cartoon series. Within two years, the high-end Brooks Brothers clothing chain had installed one of these early scanners in its flagship New York City store. Drawn by curiosity or the urge to be the first to test a cool new technology, customers marveled at the system's precision; one commented, "Every tailor who ever measured me told me I had a 15½ inch neck. With the computer scan, I now know it's 15.95 inches—so already they're ahead."[1]

What's more, the custom garments were surprisingly affordable. Brooks Brothers suits created using the new scanner were available for as little as $700, meaning that the price premium ranged between $100 and $300 over the cost of an off-the-rack model. The finished garment would be ready within three to four weeks, and once a customer's measurements were on file, new outfits could be ordered over the phone with reference to a simple swatch book.

Company officials were enthusiastic. They talked about rolling out the program nationwide, expressed hope that thousands of Brooks Brothers patrons would upgrade to the computer-designed garments, and even dreamed that the new technology might stem the gradual decline in sales of formal clothing that had depressed the company's growth in the past decade. They also forecast extra financial benefits from the new technology: If a sizable portion of their customer base shifted to custom-made suits, it might be possible to drastically reduce the number of ready-made garments in store and warehouse inventories, each representing a chunk of the company's capital tied up unproductively for weeks or months while awaiting purchase.

Five years later, those dreams appear to have stalled. The New York City store remains the only Brooks Brothers outlet equipped with a body scanner, and just a small fraction of the store's customers opt for the high-tech service. The vast majority of Brooks Brothers patrons have continued to buy their familiar off-the-rack garments. And those who need or want custom-fitted suits appear to prefer the traditional form of clothing customization, provided by a flesh-and-blood tailor equipped with chalk, tape measure, and a mouthful of pins—despite its higher cost.

What's behind the apparent failure of Brooks Brothers' much-ballyhooed body-scanning initiative? It is the kind of chicken-or-egg problem that often plagues new technologies. Customers are unfamiliar with the new system and perhaps a bit intimidated by it. (Is it really safe to have all those electronic beams focused on my nearly naked body? And do I really want an ultradetailed, lumps-and-all topographic image of my middle-aged spread on a screen for every Brooks employee to snicker at?) But until more customers decide they like the system and begin to use it, stores will be reluctant to install the machines, which makes it unlikely that customers will ever become familiar or comfortable with them.

The size and price of the scanners posed another major obstacle. The original device measured 21 by 15 feet and sold for a daunting

$125,000. That's a big investment for retailers desperately trying to squeeze profits from every square inch of floor space. With only a trickle of customers opting for the space-age system, no wonder store managers have been reluctant to install the machines.

In an effort to overcome these barriers, TC2 has been pushing the technology forward. Fourth-generation scanners are now much smaller (5 by 9 feet) and cheaper (around $40,000 per unit).[2] The new machines are also simpler to operate, taking just 200 measurements rather than the hundreds of thousands originally deemed necessary.[3] This may help matters, but it is apparent that body scanners aren't ready to become familiar fixtures in clothing stores. Customers have not yet decided that a more-accurate neck or waist measurement is worth the time, effort, cost, and (perhaps most important) attitude adjustment required to step into the unfamiliar machine.

(In response, Brooks Brothers has shifted its marketing emphasis to traditional made-to-measure suit-making, pins-in-the-mouth and all. They won't sell huge numbers of these custom garments—the premium averages a steep $700 over the off-the-rack equivalent—but the profit margins are handsome, and technology fears aren't a factor.[4])

Does this mean that technology-enabled customization of clothing is dead in the water? Not at all. Mid-range direct clothing retailer Lands' End (owned by Sears Holdings) appears to have found a better approach than Brooks Brothers. Some 40 percent of Lands' End customers are now paying $20 extra (or more) for customized jeans, chinos, and blouses, a success story that Bill Bass, the company's vice president for e-commerce, has called "the first application in a major way of mass customization of clothing."[5]

The Lands' End system is dramatically different from that employed by Brooks Brothers. Sophisticated computer software is used to develop the customized patterns needed to make made-to-order garments, but the technology is kept at a distance from the customer, reducing the fear factor that may have slowed acceptance of body scanners. Lands' End customers respond to a series of 15 to 25 detailed questions about specific body measurements and choose from pictures that represent possible shapes and sizes; for example, when designing jeans, they select the image that most resembles their own backside. Then they select from other styling options—What kind of fabric? How many pockets? What shape of collar? Based on these data, the software chooses one of 900 million different garment patterns and transmits the order to a factory in Mexico. The finished item arrives on the customer's doorstep two to three weeks later.[6]

Lands' End has continued to refine its customization technology. In 2004, the company launched an updated version of its web site feature known as My Virtual Model. (The technology, developed by a Montreal-based technology company called My Virtual Model, Inc., had originally appeared in a much more basic form as early as 1998.) It creates an image intended to mirror that of the customer. Log on to the Virtual Model page and you're asked to provide basic measurements and size data (height, weight, and so on) and even to select hair color and facial type that roughly resemble your own. Within a minute or two, you are gazing at a computerized full-length portrait of yourself that you can view from various angles and "dress" in your choice of dozens of garments.

A fun toy? Sure—but it also allows Lands' End customers to quickly and easily recognize which styles best complement their body types and which ones simply won't work on them.

Customers have responded enthusiastically to the Lands' End system. And the company has also benefited. With profit margins just about the same for custom garments as for off-the-rack products, the higher ticket prices mean more cash in company coffers. And with fewer items in inventory at the end of the selling season, costly clearance sales are reduced, improving overall margins. Best of all, buyers of custom clothes tend to become high-value customers. According to Bill Bass, when they find their perfect fit, "they'll typically buy every color in those jeans or chinos or whatever."[7] Reorder rates for Lands' End custom clothes run one-third higher than for the company's standard fare.[8]

Driven by technological breakthroughs, other intriguing customization projects are under way elsewhere in the apparel business. Nike offers custom-designed footwear in thousands of color combinations at a modest markup (around $10 more than a standard pair).

And Ralph Lauren's Create Your Own lines of polo and oxford shifts are the most popular products available on the company's web site.[9]

Meanwhile, what about TC2, whose body-scan technology appears to be floundering in the search for a mass market demand? The company is now immersed in another, very different, but almost equally ambitious project designed to improve the customization of clothing: the first major recalibration of American sizes using computer technology. The SizeUSA survey employed TC2's scanners to measure the body shapes of 10,800 volunteers of both sexes, many ages, and every possible ethnic and racial background. It's the first major collection of such data since 1941 and reflects the enormous increase in American diversity since that time.

SizeUSA promises to revolutionize the designing of clothes, making sizes more accurate and clothing more comfortable. The data will also be useful to companies in many other industries, from auto manufacturers (who want to design car seats for greater safety, comfort, and convenience) to makers of furniture and medical gear.[10]

TC2 may be on safer ground with the SizeUSA project than with its attempt to turn body-scan technology into a direct-to-consumer application. Customers are eager to have clothes that fit better . . . they just don't want to feel like lab animals to enjoy them. By providing valuable data about the *real* sizes of Americans in the twenty-first century to the companies that need to know that information, TC2 is offering the right service to the right customers and will ultimately benefit everyone who wears clothes.

YOUR BIG AHA'S

The contrasting stories of Brooks Brothers and Lands' End offer some valuable lessons about what works, and what doesn't work, when providing customized products to your customers. Here are a few of them.

People love customized products, so long as the customization process doesn't feel intrusive. Both Brooks Brothers and Lands' End recognized that made-to-order clothing could have enormous mass appeal. But the machine-centric process introduced by

Brooks Brothers has proven much less popular than the simpler, at-home process developed by Lands' End. Customization, especially of clothes that literally touch your customers, is a deeply personal, even intimate affair, and it must be managed in a way that feels easy, familiar, and comfortable rather than intimidating.

People will pay a premium for goods that are "perfect for me," even at the low- to middle-end of the market. One might assume that the typical Brooks Brothers customer—a buyer of upscale, traditional, formal attire—would be a more natural buyer of custom-made clothing than the Lands' End shopper. Yet Lands' End customers have been willing to spend an extra 30 to 40 percent on made-to-measure clothes. Customization isn't just a luxury-market strategy; it can work in any market, provided it's planned and executed intelligently.

The customer wants to be in control. The popular Lands' End clothing customization system relies on the customer's own efforts: He or she must use a tape measure, a bathroom scale, and personal judgment to develop the data that go into creating the unique clothing pattern. This is probably a little less reliable than a high-tech system using electronic sensors, and it's certainly more time-consuming and labor-intensive for customers. Yet, people like it better because it allows them to feel in control, a fundamental human need even in a simple matter such as picking out a blouse or jacket.

To be effective, technology must be subservient to human ends. The software and web site features used by Lands' End to develop custom clothing designs look simple and may even seem a little hokey. (Does it really matter that My Virtual Model has hair the same length, color, and curliness as mine?) But they help customers take psychological ownership of their clothes even before they order them, providing a sense of figurative comfort that matches the literal comfort we enjoy in well-fitting clothes. By all means, use the latest technology, but make sure the application is designed by real people for real people rather than by specialists who love technology for its own sake.

Thirty-Nine Cents' Worth of Fame: Selling Vanity Space on U.S. Postage

Other opportunities and challenges inherent in the concept of customization are illustrated in the stop-and-go experience of the U.S. Postal Service (USPS) in making a business out of offering personalized postage stamps for use on packages and letters.

The first postage stamp was issued in Great Britain in 1840. The so-called Penny Black stamp was a small square of adhesive paper adorned with an image of Queen Victoria, the reigning monarch at the time. Its fixed price was designed to promote the then-revolutionary notion of a uniform postal rate: a half-ounce letter could be delivered anywhere in the British Isles for just a penny.

The first stamps met with some consumer resistance. Loyal English citizens found the idea of licking a paper that bore the likeness of the queen vaguely disrespectful. But soon the sheer convenience and simplicity of the concept carried the day. The United States began to issue postage stamps in 1847, starting with a ten-cent stamp featuring George Washington (the first president) and a five-cent stamp depicting Benjamin Franklin (the nation's first postmaster general). (Actually, there's a Tisch family connection to old Ben: My father Bob served as postmaster general from 1986 to 1988. We're still waiting for the postage stamp in his honor!)

Thus, was launched the tradition of honoring a nation's greatest citizens by issuing postage stamps bearing their images. Stamps depicting presidents, explorers, inventors, artists, and other national heroes became a miniature portrait gallery circulated everywhere and affordable to almost everyone. In time, the concept was expanded: Stamps were issued to commemorate historic events, natural marvels, notable anniversaries, and treasured institutions, from the profession of nursing to the founding of West Point.

Millions of people around the world became stamp collectors, buying and hoarding the tiny mass-produced artworks. In the process, they created highly profitable government revenue streams, since stamps owned by collectors were usually never affixed to envelopes or packages and therefore placed no service demands on post offices. For some countries in the developing world, the issuing of hundreds of colorful stamps depicting popular themes from Disney characters to the Olympic Games became a major source of government income.

When digital technologies for photography, design, and printing became available in the 1990s, it was only a matter of time before someone would think of applying those technologies to the world of postage stamps. That time came in August, 2004, when the USPS announced a two-month-long experimental program to allow consumers to order personalized stamps, valid for use on mail.

The program was launched in partnership with a publicly traded, Los Angeles-based company called Stamps.com, which already provided Internet-based postal services such as postage metering. The personalized PhotoStamps, each imprinted with an image uploaded to the Internet by the consumer, cost almost one dollar apiece ($16.99 for the minimum purchase of one sheet of 20 stamps), although each stamp represented only 37 cents in postal fees.

Customized printing is nothing new. People have long been able to order coffee mugs, T-shirts, and calendars with their own pictures, slogans, or company logos. But in the world of stamps and stamp collecting, this was a revolutionary step. The U.S. Postal Service had formerly maintained strict standards governing images on stamps. Living persons are never depicted on U.S. stamps. (Whereas British stamps always show the reigning monarch, the United States honors its leaders only after death.) Only events and institutions of national significance are commemorated, and religious, political, fraternal, and fund-raising organizations are specifically excluded from consideration. Limited by these and other restrictions, the postal service accepts only about 35 stamp ideas each year out of the 40,000 or so submitted by citizens.[11]

PhotoStamps rewrote these rules. Pictures of living people were permitted, even encouraged—snapshots of toddlers, bride-and-groom portraits, and birthday celebrants were popular stamp concepts. Organizations of many kinds, from small businesses to local civic organizations, could use the personalized stamps to promote themselves. Suddenly, the fame and honor of being pictured on a genuine U.S.

postal stamp was within reach of anybody with a digital camera and 17 bucks to spend.

Here was a fun and original business concept—a natural and appealing use of technology to customize a familiar product. It had the potential to generate extra revenue for the postal service while creating a new kind of customer connection. But the potential for mischief was obvious. To protect itself and the good name of the U.S. Postal Service, Stamps.com created its own set of content restrictions. Consumers were warned that the images they uploaded for stamps must not be "obscene, offensive, blasphemous, pornographic, sexually suggestive, deceptive, threatening, menacing, abusive, harmful, an invasion of privacy, supportive of unlawful action, defamatory, libelous, vulgar, violent, or otherwise objectionable." Furthermore, the company prohibited stamps depicting "celebrities or celebrity likenesses, regional, national, or international leaders or politicians, current or former world leaders, convicted criminals, newsworthy, notorious, or infamous images and individuals, or any material that is vintage in appearance or depicts images from an older era." Finally, copyrighted images—the cover of a favorite record album, for example—were also forbidden.[12]

These policies were complicated, somewhat vague, and difficult to enforce. Stamps.com had to hire a staff of 35 people to screen and weed out submitted images with any questionable content. It also offered a tempting target to would-be pranksters eager to test the capabilities of Stamps.com's policing mechanism.

From a financial perspective, the pilot program was a hit. Over two million customized stamps were sold in the first seven weeks, and Stamps.com's revenues from personalized stamps amounted to $2.3 million.[13] But this success brought with it an outsized load of public relations problems. Most coverage of the program focused on snafus and embarrassments over dubious images that slipped through the screening process.

Much of the trouble was generated by William Bastone, editor of a quirky web site known as The Smoking Gun, who declared himself offended by the new, low standards for U.S. postage. "For the longest time, stamps [were reserved for] statesmen, people who helped do incredible things for the country. Now it's devolved into Daffy Duck and every manner of dopey thing." To prove his point, Bastone submitted a series of photos in dubious taste to Stamps.com and managed to get many of them approved. A mug shot of Lee Harvey Oswald, the assassin of John F. Kennedy, was caught and rejected. But photos of Serbian dictator Slobodan Milosevic and Unabomber Ted Kacynski (as a teenager) made it into print. So did a picture of Monica Lewinsky's notorious semen-stained blue dress.[14] Eventually, The Smoking Gun proudly exhibited stamps depicting convicted spies Ethel and Julius Rosenberg, Teamsters boss Jimmy Hoffa, and former New Jersey governor James McGreevey with his alleged gay lover.[15]

Stamps.com struggled gamely with the onslaught. Their staffers devoted hours to scanning newspapers, magazines, and the World Wide Web to familiarize themselves with potentially embarrassing images. Ultimately, around 9 percent of the 83,000 images submitted during the trial period were rejected. But the slipups were serious enough that the U.S. Postal Service reportedly considered scrapping the entire project.[16]

Nonetheless, by May, 2005, the decision was made to start a second test phase for personalized postage. Stamps.com geared up for a tougher screening process, hiring new employees with special expertise in world history and cultures to spot inappropriate images. A new rule was promulgated barring black-and-white photos (since these had proven to be among the most problematic).[17] And two more web-based companies—Zazzle.com and Endicia.com—were authorized to begin offering custom stamps (with the price boosted to $17.99 per sheet of 20, reflecting the new 39-cent postal rate).

Should the post office's experiment with personalized stamps be deemed a success? It is too soon to tell. Stamps.com reportedly sold some 3.5 million custom stamps during five months of 2005—not a bad number.[18] But put that into perspective: During 2004, the postage service handled some 97 billion pieces of first-class mail, a figure that dwarfs the number of personalized stamps sold.[19] To this point, custom stamps appear to be even less than a fringe product for USPS—call it the tip of the edge of a fringe, perhaps.

Setting aside the continuing potential for embarrassment and the costly challenge of weeding out offensive images, the central weakness of selling personalized stamps is that its appeal is based on the unique prestige associated with postage stamps. As prankster Bastone (and generations of stamp collectors) know, stamps were once reserved for the greatest figures in American history—hence the fun in seeing your own face, or that of your child or pet, in the corner of an envelope. But selling that sense of prestige is somewhat of a self-contradiction. How prestigious can it be, really, if anyone with $18 can afford it? And if personalized stamps become a truly popular mass phenomenon, will their ubiquity eventually make them lose the luster of exclusivity that is now their main source of value?

As the postal service has discovered, turning customization into a truly viable long-term business isn't simply a matter of getting the technology right. It's about knowing what you're marketing and finding ways to protect its value even as you make it widely available to the public.

YOUR BIG AHA'S

The saga of Stamps.com and the marketing of personalized postage offers some unique insights for other organizations seeking routes to customization. Here are a few to ponder.

Customization means ceding some control. The value of your organization's brand grows largely from the distinctive qualities of the goods and services you offer. When you allow patrons to customize your offerings, you also run the risk of watering down those distinctive qualities or even of letting your brand be associated with repugnant qualities. A customization program requires careful planning to make sure you retain enough control to protect the value and uniqueness of your brand.

Automatic technology can't be allowed to operate automatically. Digital file-swapping and printing make it possible for Stamps.com customers to design and produce their own stamps almost instantaneously. But protecting the company's reputation (and that of the USPS) has required the creation of a separate, cumbersome, labor-intensive process for screening and approving images. Don't assume that the existence of a technological fix means that human intelligence doesn't have an essential, continuing role—it probably does.

Your system needs to be continually monitored and frequently tweaked. Any system you create that allows your customers to enter into your processes for shaping and delivering goods and services is subject to abuse or gaming by patrons who are mischievous, unscrupulous, or simply want to use the system for purposes that were never intended. Changes and adjustments to minimize these kinds of problems are frequently necessary.

Merely being different isn't enough for lasting popularity. Offering a personalized product or service that is new and unique is a great way to achieve short-term recognition and success. But what happens when your unique offering becomes a fad available and familiar to everybody? Long-term success requires that you offer a product or service with inherent, ever-refreshing utility and value—one that answers a fundamental human need.

Offering a Customized Experience People Love: Build-A-Bear Gets It Right

Perhaps the best current practitioner of mass customization is Build-A-Bear, the retail chain that lets kids or adults design, create, dress, and accessorize their own stuffed bears and other toy animals. Founded in 1997 by Maxine K. Clark, a former executive with May Department Stores, the company enjoyed seven years of steady growth, capped by a sales-boosting feature on the Oprah Winfrey show in mid-2004. It went public in October of the same year. Since then, Build-A-Bear has continued to expand, now boasting over 220 U.S. stores (including a vast 22,000-square-foot flagship in New York) and locations in 12 foreign countries in Europe and Asia.

The business concept is simple and incredibly appealing. (Though Maxine Clark has added unique elements, she did not originate the "bear workshop" idea; credit appears to go to Merrilee and Eric Woods, whose Basic Brown Bear Factory has been operating on

San Francisco's historic Fisherman's Wharf since 1975.[20]) The lucky child who visits a Build-A-Bear Workshop is greeted by a Master Bear Maker who escorts her along a sort of assembly line as she creates her choice of a bear, dog, kitten, monkey, or other animal. At the glass-fronted stuffing machine, the child participates by tapping a foot pedal as balls of fluff fill the animal's body. Then she chooses a heart for her animal and performs a little ceremony, coached by her guide:

> Rub the heart between your hands to make it a warm heart. Rub it on your forehead to give your bear brain power. And rub it on your muscles so she'll be nice and strong. Then make a wish, give the heart a kiss and tuck it into your bear.[21]

Then, after a pretend bath, the animal is dressed in any of a vast array of outfits, from Disney princess to Cub Scout, from chef to ballerina to firefighter, or even a miniature replica of an NFL, MLB, or NBA team uniform. Accessories can be added—a Hello Kitty bowling bag is $5, a camouflage-fabric pop-up tent costs $10, and a bear-sized iPod-like Pawtracks Player runs $7. With all the delectable extras, the average sale comes to $32, although a toy can be had for as little as $10.

The entire "birthing" process is cleverly designed to fascinate children, entertain their parents, and produce lumps in the throats of doting grandparents. Visiting the Workshop isn't like going shopping—it's a full-blown adventure that many adults and even cynical teenagers find themselves caught up in. ("The customer likes to smile," notes CEO Clark.[22])

More important, it creates a powerful and lasting emotional bond between the child and her toy. In a world where kids are usually the passive recipients of whatever adults choose to provide them (from food at the family dinner table to the presents under the tree on Christmas morning), creating and dressing a customized playmate in the child's own choice of outfit is remarkably exciting and empowering. Other toys, including other stuffed animals, often end up forgotten and discarded after a few weeks or months of play, but the Build-A-Bear toy is more like a beloved member of the child's family.

At Build-A-Bear, customization involves more than just designing your own toy. The company uses the power of personal information to create an intimate relationship with customers that lasts long after they've left the store. Every bear is registered in the company's Find-A-Bear identification system. Its owner receives an individually printed birth certificate, and a bar-coded ID tag is inserted in the bear. The customer benefits, since it is possible to track down the owner of a lost animal and return the missing toy. But Build-A-Bear benefits, too, since the database also helps the company track the preferences, tastes, and habits of customers and invite them back for such free services as restuffing and fluffing. (And if someone in the family uses the return visit to buy another bear or two, well, that's all right with Build-A-Bear.[23])

Customers love Build-A-Bear: A company survey found that 75 percent gave their experience the highest possible rating. And they express their enthusiasm through return visits; about 45 percent of new-bear sales are to people from a household that has already bought another bear.[24]

The company's reliance on the creativity of customers extends beyond simply letting them assemble toys to their liking. CEO Clark reports that she gets many of her best concepts for new product variations direct from Build-A-Bear fans, especially the members of her "virtual cub advisory council," a database of kids she regularly e-mails. Clark credits customers with business ideas such as bear-sized mini-scooters as accessories and selling mascot bears at sporting events. "I used to feel like I had to come up with all the ideas myself," she likes to say, "but it's so much easier relying on my customers."[25] (Maybe we should call it the "Build-A-Company" strategy.)

Can the company continue to build on its success, or will it fall by the wayside like so many other toy crazes? (Think back to the faded phenomena of years past, from Cabbage Patch Kids to the Ninja Turtles.) Build-A-Bear has worked hard to adapt to changing tastes and its own growth with surefooted adjustments. As new fads emerge among kids, it rushes appropriate outfits and accessories into stores—tiny Spiderman costumes one season, giraffes and pandas marketed in collaboration with the World Wildlife Fund the next. In 2004, the company introduced a new business concept called Friends 2B Made, a store where girls up to age 12 are invited to design their own soft and poseable dolls; stores have already opened in 63 locations around the United States.

As a result, Build-A-Bear continues to outperform comparable retailers. The stores enjoy average sales per square foot of around $600, which is double the average for mall stores in the United States.[26] And the stock price, which fell for a time when analysts made oversized growth projections, appears to have stabilized around more rational expectations.

Build-A-Bear is doing a lot of things right.

Technology plays an appropriate supporting role in its customization program. Database programs track customer information, support the lost-bear ID system, and invite bear buyers to return for additional services, but customers aren't required to interface with the technology, eliminating the possibility that confusion or anxiety could dampen their enthusiasm.

Build-A-Bear pays close attention to changing customer interests and desires, frequently introducing new customization options and choices. These are often developed through partnerships with other brands that kids (and their parents) know and trust, from Disney to Sesame Street.

Most important, although Build-A-Bear offers a traditional, huggable, child-proven toy as its product, the company is built around something much bigger and unique—a remarkable, personal experience that adds immeasurably to the value of the toy in a child's eyes. Thus, the customization process isn't something mildly unpleasant you must endure to obtain a better product (as it is with the Brooks Brothers body scan). Instead, it is a delightful, essential part of being a Build-A-Bear customer and creates a memory to be cherished for years to come.

That's customization done right.

YOUR BIG AHA'S

The story of Build-A-Bear offers some practical insights into how to make customization a powerful tool for creating satisfied customers for life.

Customize the features your customers actually care about. Build-A-Bear has artfully designed its customization process to keep it simple and focus attention on a series of emotional high-lights—the intriguing stuffing machine, the heart ceremony (which bonds the child and the toy), the presentation of the birth certificate (which gives the toy an identity), and the selection of an outfit and accessories (which makes it visually unique). Other attributes that could be customized—the length of fur, the kind of stitching, the shape of ears, and so on—would only confuse and bore a small child. These features are kept standard so as not to distract from what really matters.

At least make the process easy; if you can, make it fun. The bear-building process is literally transparent, right down to the glass-fronted stuffing machine, so that even a three-year-old can understand and participate in it. The presence of the Master Bear Maker guide adds a touch of warmth and humor, and further ensures that the process will be easy to comprehend. In the end, the experience of building your own bear is at least as enjoyable and memorable as taking home the finished product—a goal that other would-be customizers should try to emulate.

Design the customer experience to appeal to everyone *who participates.* Build-A-Bear understands that their total experience must be enjoyable not just to kids between the ages of 2 and 10 but also to their parents, grandparents, or guardians (who will pay the bill) as well as to older siblings (who are likely to tag along on the store visit) and to customers of other ages (such as love-struck college students, who often buy stuffed bears as presents for a boy- or girlfriend). The workshop and product line are designed to maximize the appeal to all these groups by offering college mascot sweaters for loyal students and alumni and occupational outfits (nurse, construction worker, business bear) as gifts for colleagues or associates.

Keep customers coming back by continually refreshing your offerings. Knowing that the toy business is driven by the ever-changing tastes of fickle school-age kids, Build-A-Bear uses its close customer connections to stay abreast of trends and fads in kiddie culture. To be meaningful, customization must provide what your clientele are interested in today.

CHAPTER 9

Let Me Introduce You

Customer Communities in an Interactive World

WE LIVE IN A FRAGMENTED WORLD IN WHICH MANY PEOPLE HAVE LITTLE sense of being part of close-knit communities. There are many causes. Social and geographic mobility, job-hopping, divorce, declining membership in organized religious and civic groups, the replacement of old-fashioned neighborhoods with spread-out suburbs or anonymous apartment towers—these and other factors have combined, over the past generation, to create a society in which few people feel they have deep, intense, and long-lasting personal ties. Instead, most of us have a handful of close family members and friends, hundreds of superficial acquaintances, and a missing in-between level that ought to be (and perhaps once was) occupied by a host of meaningful friendships.

The result: A hunger for community, often unconscious, that millions of people cannot satisfy.

Companies and not-for-profit organizations that recognize this phenomenon are finding ways to address the need for human connections while pursuing their own corporate or social missions. Just as a party host wants his guests to get to know one another and become friends, organizations that understand the power of the human touch are encouraging and helping their clients to interact with one another, forming communities of interest that make life richer and more enjoyable.

It enhances the customer experience in a way that benefits everyone involved. Customers benefit from the chance to connect with like-minded individuals who share the same interests, concerns, or goals. And the organizations that provide these benefits reap rewards that include intensified customer loyalty, the opportunity to learn more about customers and their needs, and, in some cases, the ability to create entire new businesses whose value is derived from the power of the community.

The ability of organizations to create and nurture customer communities—often through new interactive technologies—is enormously powerful. But it also creates significant challenges. People take their human connections seriously; they think of the communities they join as something they *own* and ought to control. If your organization finds itself at the apex of a vibrant customer community, you're very lucky—but you also have important questions to consider about how to maintain and grow that community in a way that will benefit both its members and your organization in the long run. The organizations discussed in this chapter are addressing those questions, each in its unique way.

Hog Heaven: The Rebirth of Harley-Davidson through Customer Community

In 1982, Harley-Davidson—the classic American manufacturer of big, powerful motorcycles—was in deep trouble. Facing new competition from peppy, well-built, low-priced Japanese imports, the once-proud company found its annual unit sales slipping to a mere 32,400, just 15 percent of the U.S. total; its bottom line showed a one-year loss of some $30 million. In that year, 13 company executives teamed up to buy the ailing company, determined to turn it around. But Harley continued to struggle. Sales remained flat for several years, and 40 percent of the workforce had to be laid off. Harley, it seemed, might be doomed.

Finally, in 1989, a new leadership team was put in place, led by CEO Richard F. Teerlink. This team took two decisive steps to revive the firm.

First, they recognized that slippage in product quality had been hurting the company's image and its sales. Vowing to restore the proud tradition of American craftsmanship that had once made Harley bikes the best in the world, they worked cooperatively with their union workforce to institute a rigorous new quality-control program. Production methods that had become slipshod were revised to emphasize hand tooling of key parts and thorough inspections. Word spread among biking enthusiasts, and soon demand surged, creating waiting lists for new Harley bikes.

Second, the company created a new approach to marketing and brand-building. The change began when Clyde Fessler, the company's vice president of business development, sat down with his team and asked a simple but crucial question: What does Harley have to offer customers that Honda, Suzuki, and the other competing manufacturers can't possibly match? After much conversation, the answer emerged: It was the unique Harley-Davidson heritage that had long made Harley *the* motorcycle in the eyes of most Americans.

This heritage had been a long time in the making. Soon after the company's founding back in 1903, Harley motorcycles had begun to develop an image as symbols of blue-collar toughness, an independent spirit, and the allure of the open road. In the 1950s and 1960s, such icons of American rebellion as Elvis Presley, Marlon Brando, and *Easy Rider's* Peter Fonda had all become associated with the glamour of Harley. Even the notorious leather-jacketed Hell's Angels gang, feared by some but respected and envied by many, were part of the Harley legend. This was a mystique few other brands could match. After all, how many other company logos have ever won the honor of being tattooed on the arms of their customers?

Recognizing that the Harley heritage was the unique asset on which the company ought to build, Fessler took the radical step of focusing 80 percent of Harley's budget for advertising, promotions, and public relationships toward *existing* Harley owners rather than prospective customers. The idea: To build the powerful Harley image into a national phenomenon. "If you provide a value experience to your existing customers, they become your salespeople and brand ambassadors," Fessler says—and over the next decade, that's exactly what happened.[1]

Harley began promoting its iconic brand through several interlocking strategies. It introduced a series of offerings in new, seemingly unrelated product categories, from clothing and motorcycling accessories to toiletries, beer, and even Harley-themed Barbie dolls. It partnered with Ford to create the unique Harley edition of the F-150 truck, complete with logo, special paint and upholstery, and other flourishes to give it a Harley look.[2] The idea was not simply to create alternative streams of revenue for Harley-Davidson (although that was a welcome infusion of cash for the beleaguered company). The central concept was to promote the Harley brand as representing not just a vehicle but a lifestyle centered around values such as independence, freedom, and "cool"—qualities that millions of Americans stuck in office jobs could identify with and yearn for.

Most crucial, the company launched the Harley Owners Group (HOG), an organization designed to help educate—not to say indoctrinate—new motorcyclists into the Harley mystique and lifestyle. The club's name purportedly derives from a 1920 episode in which an early motorcycle racing team carried its mascot, a pig, on a victory lap after every race; but it also embodies the defiantly tough nickname "hog" that Harley riders had long applied to their powerful road machines.[3] Built around local chapters, HOG provided members with training in safe riding techniques, showed them how their bikes could be customized and accessorized, and gave them a venue in which to meet, swap stories about great riding experiences, and plan shared excursions on their Harleys.

HOG caught on, big time. The same instinct that had long moved motorcycle fans to form gangs and clubs drove thousands to participate in HOG activities. Spouses, kids, and friends came along for the ride, and Harley ownership was transformed into a social activity around which whole families would plan their leisure time.

Today, HOG continues to encourage motorcycle enthusiasts to gather and share their love for the bikes and for the Harley lifestyle. Boasting over 800,000 members (every new Harley owner gets a free initial membership), HOG draws huge crowds to events like the annual national rally in Sturgis, South Dakota, as well as to rides organized by local affiliates (many of them sponsored by Harley dealers) around the country. HOG has also helped to improve the once-raunchy image of motorcycle riders: HOG chapters regularly sponsor charity events and community fund-raisers; and towns that once feared and shunned motorcyclists now compete to host HOG rallies to enjoy the hotel, restaurant, and entertainment dollars they generate. The visibility that such events bring to HOG and to motorcycle riding helps boost Harley sales, an effect that's not lost on company executives.

The biggest HOG event of all was the 2003 celebration of Harley's centennial, which drew an estimated 250,000 Harley owners to the company headquarters in Milwaukee—"the ultimate party," in the words of one HOG member, "the Woodstock for the 40-year-olds and older." Those who were invited to ride in the grand parade of 10,000 bikers are still talking about the honor.[4]

As Joanne Bischmann, Harley's vice president of marketing, explains, the emphasis on brand identity continues to be central to the company's strategy. "We've changed how we educate and manage the brand," she comments. "When I came on board [in 1990], most of it was done through tribal knowledge; there was no true documentation of branding strategy hierarchy or identity." Now a brand advisory council meets twice a year to discuss crucial branding issues, always focusing on the potential impact of a proposed sponsorship, partnership, or other initiative on the community of Harley lovers and their attitude toward the brand.[5]

Harley's deliberate focus on nurturing the community of its customers was born out of necessity. The mystique attached to Harley ownership was practically the only unique asset that the company had to build on during its years in the wilderness. But it has evolved into a force in its own right, providing enormous psychic and social rewards to Harley customers even as it drives continued growth for the company and strength for its brand.

In 2004, Harley sold 317,000 bikes—nearly 10 times the 1982 total—and enjoyed profits of $889 million on record revenues of around $5 billion. It (narrowly) trails market leader Honda in its share of the overall motorcycle business, but it dominates the highly profitable large-cycle segment on which it has historically chosen to focus.

Harley's revival has been largely based on the strength of the customer community, embodied especially in HOG and its members. But community isn't a static thing; people are constantly changing and evolving, along with their needs, interests, and preferences. Today, the future of Harley's customer community is far from clear. The baby boom generation has been at the core of Harley's explosion in popularity—as sales soared, the median age of a new Harley buyer rose to 46 from 38.7 (in 1987). Now the boomers are nearing retirement age, and they can't be relied on to boost motorcycle sales for much longer. Accordingly, the company is looking for ways to shift its marketing focus with long-term growth in mind.

On the product side, Harley is introducing less-expensive models like the high-performance V-Rod and the low-priced Sportster, designed to appeal to a younger, somewhat less affluent crowd. They are also creating bikes with a lower, less bulky profile, in hopes of attracting a broader female market.[6]

Customer outreach efforts are also being adjusted to expand the Harley demographic. The new Rider's Edge training program teaches motorcycle novices how to ride their vehicles safely. Women-only classes have proven especially popular—few people like being the only person of their gender in a roomful of strangers.

The early feedback from these efforts at brand shifting is encouraging. Harley sales to Gen Xers have been growing eight times faster than sales to boomers, and the percentage of purchases by women has been inching up, from 5 percent to 10 percent. However, it will take another 5 to 10 years to determine with any certainty whether Harley will attract enough younger customers to replenish the community base on which its past success has been built—as well as modifying the HOG image and ethos so as to meet the needs of the new generation without alienating the old.

Harley's leaders are quick to emphasize that they are not abandoning their traditional customer community. To do so would make little business sense. The company's demographic analyses suggest that opportunities continue to expand in Europe and Asia, where the attitudinal, buying, and brand affiliation behaviors of the baby boomers appear to lag those in the United States by some six to seven years. Accordingly, Harley is focusing heavily on expanding sales in those regions. "If you factor in different markets at different stages of the evolution curve," says Clyde Fessler, "Harley has a bright future for the next 20 to 30 years."[7]

YOUR BIG AHA'S

Harley Davidson leveraged an existing community of loyal customers to turn around a moribund brand. Here are some of the lessons other organizations can learn from Harley's story.

Start building your future with your existing customers. Nearly every organization can point to some customers, clients, or members who are loyal and satisfied fans. Rather than chasing new customers, who are almost always elusive and expensive, why not start your marketing efforts with the people who already love you? They represent a base that is easy to reach and probably ready to buy new offerings from you, provided you appeal to the same qualities that attracted those customers in the first place.

Give your customers good reasons to enjoy and expand their loyalty. The Harley Owners Group attracts and retains members because it is not primarily a venue for selling Harley-related merchandise. Instead, it rewards and delights Harley owners with opportunities to learn about and enjoy their vehicles through road trips, rallies, and get-togethers. If you have the opportunity to create a customer community (or to support an existing one), don't just sell to the community members—provide them with rewards that will increase their loyalty and encourage them to invite others into the magic circle.

Provide happy customers with opportunities to infect and encourage one another. Through national HOG, Harley sponsors about a hundred motorcycles rallies every year, while local HOG chapters organize thousands of additional excursions, rides, and local events. Each of these gatherings deepens the bonds among Harley riders, creating lifelong friendships built around motorcycle riding, as well as their connection with the company.

Always be looking ahead to the next demographic wave. With Harley sales continuing to grow, it would be easy for company executives to rest contented with their current success. But the gradually rising age of the average Harley purchaser is an early warning sign of future trouble for the company. Harley's leaders are taking smart steps today to head off this problem by reshaping their product line and modifying their marketing to appeal to the next generation of motorcycle buyers. Communities are in constant flux; you need to be prepared to shift with them.

eBay—From Online Bazaar to Virtual Community

It is the fastest-growing business in history, reaching $3 billion in annual revenues within eight years, a feat unequaled by Microsoft, Dell Computer, or any other company. Based on the volume of goods sold, it is one of the nation's largest retailers, and if the 430,000 people it supports were all on the company payroll, it would be second only to Wal-Mart as an employer.[8] Yet it owns no stores, maintains no inventory, and doesn't manufacture, import, or market a single product. The value of eBay, one of the United States' most successful companies, lies primarily in its vast network of buyer/seller communities built around specific interests.

The company was launched in 1995 under the name of Auction-Web. Legend has it that the original motivation of founder Pierre Omidyar was to create a venue where his then-fiancée could trade her favorite collectible, vintage dispensers for Pez candy (though apparently this tale has been discredited as a "just-so story" concocted by a company publicity director).[9] In the years since its founding, eBay has become the overwhelming marketplace of choice on the Internet, used by countless individuals to auction off household items and collectibles and by thousands of retailers and wholesalers seeking markets for extra inventory. Almost anything you can imagine (and plenty of things you probably can't) has been put up for sale on eBay, from a used George Foreman grill to a seven-day vacation for 12 at the royal estate of Alltnaguibhsaich Lodge in the Scottish Highlands, auctioned off by Queen Elizabeth to commemorate her fiftieth year as Britain's monarch (proceeds to charity, of course).[10]

It is easy to take eBay's success for granted. Even Meg Whitman, the company's much-admired CEO, likes to joke that "a monkey could run this business." But the truth is much less simple. Making it easy for people to buy and sell online requires establishing a rare sense of trust among millions of strangers. One way eBay encourages that sense of trust is through its rating system. After every transaction, the buyer and seller are asked to rate one another for reliability, honesty, efficiency, product quality, and other factors. Cumulative ratings are made available on every future auction, making it easy for prospective customers to see what kind of experience past buyers have had with a particular merchant. A reputation for ethical corner-cutting or shoddy practices spreads quickly and is difficult to shake. The mere existence of this system, and the transparency it creates, adds immeasurably to the comfort level of eBay customers.

Another tool for building trust is PayPal, the online payment system that eBay bought for $1.5 billion in 2002. It simplifies online purchases by eliminating the need to mail a check or input credit card data, instead crediting funds directly to a secure PayPal account. It ensures sellers against losses from buyers who fail to pay as promised for up to $700 per year at no cost, and also offers additional coverage for a small fee.

These and other features of the eBay system—developed over time through extensive experimentation—help to explain why some 48 million active users are willing to participate in an online market with strangers they have never seen. eBay softens the anonymous, "Wild West" edges of the Internet by establishing ground rules that let buyers and sellers feel comfortable doing business with one another.

Being the first, biggest, and most popular auction site on the web has produced enormous business benefits for eBay. As auctions flourish on the site, the so-called network effect ensures that more and more buyers and sellers will continue to flock there. Since you can find, for example, more vintage movie posters for sale on eBay than anywhere else on the Internet, fans of such posters tend to gravitate to eBay first. The presence of all those eager shoppers means that individuals and companies interested in selling old movie posters would be foolish not to list their wares on eBay, which in turns attracts still more customers. The cycle is very difficult for a rival auctioneer to disrupt, and virtually guarantees continued profitable growth for eBay.

This same dynamic has also made eBay the host for thousands of online communities, each made up of people united by a common interest. It's the existence and loyalty of those communities that makes eBay such a powerful and lucrative business. This is why eBay nurtures them through events like eBay Live!, an annual gathering (in real, not virtual space) that attracts thousands of members eager to swap tips and stories about how best to buy and sell on eBay.

Thanks to the network effect, eBay's success is self-reinforcing. But this doesn't mean that the company is truly monkeyproof. Creating and maintaining a business based primarily on the shared interests of a community of customers poses some unique challenges. These are the kinds of issues on which CEO Meg Whitman spends her days.

One issue is how much control to exercise over the choices and behaviors of individual eBay members. Company founder Pierre Omidyar dreamed that eBay would be a "self-regulating" marketplace governed by few if any rules. It's a vision that appeals to the libertarian ethos of many Internet users. And much of the strength of eBay comes from the unfettered behavior of its millions of members. Without the amazing diversity, creativity, imagination, and unpredictability of the offerings on eBay, the site would be a far less compelling place to visit.

Yet, some activities by eBay members threaten to endanger the sense of safety and community that makes eBay a viable marketplace. Although fraud is an area in which eBay is constantly forced to be vigilant, there are other more basic issues such as the kinds of merchandise offered for sale on the site, some of which pose knotty legal, ethical, and cultural challenges. As eBay's millions of users have pushed the boundaries of acceptable online behavior, the company has had to make some tough choices about whether and how to police its members. Examples of the problems eBay has had to tackle include the following:

- *Pirated products:* In its early years, eBay was a popular venue for the trading of illegal copies of copyrighted materials, from music CDs and movie DVDs to pirated software. Many Internet users take the position that "information wants to be free" and advocate near-anarchistic positions on intellectual property. But creators of such property and the companies they work for have lost billions as a result of such attitudes. In response to pressure from industry organizations like the Business Software Alliance, eBay began scanning auctions for such items and removing them from the site in 2001.[11]

- *Human organs:* Trade in human body parts and remains is illegal in both the real world and cyberspace, but some eBay members have tried to take advantage of the anonymity of the Internet to evade such restrictions. One eBay member offered to sell a kidney and actually attracted bids ranging up to $5.7 million before eBay officials stepped in. The company subsequently instituted and began proactively enforcing its own ban on all human organ sales.[12]
- *Military-style weapons:* In an age of terrorism, there's the potential that eBay could be used to transfer weapons from rogue states or felonious individuals to extremist or criminal groups. On March 3, 1999, a surface-to-air missile was posted for auction on eBay. The company's associate general counsel, Rob Chesnut, who specializes in halting the sale of inappropriate items on the web site, worked with the Department of Defense to facilitate the arrest of the would-be arms dealer.[13]
- *Illegal drugs:* In September, 2005, drug enforcement officials at the state and federal levels announced that they were investigating sales on eBay of pseudoephedrine, the cold and allergy medicine used by criminals in the manufacture of methamphetamine. Small-volume sales of the drug are perfectly legal, but some sellers apparently have taken advantage of the anonymity of eBay to sell thousands of tablets at a time. One blogger reports that eBay has removed at least 40 auctions for large quantities of pseudoephedrine from its web site when asked to do so, and the company is now considering banning sales of the drug altogether.[14]
- *Offensive collectibles:* Perhaps eBay's most famous act of censorship was Whitman's 2001 decision to ban the sale of Nazi memorabilia, driven in part by the urgings of then-company-director Howard Schultz (chairman of Starbucks), who had just returned from a visit to Auschwitz. After much soul-searching and intense debate among company executives, Whitman decided to forbid

sales of almost all Nazi-related items, a choice she frankly admits was subjective and personal.[15]

Some of these decisions were easier than others. There are probably some eBay members who wish that Pierre Omidyar's dream of a completely self-regulated marketplace with total user freedom might still be realized. But it's likely that the vast majority of users prefer being part of an online community where overtly illegal, dangerous, or repellent merchandise is not for sale—just as most visitors to a real-world shopping mall would *not* be pleased to find dealers in illicit arms or drugs setting up shop in a vacant storefront.

Another challenge that eBay's leaders face is how and where to draw borders around the online community. On the one hand, eBay needs to provide its members with value-building services that will help them have fun, make money, and (if they want) build successful businesses of their own. Yet, ideally, they want to do all this without reducing the members' dependence on and devotion to eBay. It's a fine line to walk. What if a retailer becomes so successful and well-known from his sales on eBay that he can wean himself from eBay altogether, becoming a viable online retailer in his own right? Will the all-inclusive eBay community eventually fragment into many separate marketplaces?

The company has struggled to define appropriate policies to address these questions. eBay currently forbids retailers who auction items on eBay from providing links to their outside web sites. The purpose of the rule, eBay executives explain, is to support the community by keeping shoppers on site.[16] However, eBay offers members a service called ProStores designed to make it easy for small-to-midsize retailers to create their own e-commerce web sites linked to yet separate from the eBay market. Available in four tiers of service with a minimum monthly cost of $6.95, ProStores lets eBay members create their own online stores with simple, customizable designs where merchandise can be sold at a fixed price (not at auction). eBay collects a commission of between 0.5 percent and 1.5 percent on every item sold.

The reaction of eBay members to the ProStores initiative has been cautious. Ruth Lozowy, a seller of crafts and bridal supplies, sees Pro-

Stores as a potentially devious business strategy: "It sets you up to be dependent on eBay, and then they can raise the fees."[17] eBay prides itself on its mission to build and sustain an online community, but where exactly does that mission diverge from the profit motive?

Then there is the issue of online democracy. One of the attractions of eBay is the sense of equality among buyers and sellers, who interact freely in a virtual space with none of the potentially intimidating or even discriminatory trappings of big business. On eBay, a tiny retailer of (say) handbags or ceramic pottery or computer gear can compete on an equal footing against a major department store, a famous antiques dealer from a prestigious New York City neighborhood, or a big company like Dell. To maintain this sense of egalitarianism, eBay has steadfastly resisted calls from its largest accounts to provide volume discounts on fees. The company that sells a thousand items a month on eBay pays the same commissions as the hobbyist from Dubuque who sells three items a year.

Home Depot's Bob Nardelli, one of the big retailers who favors volume discounts, grudgingly admires Whitman's stand on this issue. "I admire her position," he says. "I just wish I could have convinced her otherwise." And Nardelli acknowledges that, if he were eBay's CEO, he would probably do the same thing: "Once you start [giving discounts], where do you stop?"[18]

But the pressure on eBay to provide special benefits to high-volume retailers continues. In 2004, some 100 of eBay's biggest accounts created an informal organization they call "the eBay Elite," whose goal is to influence company policies. The pressure has produced certain concessions. Those dubbed "PowerSellers" because of their large volume of sales (as well as consistently high feedback ratings from buyers) are eligible for a co-op advertising program that reimburses them for up to 25 percent of their print advertising expenses.[19] It is a modest concession that is familiar from almost every form of offline retailing. It certainly hasn't been enough to satisfy the demands of the PowerSellers, some of whom organized a short-lived boycott of eBay in 2005. Yet, some eBay purists worry that it's a portent of the growing "corporatization" of eBay and, perhaps, the ultimate demise of the sense of community that is the company's greatest strength.

Meg Whitman is determined not to let that happen. She devotes much of her time and energy to staying in touch with the passionate individuals, small businesses, hobbyists, collectors, and bargain hunters who originally built eBay into the powerhouse it is today. She walks the floor at the annual eBay Live! gatherings, listens to members' gripes and suggestions, and presides over regular "Voice of the Customer" meetings where a cross-section of eBay members are invited to air their opinions.

But keeping this unruly crowd satisfied isn't easy. Jeff Jordan, a former Disney executive who now helps run eBay's U.S. operations and often bears the brunt of customer critiques, comments ruefully about the mixed blessings of the company's egalitarian ethos: "I have never had my job performance criticized so broadly and so openly. We are trying to run a corporation that optimizes its profits at the same time we are running one of the more empowering social phenomena of the last decade."[20]

As the most successful company to date built on the basis on customer community, eBay represents a fascinating business and social experiment. How long will Whitman and her team continue to find the right balance between nurturing community and growing the bottom line? Avid students of human behavior—to say nothing of tens of millions of eBay users—will be watching future developments carefully.

YOUR BIG AHA'S

Cynics may think that "a monkey could run eBay." But the company's success didn't come as easy as that. Here are some of the lessons about community-building that the eBay story can teach.

An atmosphere of trust doesn't just happen. Millions of eBay members feel comfortable buying, selling, and trusting their prized possessions to strangers because of the carefully designed and rigorously maintained infrastructure of eBay. It includes the massive web site architecture that serves millions of browsers without breaking down, the feedback system that tracks the reliability of individual buyers and sellers, and the PayPal system that makes online financial transactions easy and secure. Trust never happens by itself; it's always a by-product of thought, planning, and hard work.

Most people will do the right thing—and they deserve to be protected from the wrongdoers. The percentage of eBay members prone to committing fraud is minuscule, but even those tiny numbers might be enough to destroy the reputation of the site and drive millions of users away. As a businessperson or organizational leader, you may not fancy the role of "policeman" over the behavior of your customers. But if you are building or nurturing a customer community, you must be prepared to establish and enforce minimal rules to protect the interests of all; otherwise, the community will be doomed to failure.

Building community sometimes means passing up easy profits. Some half a million small businesses buy and sell goods on eBay. They are the heart of the site's global Main Street, and they play a huge role in making it fun and attractive for shoppers to browse. eBay is under enormous pressure to disadvantage these small merchants by giving volume discounts to the biggest sellers, which would probably attract more large companies and boost the company's overall revenues. But eBay has resisted this temptation, choosing instead to protect the long-term health of the online community. It is not an easy choice, but it is a wise one.

Listen to community members, then do the right thing. Any diverse community of customers will contain clashing opinions and strident voices that don't necessarily represent the majority. It is imperative that you, as an organizational leader, listen to all these voices, even when they are passionately opposed to your own. But then you must make what you are convinced is the correct decision for the benefit of the community as a whole, even if it subjects you to additional abuse. That's part of the burden of leadership.

Mr. Murdoch Meets Girls Gone Wild: Online Communities for Sale

You may not think of Rupert Murdoch, the politically conservative media mogul from Australia, owner of Fox and chairman and CEO of News Corporation, as a cutting-edge pioneer of the hip and the happening. But in December, 2005, he proved that he (or someone in his company) is savvy enough to recognize a hot trend among twenty-somethings and jump on it. Murdoch paid a reported $580 million to buy Intermix Media, the company that owns MySpace, today's most popular social-networking web site. Murdoch described his latest toy to Wall Street analysts using some of the newest buzzwords: "It's sticky, it's fun, it's informative." And he added the classic appeal of any business acquisition: It's also "poised to be very profitable."[21]

Some online businesses are easy to describe and define, at least approximately. For example, eBay is like an electronic version of Sotheby's auction house. But online social-networking spaces are a little different from anything that has gone before. They're a bit like personal ads ("SWF seeks male aged 25–35"), except that they aren't focused on dating. They're a bit like the traditional printed "facebooks" created by some colleges to help freshmen find friends, except that they aren't limited to any one school or geographic location. They're a bit like the chat rooms that defined early interactions on the Internet, although they aren't focused on particular topics.

Perhaps the best comparison is to a college town's most popular hangout—the best and most crowded bar, coffee house, or campus center, where everyone goes to see, be seen, and make connections with familiar faces and new ones—except that they exist purelyin cyberspace and therefore can be national or even global in scope.

Today, MySpace is the world's biggest social-networking web site, with more than 54 million members (a number that will be outdated by the time you read this page). Members sign up and create their own personal web pages, which might include scanned and uploaded photos, links to their favorite music, a blog with current thoughts, diaries, and gossipy messages, and an opportunity for web site visitors to sign up as a "friend." Once you've gathered a list of MySpace friends, which might number anywhere from 2 to 2,000, you can quickly and easily send them all messages or invitations—"Check out this cool new video" or "Join me at my favorite band's upcoming concert." Best of all, it's all free.

Created in 2003, MySpace was the brainchild of Tom Anderson, a Santa Monica music fan who wanted to give others a way to share news about favorite indie rock bands.

Although it has since expanded way beyond that original rationale, MySpace hasn't lost its roots in the indie music world. Thousands of performers have used MySpace to build their careers and develop fan followings by using a MySpace page as a quick, easy, and free equivalent of a personalized web site. Many once-unknown bands have signed recording deals after being discovered through MySpace.

One example among hundreds: Huxley, a band out of Wichita, Kansas (not exactly an indie music hotspot), signed a deal with Rhino in a Tree Records after being scouted on MySpace by a company rep. Now when they tour, they use MySpace to find local high school kids and invite them to their concerts. Huxley recently performed in Cranston, Rhode Island, for the first time, and one band member reports, "We played a show there for 1,000 kids, and they all knew our names." MySpace was responsible.[22]

Big-name performers are also piggybacking on MySpace. Major artists including REM, Black Eyed Peas, Beck, Madonna, Nine Inch Nails, and even oldster Neil Diamond have used it to create buzz about their tours and records, often making album cuts available for downloading on MySpace a week in advance of general release.

Today, as part of the Murdoch media empire, MySpace is continuing to capitalize on its music-industry connections. Interscope Records is now distributing a MySpace record label. And the company is seeking ways to expand into other media, such as moviemaking. In March, 2006, MySpace threw a party at the Sundance Film Festival in Park City, Utah, to celebrate the launch of its filmmaker-community site with a contest that challenged members to create a video for a Beastie Boys song.[23] It remains to be seen whether MySpace becomes as great a force in Hollywood as it is in the music business, but if not, it won't be for lack of trying.

The unique character of MySpace may be shaped in part by its show-business origins. But most members aren't especially focused on music or movies. They use the site as an easy way to link up with people who share any interest of theirs or who just want someone to chat or play games with online. Some MySpace relationships turn into real-world friendships, but most don't; rather than feeding into a young person's social life, they occupy a unique and separate space of their own.

Although MySpace is the largest current business built on social networking, it's far from the only one. There are many others, each with its own target niche and specialized sense of belonging. Friendster, the first well-known social-networking web site, still has 1.4 million followers. Facebook (11 million members), the second-largest social-networking site, competes with MySpace for an audience of young people, with an especially strong position among college students; it has affiliations with some 2,200 colleges and universities around the country. Xanga.com (8 million) is primarily a collection of individual blogs—online diaries and musings shared with the world. ASmallWorld.com is an invitation-only site famous for having Paris Hilton as a member. QuePasa.com targets Latinos.[24] And Whyville.net, with 1.8 million members, is aimed at providing kids 8 to 15 with a wholesome virtual world where they can hang out, chat, play games, and learn.[25]

Many members find their favorite social-networking sites addictive. They compete obsessively with one another to post the coolest quotes, the funniest pictures, the hottest gossip, and the hippest list of music downloads and favorite TV shows. A Facebook executive reports that some two-thirds of the site's members visit it at least once a day, more often multiple times.[26]

Social networking provides a natural way of extending onto the Internet the human instinct to communicate with others. In that sense, it seems a benign, perhaps wholly beneficial trend. But is there any downside to the burgeoning social-networking movement? It's probably too soon to tell, but that doesn't stop the critics from weighing in.

A source of concern is the enormous commercial potential of social networking. The ability of the networking sites to reach millions of plugged-in young people—prime targets for advertisers and marketers—makes them very attractive as tools to manipulate customers. It is the business angle that people like Rupert Murdoch are interested in exploiting; soon after acquiring the company that runs the site, the Aussie mogul announced plans to try to build it into a rival to Yahoo! for Internet dominance. One of the 20 most-visited sites on the web, MySpace already claims to carry more than 10 percent of all the advertising viewed online.[27]

Advertisers aiming at a youthful audience are especially interested in social networking. Apple Computer sponsors a site devoted to the company's products on Facebook; Disney's Touchstone Pictures created blogs on Xanga.com that were supposedly written by characters from the movie *Hitchhiker's Guide to the Galaxy* as a way of promoting the picture; and Coca-Cola has sponsored a webpage on MySpace for a fictitious hip-hop dancer named Sprite.[28]

These efforts raise the obvious question: How long will an online community based on real human connections retain its appeal when corporations infiltrate it in hopes of creating a gloss of authenticity over what are essentially marketing ploys?

Some advertisers recognize the danger. Unilever is currently using a MySpace page hosted by the sexy, big-busted blonde Christine Dolce (alias ForBiddeN) to promote Axe, a deodorant aimed at 18-to-24-year-old males. The page has attracted some 900,000 friends. But a Unilever spokesperson notes that the company must walk a fine line: "[W]hen you deliver 18- to 24-year-old guys content they want to engage with, they don't mind if it comes from a brand. . . . [But w]e need to be engaging with them, not banging them over the head with brandalism that pollutes their space."[29]

Other observers are concerned that the networking sites may be operated with questionable ulterior motives. Intermix Media—MySpace's parent company—was sued in 2005 by New York's crusading attorney general (now governor) Eliot Spitzer for allegedly planting secret spyware and adware programs into games and screen savers. An out-of-court settlement was reached in which Intermix agreed to pay a $7.5 million fine.[30]

Then there are the psychological aspects of the social marketing. Some critics worry that young people are becoming overly accustomed to social interactions without actual connections, surfing from one instant message to another in the isolation of their dorm rooms or apartments. Others fret about the way our sense of personal privacy and intimacy may be morphing. The atmosphere on MySpace is notoriously raunchy, filled with suggestive pictures and sexual come-ons that may or may not be seriously intended—a blend of *American Pie* and *Girls Gone Wild,* as *New York Times* columnist David Brooks has commented.[31] When people post intimate accounts of their sexual encounters or drinking escapades online for anyone with a computer to read, are they exposing themselves to possible danger from those who might misuse the information? Furthermore, there have been reports of young college grads finding themselves stymied in their search for a first job when prospective employers surf the web and discover embarrassing information about them.

All these potential negatives have some people concerned—so much so that, in July, 2006, the House of Representatives passed a bill to forbid libraries and schools from allowing children to visit social-networking sites.[32] An overreaction? Probably. But it's also a clear indication of both the significance of the phenomenon and the possibility of a backlash.

It will take time for people to develop clear ideas about how far to go with the new social-networking tools and where to draw lines. Excesses will occur. But it seems clear that online spaces for making human connections are here to stay, not replacing traditional forms of community but supplementing them. As MySpace shows, enormous companies are being built around social networks that connect millions of people who are in search of one another. But the long-term future of such online communities, as well as their viability as part of our business and social infrastructure, has yet to be mapped.

YOUR BIG AHA'S

As the success of web sites like MySpace demonstrates, people are eager to find new ways of creating and joining communities. Organizations that create opportunities for doing this can attract vast numbers of followers. But there are important caveats to consider.

When customers create your business, they can vanish as quickly as they arrived. The world of online networking has proven to be highly faddish. Friendster launched the industry in 1999; it was quickly overtaken by MySpace, which in turn faces hundreds of eager challengers. Since the value of membership in any networking site is proportional to the size and currency of the overall membership roster, any shift in perceived "hipness" or "coolness" may spell a rapid decline for one site and an explosion for another.

Online communities may be prone to a race-to-the-bottom mentality. The sense of freedom and lack of censorship found at most online networking sites is part of their appeal. But combined with the relative anonymity of the Internet, this may encourage members to focus on lowest-common-denominator interests and activities—the *Girls Gone Wild* syndrome. If this mentality comes to dominate, it may spell long-term difficulties for the sites in attracting and retaining members, and, especially, in drawing advertisers.

Commerce and community make for an uneasy mix. Some kinds of business dealings seem to fit naturally into online networking; for example, the self-promotional efforts of little-known local bands seeking out fans interested in cutting-edge music. But as businesses push the envelope, seeking to use social networks for promoting products from deodorants to life insurance, it seems likely that web surfers will begin to turn off the commercial appeals, just as millions of TV viewers have learned to channel-flip or leave the room during commercials.

When the spirit of community is abused, expect a backlash. The broader society takes an interest in the large-scale social networks its members form. This is especially true when those networks focus on young people, who are perceived as impressionable and vulnerable. If your organization is involved in community-building, don't be surprised to find yourself the subject of intense scrutiny concerning the wholesomeness of the activities, information, and ideas you are promoting.

CHAPTER 10

High–Tech
Goes High–Touch

Using the Internet to Go Global
and Go Local

THE ROLE OF TECHNOLOGY HAS PLAYED A MAJOR ROLE IN THE PAGES OF this book. Organizations from Dell Computer and eBay to E-ZPass and MySpace have used the new electronic media to provide customers with experiences that make life easier, more efficient, more affordable, and more fun. And organizations like Brooks Brothers and Microsoft have sometimes stumbled in the application of technology—the one by prematurely trying to entice customers into using technology (body-scan imagery) that most find intrusive and uncomfortable, the other by being too slow to take customers concerns about online security seriously enough.

It's not surprising that technology should be such a major theme in a book devoted to customer connections. New technological applications—high-speed wireless Internet connections, streaming video, blogs and other interactive web sites, chips and tags that turn ordinary products into "smart" ones, and other innovations—are creating remarkable new opportunities for organizations to touch and be touched by their customers. No company interested in developing intimate links with its customers can afford to fall behind in the understanding and application of today's electronic connections.

In a curious way, ultramodern technology can be seen as turning back the clock. The new wave of technologically driven information management tools is making it possible for organizations and their customers to rediscover earlier norms of personal service.

A century ago, face-to-face, one-on-one service was the norm. The local merchant knew your name, your family, and your product preferences. Unasked, your neighborhood butcher would set aside a couple of steaks just the way he knew you liked them; on request, the tailor around the corner would produce shirts or dresses in your choice of styles and colors, and even deliver them to your front door. Government and nonprofit organizations often enjoyed equally close connections with their clients. The cop on the beat, the local political boss, and the neighborhood social worker weren't distant figures but family friends.

By the middle of the twentieth century, however, the world had become too big and complex to sustain that level of intimacy. Most people had gravitated from small local stores to giant shopping malls and supermarkets where the product selections were larger and the prices lower, but where no one knew their name, their likes, or their dislikes. Governments and nonprofits, too, evolved into giant, faceless bureaucracies. These changes involved trade-offs that most Americans accepted but that were far from completely satisfactory.

Now technology is redefining the terms of that compromise. The world hasn't gotten any smaller or simpler. But electronic technology is creating the possibility of a new kind of intimacy. More and more people are becoming accustomed to shopping on web sites where, at the click of a mouse, their names, addresses, credit card information, shopping history, sizes, preferences, tastes, and interests can all be instantly conjured up from an unobtrusively powerful database. It just takes a few more clicks to confirm or modify a standing order or to add something new to the shopping cart, and just as in the good old days, purchases can be delivered to the customer's front door, often within a day or two. And as examples like E-ZPass and the 311 telephone information service illustrate, a similar level of rapid, personalized service is beginning to be found in government as well. It is old-fashioned service made possible, not through a person-to-person relationship, but through millions of person-to-network connections.

In a remarkable way, then, a new generation of technology is beginning to reverse what used to be seen as the unavoidable effects of technology: impersonality, standardization, and alienation. And while we may sometimes miss the smiles, the small talk, and the sense of community that came with the old way of connecting, the new way has its advantages. Many of us *like* shopping at three in the morning without getting dressed and without having to chat with the store owner if we don't feel like it.

As a medium for communication, commerce, and community, the Internet is still in its infancy. There's no doubt that, in the years to come, new applications of electronic networking will emerge that we can only imagine today. But the first decade of Internet time has already revealed much of the potential of this powerful new tool, as well as some of the complex challenges that organizations will need to meet. How can we define and achieve the right balance among the many competing forces on the Internet, including global versus local connections, real-world versus virtual relationships, top-down versus bottom-up communications, and centralized control versus individual autonomy? There will probably be as many answers as there organizations active on the Internet. But every organization needs to be thinking about these questions as the World Wide Web continues to grow in importance.

An Electronic Handshake: The Internet Reshapes Politics

Tip O'Neill, the Massachusetts Democrat who served in Congress for 34 years and rose to be Speaker of the House from 1977 to 1987, is famous for having said, "All politics is local." O'Neill's rule, which provided useful advice for several generations of aspiring politicos, had more than one meaning.

On the one hand, O'Neill was reminding his listeners about the importance for any government official of "taking care of the home folks"; a council member, alderman, mayor, or senator who hoped to be reelected had better be sure to bring the home district a fair share of government dollars for bridges, schools, highways, sewers, and other projects.

On the other hand, O'Neill also meant that the art of winning elections was essentially about personal relationships; while TV ads, radio commercials, and mammoth rallies might be fine ways of publicizing a campaign, wooing voters was a retail activity to be conducted one person at a time. The archetypal glad-handing, baby-kissing politician is no figment of anyone's imagination—those kinds of one-on-one connections are what politics has always been about.

Today, however, as populations grow and the demands on politicians' time increase, it's becoming harder and harder for a leader to know everyone in his district personally. Technology is providing new ways for politicians to touch voters. It is also creating new ways for citizens to become involved in monitoring, supporting, influencing, and organizing political movements. Retail politics is no longer restricted to live, in-person activities; it is now increasingly being conducted electronically, as the Internet vastly extends the reach and potential power of campaigns.

Politicians have always sought to use the latest communications technologies. Seventy years ago, Franklin D. Roosevelt's campaign manager James Farley made unprecedented use of a new form of electronic information technology—the telephone—to build an unparalleled nationwide political machine:

> By the mid-1930s, [Farley] had constructed a formidable communications empire, with contacts in every town and city of note. A combination of assiduous use of the telephone, a massive correspondence, use of his scouts and informants nationwide, and regular consultations with the president, agency heads, and leading congressmen guaranteed that Farley always had the inside track on party business. Using these methods, Farley was able to treat the national organization as a city boss would treat his local turf.[1]

Farley's mastery of countless thousands of details about voters and their behavior enabled him to engineer two massive electoral landslides for Roosevelt (in 1932 and 1936), won him a reputation as the world's shrewdest political prognosticator (he predicted the details of the 1936 victory right down to identifying accurately the only two states that the Democrats would not carry), and helped craft the New Deal coalition that would dominate national politics until the 1960s.

Nor was Farley the first master of using proprietary information in politics. As far back as 1896, the McKinley campaign led to a historic election and created a generational shift in the national political landscape. The campaign, managed by the legendary Mark Hanna, identified and targeted dozens of specific demographic and interest groups using mass-produced flyers and direct mail in a process similar to the one a smart marketer uses when planning a product launch.

Later, in the post-World-War-II era, politicians recognized the remarkable impact on voters that broadcast television could have. A charismatic, telegenic young John F. Kennedy was deemed to have won the historic presidential debate of 1960 by those who saw him spar on TV with a wan, poorly made-up Richard Nixon, while those who listened on radio and could judge the two men only by their words and ideas felt Nixon had prevailed. In November, it was Democrat Kennedy—the candidate loved by the television cameras—who won the election.

Four years later, the power of television was confirmed when Kennedy's successor, Lyndon B. Johnson, won a landslide victory over Republican Barry Goldwater in part because of the effect of the shocking, controversial "daisy" commercial, which sent the implied message that Goldwater was a warmonger whose election might bring a nuclear holocaust.

Today, 40 years after the advent of televised politics, candidates and the operatives who support them are adopting the Internet and other electronic media as tools for reaching voters more directly and powerfully than ever. This is a natural evolutionary step. The power of the Internet as a communications medium for the politically involved has been soaring. A Pew Research Center study found that the portion of Americans who sought election-related news online more than doubled in just two years, from 13 percent in 2002 to 29 percent in 2004.[2] Meanwhile, other media are in decline. Between 1999 and 2003, daily newspaper circulation in the United States fell by over a million, and broadcast radio listening has experienced a similar decline. The traditional television networks are drawing an ever-declining percentage of viewers, and those who do tune in are ignoring commercial messages, including paid political ads, more and more. According to the New Politics Institute, a think tank devoted to strategizing on behalf of progressive politicians, fully 64 percent of those who use the increasingly popular TiVo or other videorecording systems skip television ads altogether.[3]

In the face of these trends, it would be just as foolish for politicians as for businesspeople to ignore the growing reach of the Internet—and they know it.

Among the first national campaigns to successfully exploit the potential of the Internet was that of Democratic presidential hopeful Howard Dean in 2004.

As all politicians had done for the past five years or more, the Dean campaign used e-mail for communications and maintained a web site to inform and educate voters. But the not-so-secret electronic weapon of the Dean campaign was Meetup.com, an online social networking service that specializes in providing opportunities for individuals to create groups based on specific interests and geographic location.

Meetup.com was founded in June 2002, by Scott Heiferman, who has said he was inspired by reading Robert Putnam's 2000 book *Bowling Alone*, an influential sociological study of how the United States' "social capital" is declining because fewer people are engaged in their communities.[4] Concerned about this trend, Heiferman decided to try to harness the power of the Internet to reverse it. Meetup.com was designed to make it easy for people to locate neighbors with whom they shared a concern, goal, or interest, and then form real-world connections with them. "The traditional logic goes that the Internet makes things less local," Heiferman has said, "but why couldn't it make things more local?"[5]

The web site allows "meetups" to be organized around almost any conceivable interest or shared characteristic, from a passion for knitting or zydeco music to being a stay-at-home mom, an Asian American entrepreneur, or a witch. Meetup members with a shared interest meet at a time and place suggested by a volunteer convener, and a new real-world community with online roots is born. Most Meetup services are free; Heiferman's company earns profits mainly from advertising on its web site.

When it was launched, Meetup had no particular association with politics. Then, in late 2002, company staffer William Finkel decided to launch an experiment by adding the topic of "politics" to the Meetup menu. Within days, an unusually large number of Dean supporters— liberal Democrats who admired the feisty underdog candidate from Vermont—started logging on to the site and using it to find one another. Many were drawn there by online publicity generated by Jerome Armstrong, one of the most prominent liberal commentators in the blogosphere.

The online Dean phenomenon exploded when Joe Trippi, campaign manager of Dean for America, got a call from Finkel alerting him to the wave of interest in Dean at Meetup. Trippi decided to make meetups an integral part of the Dean organizing campaign. Meetups centered on the Dean candidacy began to multiply in locations around the country, and participation grew monthly. By March, 2003, when a New York City Meetup for Dean was scheduled for a trendy downtown bar called the Essex Lounge, 500 people showed up—far more than the organizers expected or than the little bar could accommodate.[6] Suddenly Dean had become the hottest Democratic candidate, and the Internet was the place to learn about him. Before the year was out, Meetup's membership would include 185,000 Dean supporters, all of them meeting regularly in local groups around the United States with the sole mission of advancing their candidate's campaign.

Dean fans linked by Meetup engaged in a wide array of supportive activities. They organized volunteer teams to pass out flyers at movie openings where large crowds were gathered; they hosted debate-watching parties in supporters' homes to cheer on Dean at key moments in the campaign. They created a letter-writing program targeting undecided voters in the key early voting states of Iowa and New Hampshire that generated over 100,000 handwritten notes; they designed online posters that could easily be downloaded and printed out by any Dean supporter. And because the Internet has no geographic limitations, overseas Americans could also get involved; Dean supporters in London and other European cities held their own meet-ups to raise funds and organize absentee balloting on behalf of Dean. Just as Scott Heiferman had envisioned, Meetup was harnessing the power of the Internet to stimulate local connections in a hundred innovative forms.

Inspired by the energizing power of Meetup, the Dean campaign also developed other new online techniques, expanding the Dean for President web site with a host of creative new features. A directory of local Dean supporters, organized by zip code, made it easy for web surfers to locate the nearest Dean committee to volunteer or get information. A cadre of volunteer software engineers developed a program called DeanSpace that made it easy for local groups to create their own Dean web pages to supplement and extend the reach of the national campaign's site. "It's like having an office anybody can walk into and instantly become part of the staff," commented Zephyr Teachout, the campaign's Internet director. "We're basically using the Internet to allow us to have a 500,000-person staff."[7]

As the popularity of blogs soared in early 2003, the Dean web site launched Blog for America, which allowed readers and visitors to post diaries, comments, questions, ideas, and reactions to others' posts, all without editing or censorship. The degree of citizen response to the blog's availability was impressive. During the second half of 2003, well over 100,000 comments were posted on Blog for America, the vast majority of them from Dean supporters eager to air their ideas about the campaign.

A culture of self-policing quickly developed. When the blog was infested by "trolls"—hostile anti-Dean activists who posted attack diaries just to distract and annoy the other participants—a clever Dean supporter suggested that visitors to the web site pledge an additional financial contribution to Dean for every troll posting that appeared. Realizing that their attempts to sabotage the web site would end up strengthening Dean, the trolls soon vanished.[8]

The Dean campaign also developed the art of online fund-raising into a powerful tool. Rather than simply asking web surfers who visited the site to send a check (as past campaigns had done), the Dean campaign hosted online telethons, with posted financial goals, deadlines, and tickers that added up the moneys donated on a minute-by-minute basis. Traditional political fund-raising campaigns had rarely disclosed their goals to avoid the embarrassment of publicly falling short, but the excitement of the online telethons generated widespread interest, enthusiastic participation, and unprecedented success.

The Dean team took advantage of the Internet's speed to develop rapid fund-raising responses to news events. When former vice president Al Gore made headlines by endorsing Dean on December 9, 2003, within minutes the Dean web site sprouted a special button encouraging visitors to "Donate to thank Al." Four days later, clicks on that button had generated over half a million dollars in donations.[9] When Vice President Dick Cheney hosted a pricey fund-raising dinner for well-heeled Republican contributors, the Dean web site responded with a photo of their candidate scarfing down a turkey sandwich—and raised $250,000 in three days.[10]

Using innovative online techniques like these to connect with a nationwide network of supporters, Dean raised $41 million during 2003, most from small donors and first-time political contributors. This sum surpassed all of Dean's Democratic party rivals and broke the old party record, held by Bill Clinton, for money raised in a single quarter.[11]

As you might expect, other campaigns sought to imitate Dean's success with Internet-based organizational tools. Wesley Clark, the retired general who competed with Dean for the Democratic presidential bid, used Meetup.com to foster connections among his supporters just as Dean had done. By December 2003, Clark supporters were hosting some 300 meetups around the country (about one third the total of Dean meetups during the same month).[12] Rival candidate Dick Gephardt, whose campaign line describing Bush as a "miserable failure" as president briefly seized the media spotlight during the primary race, tried to parlay that publicity into votes by creating a special campaign web site with the memorable address of www.AMiserableFailure.com.[13]

Perhaps most significant, the 2004 campaign demonstrated the unusual degree of involvement and commitment that members of an online political community can share. Internet-based supporters devoted hours to communicating on behalf of their candidate, raising money, canvassing for votes, planning rallies, and exchanging ideas about strategy. The easy accessibility of the Internet turned many once-lukewarm citizens into local activists. Being able to log onto a campaign blog or send e-mails at any hour of the day or night promoted involvement among people who might once have been unable to participate in a political campaign, including full-time parents, the elderly or infirm, and those whose only free time was late at night or early in the morning.

Leah Faerstein, a 50-year-old New York City mom says she used to be politically uninvolved. During the 2004 campaign, she became an avid Wesley Clark supporter via the Internet, and was very excited when the candidate used a phrase she suggested on the official campaign blog in a speech. For Faerstein, this was the ultimate reflection of the power of the Internet to foster a personal tie between a candidate and the citizens. "I'm not going to take the credit," she commented, "But I think it's osmosis. There's a back and forth between us and the campaign. I couldn't feel more connected."[14]

Blanche Ramirez, a 27-year-old Californian, got married during the Dean campaign. She asked her wedding guests to forgo conventional gifts ("We didn't need anything. We had two blenders already") and instead make donations to Dean through her personal Dean Team web page. Now *that's* a personal connection.[15]

In the end, Howard Dean did not succeed in capturing his party's presidential nod. In an ironic twist, the candidate who had shown the world the enormous potential of the new electronic media was undone, in large part, by the power of an old medium—television. A brief video clip from an overly enthusiastic campaign appearance by Dean in January 2004, was isolated and repeated endlessly on TV news and opinion programs, usually accompanied by commentary suggesting that the "screaming" Dean appeared emotionally unstable, if not downright crazy. Dean's poll numbers fell, and rival John Kerry captured the nomination.

However, the broad base of support Dean had built with the help of the Internet didn't evaporate. Thanks in large part to lobbying by his passionate, committed followers, Dean was elected national chairman of the Democratic party in February, 2005. He is now working to revitalize the party's grass roots using some of the same electronic organizing techniques for which his presidential bid became famous.

As it happens, Meetup.com has also profited from its association with the Dean campaign. The publicity associated with the Dean connection helped boost Meetup's membership above two million. What's more, as politicians of all stripes have come to recognize the power of online networking, Meetup is capitalizing financially from their newfound interest. For campaigns that want to go beyond the free services available to anyone on Meetup.com, the company now offers paid organizing and communications tools at rates starting at $750 per month for congressional candidates and $1,500 per month for senatorial and gubernatorial candidates.[16]

Today, the innovations of the Dean campaign are being copied and expanded by many other groups and individuals, who are developing and experimenting with a host of new electronic methods for connecting with citizens. Here are some examples:

- *The blogosphere flexes its political muscle.* With daily visits to the most popular political blogs having soared past the three million mark, bloggers on both the left and the right have been using their growing influence and visibility to launch campaigns aimed at promoting specific policy goals.[17] During the 2004 election cycle, conservative bloggers helped spread the anti-John Kerry message of the Swift Boats Veterans and discredited CBS News's story about President Bush's National Guard service, a controversy that ultimately forced the resignation of anchor Dan Rather. The following year, liberal bloggers such as Josh Marshall of the web site TalkingPointsMemo played a major role in helping to derail President Bush's program for restructuring Social Security, targeting wavering Democratic representatives and senators for pressure from constituents and spreading data and arguments for use on call-in radio shows, letters to the editor, and word-of-mouth campaigns.
- *Political meetups, Round Two.* Across the country, groups that originally coalesced around the Dean candidacy—often through connections forged by Meetup.com—have been transformed into

permanent organizations focused on liberal or Democratic party issues. Many operate under the rubric of "Democracy for America." The St. Louis chapter of the Dean for President organization has morphed into the St. Louis Democracy for America Meetup Group, which boasts over 1,200 members.[18] A similar group in Austin, Texas, has 2,300 members; downtown Manhattan, over 6,000; and Raleigh, North Carolina, 110. In all, over 155,000 Meetup members are organized around the Democracy for America concept, forming a rich potential base of support for candidates and activists with compatible philosophies. On the other side of the political fence, over 10,000 Republican activists are using Meetup in much the same way.

- *Local political organizing via the Web.* Inspired by the Dean campaign, liberal advocacy group ProgressNow, based in Colorado, has created ProgressNowAction.org, a web site designed as an online forum where like-minded activists can find one another, plan organizing efforts, mobilize action around specific legislative initiatives, and coordinate fund-raising and get-out-the-vote efforts. Visit the site and you can hook up with any of almost 150 local groups around the state that meet regularly to plan strategies for promoting their favored causes. ProgressNow resembles such national organizations as MoveOn.org, but its goal is to focus on local issues that often galvanize voters in ways that global concerns fail to do. If it is successful, ProgressNow could become a template for similar groups around the country.[19]

- *Connecting with voters using streaming audio and video.* Candidates are now spreading their messages via the Internet using new media that go well beyond the traditional text-and-picture format of web pages and blogs. John Edwards, who ran for vice president on the Democratic ticket in 2004 and is a potential presidential contender for 2008, is now devoting several hours a week to recording video exchanges with voters for downloading and viewing from his personal blog (http://blog.oneamericacommittee.com/). Other activists are creating daily podcasts, audio recordings direct from political leaders that supporters or others interested in politics can listen to via their computers or MP3 players and pass along to friends. Still others are investigating the possibility of beaming video campaign ads to supporters' cell phones.[20]

- *Going negative on the Web.* Perhaps inevitably, campaign attack ads have also migrated to the Internet. The anonymity of the Internet makes it an attractive venue for campaigns to post embarrassing or damaging accusations about opponents without being publicly linked to the mudslinging, and both major parties have engaged in this practice. Tennessee Republicans created a web site called www.fancyford.com whose sole purpose was to attack the supposedly excessive spending habits of Democratic Congressman Harold W. Ford Jr. Meanwhile, Democrats were said to have launched a site at www.capitolbuzz.blogspot.com to describe sightings of Republican Senator Rick Santorum of Pennsylvania parking his car in a handicapped spot.[21] Cause and effect are always hard to demonstrate, but both Ford and Santorum lost their senatorial races in the 2006 elections.

What all these disparate trends make clear is that politicians and political operatives of every stripe are now recognizing the power of the Internet and other new media to revive and revitalize the locally based, one-on-one connections between leaders and followers that have always been at the heart of the electoral process.

"It's ironic," says Ralph Reed, the veteran conservative organizer, "that the technology of the twenty-first century is taking us back to the politics of what most thought was a bygone era, which is grass-roots. . . . Grass-roots work."[22] And today, the best way to nurture those roots is through the new electronic technology.

Thus, the World Wide Web is more than just a great way to transmit a message to people around the country and the world. It's also a great way to reach out to individual cities, towns, villages, and districts, providing people with tools to forge strong local connections. Electronic networking is a multilayer phenomenon that can help make the activist slogan, "Think globally, act locally" into a powerful reality.

YOUR BIG AHA'S

In today's high-tech era, both individuals and organizations are badly in need of the personal connections that once made life richer and more meaningful. Now electronic communications tools, especially the Internet, are making such connections possible again. Here are some of the lessons about high-tech/high-touch communication that any organization can glean from the experiences of political organizers on the Web.

The Internet connects people at many levels. Mass media like newspaper, television, and radio are great for top-down, global communications. But often your organization may need to supplement these with bottom-up, locally-based communications that foster connections among people at a grassroots level. The Internet can be a powerful ally in your efforts to create such connections, provided you give people the tools to find one another and link themselves appropriately, even as they remain in touch with the goals and directions of the broader organization.

Investigate preexisting tools that can help you spread your message. Your organization should have a great web site loaded with interactive tools for customers and your own staffers to use. But outside web sites, forums, blogs, and networks may serve to supplement your own Internet presence, potentially reaching thousands or even millions of individuals who may never visit your organization's own site. You should continually monitor the Web in search of sites that can do for your organization what Meetup.com did for the Dean campaign.

New ways of connecting with customers may require new rules of communication. One secret of the Dean team's unprecedented online success was its willingness to break with traditional norms of political campaigning. Previous campaigns had shied away from announcing fund-raising goals, but the Dean campaign recognized the emotional appeal of posting a goal on their web site and allowing supporters to watch as, minute by minute, their efforts allowed that goal to be met and surpassed. Similarly, a traditional campaign would probably not have struck the irreverent note of Dean's online "chicken salad" fund-raising dinner; few past candidates have been comfortable with this self-mocking humor. But in the blogosphere, freewheeling satire is viral and energizing, a fact the savvy leaders of the Dean campaign recognized and successfully exploited.

Find ways to link the virtual world with the real world. It is easy to think of the denizens of the Internet as technophiles isolated at their computers. In reality, they are real people—moms and dads, students and workers, homemakers and business owners—who are ready to translate their online interests into real-world activities. Your job is to provide ways to make it easy and enjoyable for them to do just that, as the Dean team did through Meetup.com.

CHAPTER 11

Everyone Is Welcome

The Challenges of Customer Diversity

MAKING POWERFUL CUSTOMER CONNECTIONS WOULD PROBABLY BE easier if all your customers were more or less the same. Imagine a world where everyone was created in your image. All your customers would be the same sex as you, the same age, the same race and religion. They would share your interests, your values, and your tastes. They would want the same things from the products and services they buy, respond in the same way to advertising and marketing and sales appeals, laugh and cry and applaud at the same things on television and in the movies. In this standardized, uniform world, all you'd have to do to connect with customers would be think about what you like and provide it exactly the way you prefer.

How very comfortable, convenient, and profitable such a world would be—and how excruciatingly boring.

In the real world, a central challenge for all leaders that is only growing in importance with each passing generation is the challenge of diversity. No two people are the same. This truth applies to business managers, the employees who work for them, and especially the customers they serve. If you reach out only to people who are the same as you, the chances are good that your clientele will end up being disappointingly narrow. Thus, effective leadership today requires that you inspire your organization with a spirit of openness and respect for all customers, no matter how they vary. That means developing training procedures and managerial processes to ensure that your organization responds to the needs of clients of all races, genders, cultures, religions, and personality types.

Diversity—Waves of the Future

You will want to conduct your business this way simply out of sympathy for your fellow humans. Think about the last time you were snubbed by an arrogant *maitre d'* or night club bouncer, or the way it felt to be the rejected outsider at school or camp. Life has enough pain—we don't have to go out of our way to inflict more of it by excluding one another from a place at the table. But companies that reach out to all their potential customers also enjoy definite business benefits.

For one thing, ethnic and social diversity is an increasing fact of life. Any organization that hopes to grow with evolving markets must learn to cope with diversity. It is true on a global scale, as vast new middle-class cohorts emerge in countries like China, India, Indonesia, Nigeria, and Brazil. Hundreds of millions of newly affluent customers who are probably quite different from your current customer base in cultural, linguistic, ethnic, and social terms hold the key to global economic growth in the next century. For the past 150 years, American firms have enjoyed the advantages of serving a vast, rapidly growing, relatively homogeneous continental marketplace right here at home. International expansion was gravy. Now the situation has changed. The United States is a mature market. Over the next 50 years, the most successful companies will be those that literally know how to speak the languages of overseas markets, from Mandarin and Hindi to Spanish and Farsi, because that's where the economic growth will be.

What's more, the growth won't be restricted to a Western-style middle class that will be satisfied with slightly modified versions of the same goods and services we sell here at home. Vast opportunities exist among customers traditionally assumed to be unprofitable and unreachable by conventional marketing methods who require seriously new forms of thinking if they are to be turned into consumers. Companies like Procter & Gamble are creating new markets worth billions by focusing on the "bottom of the pyramid"—the four billion people living on less than two dollars per day, who collectively represent enormous untapped buying power. Companies that figure out how to sell goods and services to this burgeoning market will reap huge rewards in the decades to come.

Business consultant C. K. Prahalad has studied the business opportunities at the bottom of the pyramid. He shows how companies that adapt to the specific needs of low-income consumers can build great businesses. Among the examples Prahalad cites are Casa Bahia, a Brazilian retailer with sales of over $1.2 billion and over 20,000 employees, which operates exclusively in the *favelas,* or shantytowns, where the poorest people of Brazil are found; Annapurna Salt, a Unilever subsidiary that has captured a significant share of the market in India, Ghana, Kenya, Nigeria, and other African nations with small, low-priced packages of iodized salt specifically designed to help combat rampant iodine deficiency disorder among the poor; and Hindustan Lever Ltd., the largest soap producer in India, which has achieved sales of over $2.5 billion through innovative production, packaging, and marketing techniques that reach into many of the smallest and poorest villages in the subcontinent.[1]

It takes ingenuity and creativity to find ways to reach bottom-of-the-pyramid customers. But the effort is important, not just because of the short-term profit opportunities but because of even greater long-term benefits to companies that win the patronage and loyalty of this huge group of consumers at the start of their march toward middle-class status—a transition that bottom-of-the-pyramid business programs will help to accelerate.

Reaching out to diverse customer groups around the world is a key to success in the years to come. This is one reason many U.S.-based business groups are developing programs of research and outreach designed to improve our nation's image abroad and our relationships with peoples around the world. Organizations like the Travel Business Roundtable (which I happen to chair), the Travel Industry Association, the Discover American Partnership, and Business for Diplomatic

Action have been raising concerns about the problems of worldwide anti-Americanism and are striving to create new forums for cooperation and dialogue across cultural and political borders. We can't leave these issues to be dealt with by government alone; leaders of businesses and not-for-profit organizations, as well as ordinary citizens, have important roles to play as well.

At the same time, ethnic and social diversity is exploding even within the countries of the developed world. Western Europe has long been thought of as relatively homogeneous in ethnic, racial, and religious terms. Yet, thanks to accelerating immigration and striking differences in birth rates, Europe's Muslim population is skyrocketing, having already reached an estimated 50 million—nearly 7 percent of the continent's total.

And in the United States, the buying power of ethnic minority groups is huge and growing. Does your organization do any business in the state of New Mexico? Latinos represent almost 30 percent of the economy there. Do you operate in the District of Columbia? African Americans command over 32 percent of buying power in DC. What about Hawaii? Asian consumers of various stripes—Japanese, Chinese, Filipinos, and many others—make up over 50 percent of the marketplace there. You ignore the demands of ethnic diversity at your peril. By 2010, it's estimated that African Americans will wield over a trillion dollars in economic purchasing power. So will Hispanic Americans, while Asians will have at their disposal almost $600 billion. Any organization that wants to claim its share of that vast pool of spending money needs to be prepared to reach out to these expanding customer communities—or get left behind.[2]

And ethnic variation is only one strand in the ever-evolving tapestry of human diversity. A generation or two ago, businesses and other organizations tended to think of their customers as middle-class white males (except for packaged-goods companies, which assumed that their customers were the wives of middle-class White males). Today there's a long-overdue recognition that human beings come not only in several colors but in many other varied forms. The new forms of diversity that every organization must recognize include:

- *Gender:* In one business after another, old assumptions about which sex makes up the market are being eroded. Across the country, millions of men are doing laundry, changing diapers, and fixing lunches, while millions of women are buying cars, managing the family investments, and launching businesses. As a result of these shifts, the arts of selling are being redefined.
- *Age:* The progress of the baby boomers through midlife and dramatic changes in family structures and conventions are both altering traditional age-related patterns of behavior. Many kids have large disposable incomes and have taken on responsibilities once reserved for adults such as getting dinner on the table. Meanwhile, many elders are returning to school, starting new careers, and getting (re)married.
- *Sexual orientation:* Gays, lesbians, and the transgendered have emerged from the closet and are demanding recognition as the powerful, influential, and relatively affluent voters, citizens, and consumers they are. Openly gay entertainers like Rosie O'Donnell and Ellen DeGeneres are among the most popular figures in show business; and causes like same-sex marriage, once an almost unthinkable concept, are winning approval from growing numbers of Americans.
- *Physical status:* The handicapped, those with sight or hearing disabilities, and those who are physically out-of-the-average—the very large or small, the overweight—are all more visible and vocal than ever. Laws and regulations like the Americans With Disabilities Act (ADA)—as well as evolving social mores—have encouraged thousands of institutions to find ways of accommodating the differently abled, from wheelchair ramps and special seating areas in theaters and stadiums to ATM machines with instructions in Braille.
- *Religious and cultural variation:* For generations, mainstream Americanism included Protestant Christianity and a kind of "white bread" culture represented by popular TV shows hosted by the likes of Lawrence Welk. It is hard to believe, but less than 50 years ago the idea of a Roman Catholic president struck many Americans as controversial, even threatening. Today, acceptance of varied religions and cultures is the norm. Young Americans revel

in music from every corner of the globe. One major political party recently nominated an observant Jew (Connecticut's Joseph Lieberman) for vice president; a Mormon (Mitt Romney of Massachusetts) is now being mentioned as a potential presidential candidate of the opposing party; and a Black Muslim (heavyweight boxer Muhammad Ali) is often cited as the most widely admired and beloved figure in the world.

- *Linguistic diversity:* The English language is still the dominant tongue of American popular culture, and hundreds of millions of people around the world have mastered English simply to participate in that culture. But toleration of other languages within the United States has also increased, as evidenced by signs, TV and radio broadcasting and cable networks, and government information provided in languages from Spanish and Chinese to Russian and Vietnamese, for the benefit of the many talented and energetic immigrants who come to our shores every year.

Each form of diversity represents how groups once considered outside the American mainstream are joining the national dialogue and making it richer and more interesting in the process.

For organizational leaders who haven't previously had to deal with so much diversity or with so many forms of diversity, the changes can be challenging, even confusing. Just keeping straight the adjustments we need to make can be difficult. R. Roosevelt Thomas Jr., a Georgia-based diversity consultant, describes being called in to deal with conflict between two groups of sheriffs in the Fulton County police department. One group was mainly Black, while the other was mainly White, and the departmental leadership assumed that the tension was racial in nature. But when Thomas investigated, a different story emerged. In fact, the department was split between one group of sheriffs who worked primarily during the week (and were mostly Black) and another group who worked on weekends (and were mostly White). The full-time "weekers" considered themselves more committed and professional than the part-time "weekenders," and the disparity produced resentment and hostility on both sides—which had little or nothing to do with race.[3]

Diversity, then, is much more than skin deep. It can be about color; but it can also be about gender, sexuality, religion, language, educational background, and even (as Thomas discovered) the days of the week people work. Which means that understanding the new diversity and dealing with it takes extraordinary openness, sensitivity, and judgment on the part of organizational leaders.

What's more, as our world evolves to become increasingly global, interconnected, and complex, diversity becomes harder and harder to ignore. Not very long ago, the customer base for pharmaceutical companies was reasonably monolithic. It consisted of physicians who prescribed medications for their patients. And in the United States, these doctors were overwhelmingly affluent white males. Selling and marketing to this group wasn't always easy, but at least the challenges were clear, consistent, and predictable.

Today, all this has changed. Enrollments in U.S. medical schools have changed dramatically; women make up a larger percentage of the classes, as do international students from Asia, Latin America, Eastern Europe, and Africa. Also, more and more groups, including patients, are getting involved in influencing doctors' choices of medications. As a result, customer diversity is suddenly an issue for pharmaceutical companies like Pfizer. In the words of Yvonne Jackson, Pfizer's senior vice president for human resources, "We no longer sell to doctors alone. Now we sell to governments and to employee groups and similar organizations. We often work with heads of human resources of employee benefits, who are mostly becoming women." In response, Pfizer is hiring more women and minority-group members, as well as training all its employees in the art of communicating across gender, race, and ethnic lines.[4]

Maybe your organization has already tackled the same diversity challenges as Pfizer. If not, you soon will.

The Multicultural Welcome

On the most basic level, respecting customer diversity begins with your front-line employees. Those involved in sales, marketing, service, and other customer-facing functions need to learn the art of recognizing and respecting cultural, ethnic, and other differences and treating all customers with the kind of respect they themselves would want to receive.

You might assume that this kind of behavior doesn't need to be taught. "Isn't treating people with respect a matter of simple etiquette? That's something they should have learned as kids."

This is a shortsighted assumption. Understanding and respecting diversity takes knowledge, sensitivity, and self-awareness—none of which necessarily come naturally or easily to any of us.

Many American companies rely heavily on customers who are Asian or of Asian descent (e.g., retailers and hospitality providers in cities like New York, Los Angeles, San Francisco, and Honolulu, where Japanese tourists are frequent and welcome visitors). Many of these organizations explicitly teach their employees the following basics of Asian culture that could help them avoid needless mistakes and embarrassment:

- In many Asian cultures, the number four is considered bad luck. Thus, a Japanese tea set would never be packaged with four cups; instead, five would be included.
- Personal space and physical gestures are interpreted differently by Japanese and Americans. When presenting a business card, a Japanese visitor will offer it with both hands (never with just one), then step back to a distance of around four feet. This might seem cold and unfriendly to an American; to a Japanese, it is simply respectful.
- Among Japanese, responding to a request with a blunt "No" is considered rude. It is more polite to respond with a circumlocution such as, "It would be very difficult," or "Perhaps we can consider this another time." An American who doesn't understand this style of communication may find it dishonest or evasive.

As these examples illustrate, respecting diversity doesn't happen automatically; it requires thought, training, and commitment. This isn't about pandering to a different culture—it's about treating people as you would like to be treated, with respect and consideration for the things that make you unique. As one diversity expert has pointed out, "treating everyone the same" may sound egalitarian and fair. But if a blind customer walks into your business, would you simply hand him a brochure to read and walk away? "Treating everyone the same" can sometimes be wildly inappropriate.

What's worse, many organizations actually send their employees misleading signals about their attitude toward diversity. Most companies have a "target customer"—a typical customer that they assume represents the heart of their market and the source of most revenues and profits. If you manage a high-end jewelry store, your target customer is quite different from that of a fast-food outlet, a chain bookstore, or an electronics shop. Many companies make a conscious effort to think about their target customer and to make key business decisions with that image in mind. It is a natural and useful tactic.

Whether you recognize it or not, you are probably training your front-line employees to focus on the target customer. You do this through clues as subtle yet obvious as the posters on display in your store—the models depicted in the posters in an Abercrombie & Fitch store won't look the same as the ones in an Ann Taylor or Gucci boutique.

Such targeting, however, has a downside. It may lead your sales and service staff, probably unconsciously, to ignore or mistreat customers who don't fit the target customer mold.

Imagine a store that sells expensive women's shoes and handbags. The typical target customer may be a well-dressed middle-aged woman, and your staff is probably primed to give such a customer thoughtful and courteous service as soon as she appears. But they may give short shrift to a 17-year-old girl or a middle-aged man in jeans and T-shirt.

This is a dangerous mistake. For one thing, the customer they disdain may in fact be primed to make a major purchase. The 17-year-old may be looking for an expensive handbag to buy with the money she and her siblings have pooled for Mother's Day; the T-shirted man may be a successful building contractor shopping for a gift for his wife on his way home from a job site.

Even if that's not the case, in a society as mobile as the United States, the customer you scorn today may be a major customer tomorrow.

Furthermore, every such mistake has a multiplying effect. Studies show that the typical customer who receives negative treatment in a retail store not only refuses to return but also tells an average of 10 friends or acquaintances about the experience. At that rate, it doesn't take many unfortunate incidents to ruin your organization's reputation throughout the neighborhood.

What's more, it doesn't take overt rudeness (much less out-and-out meanness or racism) to drive away a customer. In another study, 68 percent of customers who reported choosing to avoid a particular sales or service establishment said they did so "not because of negative treatment, but because they were treated with ambivalence."[5] Such subtle cues as a hurried and indifferent "Hello" instead of a warm and friendly one, or a disdainfully wrinkled nose on the face of a salesperson, can be enough to turn a possible customer into a hurt and resentful spreader of bad news about your company and its "not-very-nice" people.

The moral: Awareness of customer diversity on the part of your front-line employees can't be taken for granted. It needs to be made a part of their training so they will consciously focus on their own attitudes, assumptions, and behaviors about *every* customer who every walks through your front door.

Of course, the diversity challenge goes much further than just training your sales and service staff. It also includes adjusting your company's policies so that the needs and interests of diverse customer groups are recognized and addressed through decision making at every level.

The revolution in hospital food service was discussed earlier in the book. One element in that revolution has been a long-overdue recognition of the need to adjust hospital menus to accommodate the varying tastes and needs of diverse patients and their families. Some hospitals are now offering traditional dishes designed to appeal to the palates of ethnically and culturally diverse patients—halal meat dishes for Muslims, fish soup and bison for Native Americans, jook (a traditional rice porridge) for Chinese-Americans. The variations are as numerous as the ethnic heritages of Americans. Patients at the Alaska Native Medical Center in Anchorage may dine on such traditional American Indian fare as caribou stew, boiled fish, and berries.[6]

Is this merely a bow to political correctness or a sop to local ethnic power brokers? Not at all. It is about considering the needs of customers (in this case, patients) in a deeper and more thoughtful way than is usually done. Nutrition is an essential element of good health—an undernourished patient takes longer to heal and is prone to developing new health problems during a prolonged hospital stay. But food is also a basic component of normal life, deeply intertwined with family, culture, tradition, memory, and personal taste. Researching and preparing ethnic menus may cost a little more than simply serving the usual grayish "mystery meat" found in old-style hospital dinners. But it leads to more cleaned plates; fuller, healthier, and happier patients; and shorter, less-costly hospital stays. That's the kind of value that honoring diversity can produce.

Acknowledging diversity also means developing marketing programs tailored to specific categories of customers rather than assuming that a single set of product and service benefits will appeal to everyone. Here's an example from the world of hospitality.

Like other hotel casinos, the Venetian Resort in Las Vegas (best known for its store-lined "Grand Canal," complete with strolling street performers and floating gondolas) has long maintained an extensive database tracking the interests and activities of its frequent customers. Now the Venetian is working with a marketing firm called Cohorts to develop segmented marketing programs for a range of subgroups from among those frequent customers. Each segment is given a name and a definition. The "Jonathans" are defined as "elite single men" (I don't think the group is named after me), as opposed to the "Ryans," who are energetic and sports-minded men. The "Jeffreys and Ellens" are affluent married couples with children, while the "Burts and Marilyns" are mature couples with empty nests. Each group receives tailored mailings and offers designed to appeal to their specific interests and preferences.[7]

Is this kind of categorization a little simplistic? Maybe so—I'm sure that not every guest at the Venetian fits neatly into any single segment. The groupings used by the marketers need to be continually tested against real-world experience and in-depth research into the needs and interests of individual customers; otherwise, they may degenerate into unhelpful, superficial stereotypes. But thinking about customers in terms of several varying groups, each with a different set of characteristics, needs, and interests, is a valuable exercise. It helps to break down our image of the customer base as monolithic—an image that is far more simplistic and much less effective that even the simple set of categories that the marketers at the Venetian use.

Diversity is largely about changing how you think. It means getting past the natural tendency to look at your customers and your organization from your own point of view and learning to see the world through other people's eyes. It is not easy, but it's an essential discipline for anyone managing an organization in today's complicated world.

Your Big Aha's

In an increasingly diverse world, the art of creating strong customer connections offers new challenges. Here are some lessons that today's best-run companies are practicing to transform a diverse customer base into an asset instead of a liability.

Diversity operates along many dimensions. Some managers think of diversity almost exclusively in terms of race. Today, your customers are becoming sensitized to differences of many other kinds, from gender and sexual orientation to language, religion, and physical status.

Changing customer attributes create selling challenges—as well as opportunities. As the social and economic patterns of our lives evolve and become more varied, you and your organization may need to change the assumptions you make about who your customers are and how they want to be treated. Adjustments in how you sell may be necessary, as Pfizer has found with the growing number of nonphysicians, including many women, among their changing customer base. But don't view these changes as purely a problem to be solved—recognize them for the opportunity they are, since the first organization in an industry to adapt to changing customer demographics can seize a lasting advantage over its rivals.

Respecting customer diversity is more than simple good manners. Understanding and responding appropriately to the preferences of customers from varying ethnic, social, and economic backgrounds doesn't always come naturally. Employees charged with customer service may need training by an expert in the special characteristics of their out-of-the-mainstream customers to avoid inadvertently signaling that your organization is less than welcoming.

Targeted marketing and service efforts aimed at diverse customer groups can pay big dividends. Sometimes it takes out-of-the-box thinking to understand the varying segments of your market; key customer groups may be defined by many demographic and social characteristics, from age, gender, geography, and race to income, education, marital status, and more. Devote time and energy to open-ended brainstorming about your customer subsets as well as to quantitative research into their needs and wants, and then develop programs to attract and satisfy those preferences. Your organization may be able to build a significant new business base among once-neglected customer groups.

CHAPTER 12

Your Best, and a Little Bit More

Offering Something Extra to Your Customers

Most great companies are best known for a particular product or service. For Coca-Cola, it's a sweet, brown, sticky beverage that refreshes millions of people every day; for McDonald's, it's a hamburger and french fries served quickly and affordably at thousands of locations worldwide; for Federal Express, it's reliable overnight delivery service for letters and packages. You can scarcely think about these famous brand names without immediately recalling the specific offerings that made them successful.

Something similar applies to great organizations outside the business world. Think of the Red Cross, and you think of workers with blankets and coffee, comforting victims of a hurricane or flood; think of the Public Broadcasting Service, and you picture Big Bird and the rest of the beloved cast of *Sesame Street*; think of the National Park Service, and you visualize the Old Faithful geyser or some other sight from Yellowstone.

If you own a brand name that is closely associated with an iconic product or service, you're very lucky. It gives you a vivid brand image that customers and potential customers aren't likely to forget. But it also poses a challenge. The link to a single offering can limit what an organization is permitted to do, thereby stifling long-term growth. (Look at how

McDonald's has struggled in recent years to get beyond the burger, experimenting with tacos and chicken and salads in an effort to convince customers they're about more than Happy Meals.) It can also make it hard for you to break out of traditional channels for sales and marketing.

By contrast, expanding the products and services you offer through brand extensions can be a great way to nurture growth for your organization. But it's essential that your new offerings be organically connected to your traditional product line and your existing brand image. If not, customers may feel exploited or confused, as if you are simply "trying to sell them"—and the connection they feel to your organization may grow weaker rather than stronger.

Some of the world's most successful, longest-lived organizations have benefited from just this sort of diversification. They have found ways to offer customers something extra that is deeply compatible with their traditional brand image and that expands their marketing reach without diluting their identity. Think about Disney—a company that started out as a maker of animated films and eventually expanded into theme parks, broadcasting, cruise lines, publishing, and many other ventures, all centered around the unifying theme of "family entertainment fueled by the power of imagination." More recently, Apple Computer has successfully expanded beyond its classic line of personal computers into such high-tech items as the iPod portable music system, a natural extension of the company's public image as a master of hip, stylish technology that is easy and fun to use.

For most organizations, finding ways to expand their offerings beyond the basic product or service they're famous for is a crucial challenge. Some have handled it brilliantly; others have stumbled. This chapter explores examples of each and provides lessons from which other organizations can benefit.

Welcome to the Twenty-First Century, Herr Gutenberg: Publishers Look beyond the Book

Book publishers have long been among the world's most traditional, conservative businesses. Perhaps that's not surprising. After all, the book industry is one of the world's oldest, having been founded around

1440 with the invention (or reinvention) of printing using movable type by the German craftsman Johannes Gutenberg. The breakthrough launched a technological and cultural revolution. Within a generation, book publishers were in operation in several European countries. They flooded the world with quantities of books that would have been unimaginable in the old days of handwritten manuscripts and dramatically increased the accessibility of knowledge for all.

As a communication medium, the book hasn't changed much since the days of Gutenberg. If you can read the language, you'll have no difficulty understanding the format and contents of a book printed four or five hundred years ago, and books by the classic authors of past eras continue to move and enlighten readers of today.

Until recently, the sales and marketing methods of publishers remained largely unchanged as well. The business approach has been pretty rudimentary: Print a few thousand copies of a book, persuade a group of bookstore owners around the country to stock it on their shelves, and wait—and hope—for customers to show up and buy it.

No wonder most books die a quick death, finding their way to the three-for-a-dollar remainder tables and then vanishing forever. Even the few titles that become best sellers reach surprisingly modest numbers of readers. A book can reach the prestigious *New York Times* best-seller list with sales of just 100,000 copies or so (depending on the week-to-week rate of sale, time of year, and other factors), while only a handful of mega-best sellers (books like *The Da Vinci Code*) ever attain sales in the millions. These quantities are dwarfed by the numbers of viewers who watch even the most mediocre network sitcom.

Contemplating facts like these, scholar Jacques Barzun wrote:

> The phrase "marketing of books" is itself a paradox, a rebuke to sanity. *What* marketing of books? Tradition and a faith in things not seen maintain the bookstore, which the trade calls an outlet; actually, it is a bottleneck, a plugged-up medicine dropper. . . . The trade consoles itself with the axiom that the United States is "not a reading country." If hamburgers were as inaccessible as books, the United States would have to be put down as "not an eating country."[1]

Barzun was writing in the late 1950s, but ask most authors and they will tell you, with a sigh or a scowl, that the story hasn't changed much in the past 50 years.

My own experience as an author has been happier than most. When my first book, *The Power of We,* was published in 2004, I had the opportunity to devote a fair amount of my own time and energy to promoting it, and thanks to my experience in the business world, there were groups and organizations ready to absorb the message I had to offer. In the course of a 12-city publicity tour, I spoke before gatherings ranging from 25 people in Seattle to over 7,000 at a conference in Toronto. And in October, 2006, I shared the stage at New York's Javits Center with such luminaries as Disney's former chairman Michael Eisner, cycling champion Lance Armstrong, and former president Bill Clinton. (No, I didn't get top billing at that one.) These speaking engagements certainly did a lot to boost interest in the book.

But as with almost every author, my days on the road included a fair share of weird and funny mishaps. For example, my first big TV appearance was scheduled for NBC's *Today Show* the week of the book's release in September. "You'll be on at 9:40," I was told when I arrived, "Our hair and makeup people will get you ready."

At 9:35, host Matt Lauer (whose portion of the program had ended) visited me backstage. "Shouldn't you be on set by now?" he asked, puzzled.

"Maybe so," I replied, "but no one's come for me."

More minutes passed, as Matt and I wondered what was happening. When the show ended on schedule at ten o'clock, I realized I'd suffered every author's nightmare—I'd gotten bumped. "Oh, well," I said philosophically, "There must have been some kind of huge breaking news story that squeezed me out of the schedule."

Just then, the producer burst into the room. "Oh, Mr. Tisch, I'm so sorry we had to bump you! But it was just unavoidable. You see, Britney Spears got married over the weekend, and we had to give that story extra coverage. And since this is Advertising Week here in New York, we ran an extra segment about the Aflac duck. I'm sure you understand."

Matt Lauer was cracking up. No one could complain about getting bumped for something like a visit by the Pope or a presidential news conference—but for Britney Spears and a duck? Nothing could express more clearly the humble place that we authors occupy in the modern media food chain.

Actually, it wasn't a total loss. News anchor Ann Curry taped a very nice interview segment with me before I left the studio, and it aired on *Today* the next morning.

Even funnier was my experience two weeks later in Miami. I was scheduled for a 10 o'clock appearance on the local *South Florida Today* show on WTVJ. A few minutes before seven o'clock, I was sitting in my bathrobe in my room at the Loews Miami Beach Hotel, drinking coffee and watching the local anchors chatting about the upcoming high-lights of that morning's program. Imagine my feelings when I heard one say, "Here's some exciting news. We're going to have John Tesh live here in our studio!"

Her colleague responded, "Oh, I'm a big fan of his from his years on *Entertainment Tonight*. I hope he'll play the piano and sing a song or two!"

When I showed up on the set a couple of hours later, those poor anchors couldn't have been more embarrassed and apologetic. They graciously explained their mistake on air and conducted a very good interview. And luckily for them, I did *not* sing a song.

As you can see, reliance on unpredictable media like morning TV news programs to promote new books can be a source of frustration for authors and publishers alike. For decades, as big corporations and new business methods have broken barriers into the traditional world of publishing, experts and industry professionals have vowed to finally break the book marketing bottleneck. Trends like the emergence of the book superstores (which, for all their faults, have brought modern book retailing into hundreds of communities where it never existed before) and giant online retailers like Amazon.com have brought hope to authors and publishers. And phenomena like the massively popular *Harry Potter* books for kids and the enormous sales enjoyed by titles recommended as part of the Oprah Winfrey television book club have reaffirmed the potential of books as powerful forms of education, entertainment, and fun. They play an important role even in a world of movies, television, video games, and the Internet.

In the early years of the twenty-first century, momentum is finally building behind the forces of change. Book publishers are learning how to add value for their loyal customers and attract new ones through new product and service offerings, and in the process, they are developing new tools for marketing books. They have finally accepted that it's not enough merely to edit and produce fine works of literature; the books must also be surrounded by ancillary products and services that multiply their appeal to possible readers. If the potential of these recent developments is realized, book publishing may yet enjoy the kind of cultural and economic resurgence that bibliophiles have long dreamed of.

Here are some examples of how book publishers are learning new ways to add value to the products they sell:

- *Help in launching reading programs:* One of the most popular ways that book-lovers enhance their own experience in reading is by forming book clubs; groups of five to a dozen friends, neighbors, or colleagues meet regularly to discuss books they've read. Publishers have discovered that book clubs encourage reading and make it more enjoyable and have worked to support the formation of such clubs in a variety of ways. Many books deemed suitable for book-club selection—including nonfiction books with timely topics or strong human-interest appeal, and novels with complex social or emotional resonance—are now printed with guides for book-club discussions, author interviews, suggestions for additional reading, and other resources. On a larger scale, entire cities have created reading programs centered around thought-provoking classics such as *To Kill a Mockingbird* and *A Lesson before Dying,* stimulating civic engagement and conversations around important issues. To encourage this trend, Random House (the venerable U.S. book publisher now owned by the German media conglomerate Bertelsmann) offers advice on its web site for librarians and citizens' groups on how to launch similar citywide reading and discussion programs.
- *Opportunities to interact with authors:* New technologies like the Internet are making it possible for readers and authors from far-

flung locations to connect more directly than ever before. To promote themselves and their work, many authors have created their own web sites and blogs where readers can learn more about their favorite books, e-mail the authors, trade observations with other fans, and learn about upcoming author lectures or other appearances. Most major publishers now provide links on their own web sites to author blogs, and some even host author blogs directly. And at least two of the biggest publishing firms, Random House and HarperCollins (a division of Rupert Murdoch's News Corporation), have gone a step further: They offer local book clubs an opportunity to request a live or by-telephone chat with a favorite author. The ultimate in interactivity, these 30-to-60-minute encounters give readers an opportunity to ask authors the kinds of questions they've often wondered about: "Was your novel really autobiographical?" "Who are your own favorite authors?" "How did you get started as a writer?"—and help turn one-time readers into lifelong fans.

• *Advance news about books:* At one time, the relatively small coterie of serious readers relied on informal chats with their local independent bookseller to learn about new books of interest. Today, with independent booksellers slowly dying out before the advances of the superstores and the online retailers, this channel of communication is vanishing. The Internet has made it easy for publishers to communicate directly with book lovers about forthcoming books and related events simply by inviting fans to sign up for online newsletters, e-mail alerts, and similar informational programs. HarperCollins offers newsletters that focus on specific literary genres providing book excerpts and author interviews; an "AuthorTracker" program that sends e-mails to fans when a favorite author plans a speaking tour or releases a new title; an "Authors Near You" program that highlights author appearances in a particular state or region; and "First Look," which lets avid readers see advance copies of books before they reach the stores. Programs like these make readers feel more connected to their favorite writers and to the publishers who market their works.

New technologies and methods of communication are creating other, more indirect opportunities for publishers to improve their antiquated marketing programs. Consider the issue of coordinating book-related publicity (such as reviews and author interviews) with official "publication" (i.e., the availability of the book in local bookstores). For decades, publishers assumed quite correctly that publicity predating bookstore availability would be useless or even counterproductive, since would-be book buyers who visited a store only to be told that the book they'd heard about was not yet available would probably be turned off for good.

The advent of online retailer Amazon.com has changed all that. Amazon allows customers to place advance orders for forthcoming books, which are then fulfilled as soon as the books are available. In the words of Paul Bogards, a spokesperson for Alfred A. Knopf (the distinguished publishing imprint now owned by Bertelsmann), this "ability to capture a sale before a book is officially on sale has had a profound impact on our business." Knopf and other publishers are now borrowing a page from the Hollywood movie studios, deliberately setting out to create customer buzz months in advance of the release of a book, just as the studios have long done for their biggest pictures.

For *The Number,* by Lee Eisenberg, a book of financial advice for baby boomers that was published in early 2006, Knopf took several steps that would have been unheard-of five years ago. The company sent 300 advance copies to bloggers who specialize in financial topics; hired BzzAgent Inc., a Boston-based marketing firm that specializes in creating word-of-mouth discussion about a new product using a nationwide network of volunteers; and sent advance bound galleys of the book to influential readers a full eight months prior to publication (rather than the traditional three to four months). As a result, thousands of potential readers heard about *The Number* long before it was available, and many preordered the book online. Other publishers are using similar early-bird tactics for marketing books ranging from controversial political treatises to novels.[2]

An even more striking innovation—still experimental at this point—is the use of streaming videos on the Internet as book marketing tools. The videos have been running on popular web sites such as

MSN, YouTube, and Yahoo! that draw hundreds of thousands of visitors in search of the latest funny, weird, or intriguing images, and they vary as widely as the books themselves. In one video produced for Random House, best-selling thriller author Dean Koontz recounts funny anecdotes about his experiences as a writer. In another, famed children's book author and illustrator Maurice Sendak describes the process of creating his forthcoming pop-up book *Mommy?* for Scholastic. Still others have the look and feel of movie trailers, depicting chilling, moving, or suspenseful moments from novels or memoirs.[3]

It remains to be seen which of these innovations will become permanent parts of the book-publishing scene. The specifics of any one program are not as significant as the shift in mind-set they reflect. Publishers now recognize that their mission doesn't end with simply creating great books (difficult and important as that is). If they hope to create and nurture new generations of avid readers who are deeply and loyally connected to their favorite authors and the publishers who market their works, they must enhance the value of the books with ancillary products and services—from book club guides and author chat programs to advance publicity and video trailers.

YOUR BIG AHA'S

At long last, the once-stodgy book publishing industry is creating new ways of reaching out to its traditional customers as well as connecting with new ones. Here are some of the lessons that leaders in any industry can learn from their experiments.

Your most loyal customers are looking for new ways to connect with you. Book-lovers have always had intense feelings about their favorite authors and genres, from mysteries and romances to books about the Civil War, baseball, or Italian cooking. Yet the efforts by publishers to reach out to these devoted customers have been fragmentary at best. Leaders of every organization need to strive to identify their most loyal customers and find ways to enhance the connection with them. This is at least as important—and far more efficient—than struggling to find and attract new customers.

New forms of communication can be used to create deeper, more continuous streams of information between you and you customers. Many organizations rely on middlemen—retailers, agents, professional services providers, or local representatives— to communicate with their ultimate clients, much as publishers used to rely on independent booksellers to keep avid readers informed. But today the Internet makes it possible for organizations to remain in close, direct touch with their most loyal customers. Don't pass up the opportunity.

As technology changes, traditional assumptions about marketing may need to change, too. Even technologies that don't directly affect your products and services may have a profound impact on how your organization operates. Traditional processes for publicity, promotion, and marketing in book publishing were based on the technologies of the 1920s: newspaper ads and reviews, networks of independent bookstores, shipping supplies of books by truck. Today, publishers are working to adapt to the technologies of the early 2000s: blogs, Internet retailing, instant content downloads, video streaming.

When seeking new ways to serve customers, tap the creativity of all the people connected with your organization. The efforts of book publishers to deepen their connection to readers would be severely limited if not for the creativity and energy of authors, who are not employees of the publishers yet are profoundly committed to the success of the publishing enterprise. Look around your organization, both inside and out. Can you identify constituencies of individuals who care about your success and may be willing to offer their talent to help make it happen?

The New Museum: Satisfying the Senses as Well as the Soul

Ever since they were first created during the late Renaissance, museums have been important centers for the preservation and transmission of culture. As museums multiplied and spread throughout the developed world, they provided middle-class and working-class people with access to fine art as well as natural and scientific wonders that were formerly available only to royalty or the very rich, or in a religious setting. Many great artists have found their first inspiration during a visit to an art museum as a child, and countless ordinary citizens derive pleasure, education, and enlightenment from periodic trips to their local museums. Today, as social amenities and sources of local pride, museums are generously supported by private donations as well as by grants from city, state, and federal government agencies. Establishment of a first-class museum is often viewed as a crucial step in the development of a modest town into a great city.

But in the early years of the twenty-first century, museums face unprecedented challenges.

First, like sports arenas and shopping centers, museums are expected to play a major role in local economic development. Public funding of museums is increasingly predicated on the notion that the museums will attract out-of-town visitors, lure ancillary businesses, and enhance the image of the area, serving as an anchor and a spur to growth. This puts added pressure on museum directors to achieve ever-increasing levels of public interest and support.

Second, in their roles as educators, entertainers, and purveyors of culture to the masses, museums face far more competition than in the past. Television networks from the Public Broadcasting Service (PBS) to the History and Discovery Channels now introduce viewers to the wonders of human creativity. Learning programs offered by community colleges, online universities, parks departments, and private organizations have multiplied. And the leisure activities available to middle-class and working-class people have grown exponentially, drawing time and attention away from museums. The same days that a middle-class family might once have spent in a museum might now be spent surfing the Internet, visiting a theme park, strolling a massive shopping mall, attending a sporting event, or participating in community events at a multi-activity megachurch.

Finally, American and world cultures have subtly shifted in ways that weaken some of the allure once characteristic of great museums. A generation or two ago, a powerful sense of hierarchy separated high art from everyday experience. The works of geniuses like Leonardo da

Vinci, Rembrandt, and Picasso were taught in schools, celebrated in reverential television specials and glossy coffee-table books, and held up as unique exemplars of the highest in human achievement. This approach had its disadvantages. It created a gulf between real life and the world of art that probably discouraged many people from becoming deeply engaged with it. But it also made the museum a special place that parents felt they should expose their children to and one that every educated person felt obliged to honor.

Today, the gulf between high art and the everyday world of pop culture has almost disappeared. Ironically, this change was begun largely by artists from what once was considered the high art world, as movements like Dada (in the 1920s) and Pop Art (in the 1950s and 1960s) deliberately undercut the pretensions of high art. The trend was accelerated by the growing appreciation among artists, critics, and educators for the vibrancy and creativity of popular culture, folk art, and non-Western art. Today, few people would deny that moviemakers, jazz and rock musicians, quiltmakers, potters, and cartoonists can create art of lasting value. As a result, people who are passionate about human creativity seek it not just in museums but in many other venues, from the crafts gallery and the coffeehouse to the movie multiplex and the underground newspaper.

In this new, more open art world, museums must find new ways to define what makes them special and draw visitors through their doors. The old model of the museum-going experience is no longer adequate:

- The hushed, reverential tone that once symbolized the importance of high art is now constricting and uncomfortable for many visitors.
- The "hands-off-the-art" and "no food or drink" policies designed to protect precious works and to emphasize the specialness of art make visitors accustomed to interactive experiences feel distanced and uninvolved.
- The austere architectural design in traditional museums (marble walls and floors; high ceilings; vast, echoing, empty spaces) further alienates visitors.

• The relative monotony of the traditional museum experience— look at one painting or sculpture, read the brief accompanying label, then move on to another painting or sculpture—seems boring to many visitors from the channel-surfing era.

As a result, old-fashioned museums have an image in the minds of many potential visitors as irrelevant and uninviting. When they visit a museum, they are apt to leave after just an hour or two, feeling relieved to get back into the real world where they can talk loud, eat and drink as they please, interact with things in a tactile, multisensory fashion, and generally be themselves. Why stare at fine art behind glass in a museum when we can heft pottery in a crafts store, touch fine fabrics in a shop at the mall, or run our fingers over sculptures on display at a local studio?

Most museum directors recognize these challenges. They're not content to allow themselves and their institutions to become gradually more and more irrelevant to the lives of their communities. Instead, they've been experimenting—especially in the past two decades—with inventive ways to reimagine the museum experience, offering new, unexpected, varied, lively, and interactive displays calculated to attract and retain the interest of new generations of museum-goers. Their efforts may be unsettling to old-school types for whom the traditional museum model will always be the only real way to experience high art, but for millions of average Americans, the museum directors are breathing fresh air into an experience that had become stale and uninteresting.

Interactivity is one of the chief techniques by which museums have been expanding and redefining the visitor experience. Many cities now have hands-on science museums designed to let people of all ages, but especially kids, learn about physics, chemistry, astronomy, biology, and other scientific fields through simple experiments, demonstrations, optical illusions, constructions, and other activities.

Now the same philosophy is being expanded to other types of museums. For the 1993 centennial of the Denver Art Museum, the curators redesigned much of the exhibit space to include multiple viewing angles for individual artifacts (instead of restricting visitors to a single head-on glimpse at traditional glass cases); audiotapes in Spanish and English to explain the origins, style, and meaning of the art works; and touchable objects designed to break down the traditional barriers between patrons and exhibits.[4]

At the Children's Museum of Manhattan, a new 4,000-square-foot exhibit is being developed to draw kids under five into a direct relationship with the world of high art. Hands-on experiences will be the rule, not the exception. "PlayWorks" will feature a huge transparent wall for fingerpainting, designed to be washed periodically by a floor-to-ceiling water cascade; touchable, three-dimensional renderings of cave drawings, Egyptian paintings, and works by Leonardo da Vinci and Jackson Pollock; and a sand laboratory in which kids are encouraged to dig for buried treasures. (Accompanying parents are likely to be as intrigued and delighted by the exhibits as their toddlers.[5])

Live human interactions offer yet another way of enhancing and expanding the museum experience. When mounting a show about life on the railroads, the Festival of American Folklife used retired railroad workers talking about their work experiences to create a living museum exhibit that was far more compelling than the usual static displays of pictures, artifacts, and wall texts.[6]

One of the most popular ways that museum directors are adding a new dimension to the museum-going experience is by introducing great food. In one museum after another, the old cafeteria-style eatery is being replaced by a temple of *haute cuisine* designed to appeal to the refined palates of art lovers.

Offering a first-class restaurant does more than simply make a museum visit more enjoyable and memorable. It also generates additional revenue for the cultural institution and provides an attractive venue (and a top-notch catering service) for corporate or fund-raising events. Most important, it encourages visitors to prolong their stays. Too often, notes consultant Art Manask, museum patrons "go out to lunch and don't come back."[7] Give them a nice place to eat and they will spend their lunch break poring over the museum floor plan, probably discovering several additional galleries they want to visit during the afternoon. The strategy isn't unlike the one used by theme park companies, which keep adding new attractions to encourage tourists to extend their stays in Orlando, Anaheim, or Hershey from three days to four or from five days to seven.

There are many examples of this powerful new trend. The February 2005 reopening of the expanded Museum of Modern Art in New York featured the launch of *The Modern,* a sleek, lively restaurant run by renowned restaurateur Danny Meyer. The restaurant has its own entrance, and the food is prepared by star Alsatian chef Gabriel Kreuther.[8]

Other well-known restaurateurs are getting involved in the museum scene. Wolfgang Puck Catering (WPC) operates dining spots in museums in Boston, Chicago, St. Louis, Indianapolis, and Minneapolis, and is working on new museum venues in Washington, DC, Atlanta, and San Francisco, as well as providing the food at the newly renovated Griffith Observatory in Los Angeles and Benaroya Hall, home of the Seattle Symphony. Company officials relish the favorable publicity that accompanies well-received museum openings in new cities, as well as the opportunity to use the beautiful and historic buildings for all kinds of catered events.[9]

Many of the new upscale museum restaurants serve dishes cleverly keyed to fit the art on view in the gallery spaces. The menu at the O'Keeffe Café in the Georgia O'Keeffe Museum in Santa Fe, New Mexico, was created by chef Mike Dyer and local foodie Deborah Madison, author of *Vegetarian Cooking for Everyone* and a board member of the Santa Fe Area Farmers' Market. It features vegetarian dishes, fresh local produce, and homestyle cooking in the style that the artist favored during her years in the American Southwest. When the Denver Art Museum hosted an exhibit titled "Searching for Ancient Egypt," chef Kevin Taylor added Egyptian couscous and roasted vegetables with spicy harissa to the American-style menu at Palettes, the museum's eatery.[10]

In some cases, specific works of art inspire whimsical dishes. After viewing pop artist Claes Oldenburg's monumental sculpture *Spoonbridge and Cherry* at the Walker Art Center in Minneapolis, you can stop by the center's handsome new 20.21 restaurant (named to commemorate the museum's emphasis on art of the twentieth and twenty-first centuries) and sample "Spoon, cube, and cherry," a tower of chocolate mousse and ice cream topped with a spoon carved from chocolate and holding a cherry. When the Philadelphia Museum of Art hosted an exhibit highlighted by a Salvador Dali sculpture of a telephone, the museum restaurant produced a dish of chicken topped by a red lobster shell positioned to resemble a phone receiver.[11]

Some museums are experimenting with multiple food-service styles. The Boston Museum of Science has a food court that includes a concept restaurant called Taqueria, Puck's café, a Starbucks, an Au Bon Pain, a Boston Fish Market, and a Ben & Jerry's.

Museums are also devising still other ways of using their spaces beyond food service. The Walker Art Center in Minneapolis, the Indiana Museum of Art in Indianapolis, and the aquarium in Atlanta all have ballrooms for major entertainment events.[12] And even as museums are bringing nonmuseum activities within their once-sacrosanct spaces, they are also bringing their collections of great art to locations that might once have been unimaginable. After decades of successful operation in its classic Frank Lloyd Wright building on New York's Upper East Side, the Guggenheim Museum expanded during the 1990s to include galleries in Manhattan's Soho and the Unter den Linden area of Berlin, Germany, as well as a great new museum in Bilbao, Spain. Perhaps most remarkably, in 2001 the Guggenheim opened two museums in the world's Mecca of glitz and decadence, Las Vegas, including one at the Venetian Resort and Casino. Now plans are in the works for a Guggenheim in Abu Dhabi, the capital of the United Arab Emirates.

Today's newly designed museums aren't losing sight of their raison d'être. Great works of art, natural mysteries, and scientific marvels remain the central attraction for local visitors and out-of-town tourists alike. But museum directors have learned that expanding the museum experience through hands-on, interactive activities, as well as offering delightful ancillary services that prolong and enhance the museum visit, can draw more visitors and encourage repeat visits. In this way, these extra goodies don't detract from but strengthen the museum's primary mission of educating, entertaining, and enlightening average citizens.

The museum industry—once a stodgy realm restricted by traditional notions about how to provide access to high culture—is being transformed by new ideas about marketing and enhancing the customer experience. Here are some things you can learn from the new world of museum management.

Tradition is great, but so is (occasionally) overturning tradition. Museum directors are generally drawn from the population of people who, as children, loved the traditional museum experience—the sense of awe, mystery, and hushed expectation that pervaded a visit to a great, imposing temple of high art. But these same directors are increasingly aware of the need to tweak that experience to make it more relevant to a younger generation of art lovers, whatever their personal inclinations might be.

Broaden your focus to take in the whole customer experience, not just the parts you've traditionally emphasized. Leaders of cultural institutions like museums need to remain focused on their traditional areas of expertise, such as mounting blockbuster exhibits devoted to major artists, themes, or periods. But if they hope to establish deep and lasting connections with their clientele, they also need to consider every aspect of the museum visit, from traveling and parking to shopping and dining.

When you expand the goods and services you offer customers, your core business will also benefit. Devoting a portion of the museum space to a wonderful gift shop, a fine restaurant, or a ballroom may appear to detract from the exhibit of works of art. The same might be said about making the museum available during off-hours for catered corporate events or parties. But if these ancillary attractions are tastefully planned and managed, the museum's cultural role can be enhanced, not weakened. Visitors who enjoy the restaurant are likely to spend longer touring the galleries; guests at a Saturday-night fund-raising gala will return on Sunday morning to study the works of art they glimpsed the night before.

> *If you are great at what you do, your reputation is a valuable commodity in its own right.* The value added by the ancillary services provided at a great art museum derives in large part from the prestige of the museum. A scarf from a museum gift shop may be sold at a price premium because of the aura of artistry and class it exudes; a catered party in a marble exhibit hall may be sought after by events planners because of the grandeur of the museum and the works of art it contains. If you help to lead an organization with a great reputation, you should look for opportunities to capitalize on that reputation through new product and service offerings—but never do anything to compromise that reputation, which is the source of your credibility and value.

Starbucks and the Tricky Art of Brand Extension

We've looked at how organizations like book publishers and museums have been adding new products and services to broaden and enhance the customer experience. When these are well-planned, natural extensions of an organization's mission, they can greatly deepen and enrich your relationship with your customers. But this doesn't mean you can simply tack on new offerings to your existing menu and assume they will delight customers. Goods and services that don't fit your organization's existing mission may confuse customers and end up weakening instead of enhancing your brand.

An organization that is currently hard at work looking for ways to extend its brand is Starbucks, the enormously popular coffee shop chain. Starbucks has already done a phenomenal job of connecting to customers. There are lots of places where you can buy a good cup of coffee, but Starbucks has created a unique phenomenon with its ubiquitous storefronts, whose relaxing decor, comfortable chairs and tables, and (in many locations) wireless Internet access have made them a favorite hangout for anyone with a few minutes or an hour to kill. Millions of fans around the United States and in 21 countries overseas now seek out the nearest Starbucks both for their regular shot of caffeine and for a few minutes of peace and serenity in the midst of a hectic day.

But despite the huge success that Starbucks has enjoyed, the leaders of the company are eagerly searching for new ways to serve and connect with their customers. The reasons aren't hard to find. There is still plenty of room for Starbucks to expand into new territories, both in the United States and abroad—one estimate holds that the company currently reaches just 7 percent of the coffee shop market. But it's obvious that there are limits to the number of Starbucks outlets that the world can support. What will Starbucks do to ensure future growth and ever-deeper customer connections once they have a shop on practically every block?

To their credit, CEO Howard Schultz and the rest of the leadership team have been thinking about this challenge for some time. However, their initial attempts to answer the question by broadening Starbucks' offerings into new, fundamentally unrelated product and service offerings have met with mixed success.

Schultz has always maintained that Starbucks is not fundamentally about coffee. In the words of the CEO, "It's the experience"—the availability, for a few bucks, of a relaxing respite in the midst of a busy day, a comfortably furnished "third place," neither work nor home, where people can gather to chat, read, listen to music, or simply chill out over their favorite beverage.

While this is a vision that millions of people can appreciate, the Starbucks promise has always had special appeal to a specific demographic—moderately upscale, moderately hip, youngish urban professionals, for whom a $4 latte represents an affordable self-indulgence. For people like this, the Starbucks ambience represents an attractive throwback to college days or perhaps a memory of a great old-world coffeehouse from a vacation in Italy or Spain. This is the experience that Starbucks is meant to evoke, and it's what Howard Schultz is selling. The company's challenge: How to embody that experience in more than just a great cup of coffee?

In search of answers, Starbucks first made forays into the world of print media. In some ways, it was a natural brand extension; historically, coffee and literature have long been linked, from the very first coffeehouses in eighteenth-century London, where writers like Samuel Pepys and Dr. Johnson conducted informal salons, to the hangouts of the 1950s, where Beat writers like Jack Kerouac, Lawrence Ferlinghetti, and Allen Ginsberg gave readings timed to the pounding of bongo drums.

In an effort to continue and update that tradition, Starbucks has created links to popular literary efforts from outside the world of retailing. In 1996, it began offering a printed version of the online magazine *Slate* for sale in its stores. A lively, quirky, opinionated journal of culture, politics, and the arts edited by well-known journalist Michael Kinsley and sponsored by Microsoft, *Slate* seemed a likely fit for the Starbucks customer. After a few issues, however, it became clear that the scanty sales of *Slate* didn't justify the store space devoted to it. The Slate.com web site is still going strong, but the print version no longer exists.

A year later, Starbucks launched an effort to sell books, including a selection of titles chosen by TV talk show host Oprah Winfrey—a famous maker of best sellers—in its stores. This, too, fizzled.[13]

Starbucks wasn't through trying to make inroads into the world of literature. In June 1999, the company teamed up with the editorial forces of Time, Inc. to launch *Joe,* a quarterly magazine priced at $2.95 and featuring lifestyle articles by some of the United States' hippest young writers, including Douglas Coupland and Pagan Kennedy. Magazine racks were installed in 1,900 Starbucks outlets, and a web site containing excerpts from the print version was installed at Joemag.com.[14]

After three issues, however, the venture was defunct. The magazine failed to gain any real traction in the notoriously competitive world of magazine publishing; its articles never generated much buzz; and in the end, *Joe* simply didn't sell very well. The magazine racks were retrofitted to display Tazo teas instead.

By 2006, Starbucks' efforts to purvey great writing had been reduced to a series of coffee cups containing inspirational quotations from well-known authors and, occasionally, other celebrities—the likes of Armistead Maupin, Rick Warren (*The Purpose-Driven Life*), and civil-rights attorney Morris Dees.[15] The cups generate no revenues for Starbucks, and it's doubtful how significantly they contribute to enriching the Starbucks experience for customers.

Starbucks also embraced the world of electronic publishing. At the height of the dot-com craze, it invested in Living.com, an ambitious Internet lifestyle portal that it hoped would become one of the most popular home pages on the World Wide Web. Unfortunately, coffee lovers who visited their neighborhood Starbucks every day didn't feel compelled to do the same with Living.com. By 2000, the company had shut down the web site and written off $20.6 million in expenses derived from it.[16]

Meanwhile, more traditional coffee-product spin-offs were performing profitably for Starbucks. Sales of bottled coffee drinks and coffee-flavored ice cream in supermarkets and convenience stores were brisk. And a new ancillary service—wireless Internet access at Starbucks stores that established "hot spots" for laptops computers—proved surprisingly popular. It offered several interlocking benefits for the company: fees from access charges (ultimately dropped as free wireless access became the norm); enhancement of the customer experience; and more frequent and longer visits to Starbucks stores by customers looking for comfortable places to surf the web while sipping a favorite drink.

But CEO Howard Schultz remained determined to find ways of linking Starbucks to a broader world of culture and lifestyle. In 1999, he discovered a promising new direction—music. That was the year he first walked into a Hear Music store.

Hear Music was a small record chain that had developed a devoted following in the San Francisco area. Its special attraction: the so-called listening station, which permits customers to listen to CDs over head phones before deciding which albums to buy. Hear Music was among the first music stores to offer this now-common service, and its clerks—chosen from the ranks of passionate music lovers—prided themselves on their ability to recommend off-the-beaten-track music to customers in search of something more adventurous than classic rock or current top-40 hits.

Schultz was impressed by the quality of the customer experience Hear Music offered and vowed to find ways to link it with his own company. Again, the connection must have seemed natural—coffee-houses in cities like New Orleans, New York, Chicago, and San Francisco have long been venues for performances by up-and-coming jazz, blues, folk, and rock performers. Starbucks purchased Hear Music later in 1999.

Working with company founder Don MacKinnon, now a Starbucks vice president, and Ken Lombard, president of Starbucks Entertainment, Schultz set about finding ways to update that tradition for the electronic age. The company wasn't eager to repeat its failures from the print media. "We feel that we've got one shot to get this right," Lombard admitted.[17]

The first experiment involved selling Hear Music compilation CDs in Starbucks stores. (This was not an entirely novel effort—other retailers had previously tried selling CDs of mood music played in their stores—some quite successfully. Starbucks itself had sold CDs of jazz selections starting as early as 1995.) Starbucks then launched a series called "Artist's Choice," for which popular musicians selected their own favorite songs by other artists. And in 2003, it felt ready to begin creating original content for music CDs, starting with *Genius Loves Company,* a collection of duets between blues legend Ray Charles and such contemporary artists as Elton John and Norah Jones.

Suddenly Starbucks became a force in the music business. *Genius Loves Company* was a massive hit. It became Ray Charles's first album on the Billboard Top 100 in 40 years, and in February 2005, it won six Grammy awards, including album of the year and record of the year. (The coincidental outpouring of love for Charles following his death in June, 2004, and the release of Taylor Hackford's acclaimed biopic *Ray* undoubtedly played a role in the record's success.)

By 2004, the company had created a new "Hear Music Debut" series, in which new artists were showcased in CDs launched exclusively at Starbucks stores. The first album in the series featured live tracks by an all-female folk-rock band called Antigone Rising. During the four-month period of Starbucks exclusivity, *From the Ground Up* sold a highly respectable 94,251 copies.[18] Later in the same year, Starbucks Hear Music announced the creation of a 24-hour digital music channel, to be distributed by XM Satellite Radio.

The newest incarnation of music at Starbucks is an experiment with CD-burning stations in coffee shops. Launched in March, 2004, in a Starbucks outlet in Santa Monica, California, Hear Music Coffeehouses offer hundreds of thousands of different music tracks stored in a computer database for customers to browse, sample, and choose from. For a price of $8.99 for the first seven tracks and 99 cents for each additional song, the customer can create a personalized selection of old favorites or new discoveries, pick cover art, and have a CD complete with liner notes prepared to take home inside five minutes.

By the end of 2005—several months behind their own previously announced schedule—Starbucks was sufficiently pleased with the sales results to open new Hear Music Coffeehouses in San Antonio and Miami Beach, each boasting an expanded inventory of over a million tracks for download.

Schultz views the new push into music as more than just a pleasant amenity to enhance a coffee shop visit. "We are the most frequented retailer in the world," he notes:

> With hundreds of thousands of songs digitally filed and stored, these Hear Music Coffeehouses combined with our existing locations can become the largest music store in any city that we have a Starbucks in. And because of the traffic, the frequency, and the trust that our customers have in the experience and the brand, we believe strongly that we can transform the retail record industry.[19]

Ken Lombard adds that the profile of the Starbucks customer fits perfectly into a niche that is underserved by the music business:

> The Starbucks consumer is part of that huge component of the music consumer that has become disenfranchised and disconnected from the music experience. If you asked 100 of them where they go to buy their music, the majority of them will tell you they don't really know.[20]

Meanwhile, Starbucks hasn't given up on its literary ambitions. In August, 2006, the company announced plans to create a new bookselling program, centered initially around a new novel by best-selling author Mitch Albom (*Tuesdays with Morrie*; New York: Doubleday, 1997, spent an astounding 363 weeks on the *New York Times* best seller lists).

Can Starbucks realize its dream of broadening its identity as a cultural concierge to its millions of loyal coffee-loving fans? The business world is rife with skeptics. Geoffrey Moore, a partner at the venture-capital firm of Mohr, Davidow and author of *Crossing the Chasm,* a well-known study of how entrepreneurial firms achieve lasting success, calls the music foray, "a very interesting experiment," but he cautions: "[I]f I was on [Starbucks] board of directors, I'd be more concerned that they not corrupt the brand. . . . If Starbucks is just trying to find more ways to monetize the traffic that comes through, this is a bad idea. At some point the customers will start to feel abused."[21]

So far, the financial results posted by the Hear Music Coffeehouses have been modest. Restaurant analyst John Glass of CIBC World Markets pegs annual revenues from music sales at a maximum of $120 million, just 3 percent of Starbucks U.S. sales—nowhere near enough to have a transformational impact on the business.[22] Even the acclaimed Ray Charles album produced only minor revenues. And many of the young customers Starbucks is targeting with its Hear Music Coffeehouses have moved beyond the era of CD-burning, keeping their personal music collections exclusively on their iPods, the portable music players created by Apple Computer. So far, Hear Music does not permit downloading of MP3 files for iPods or other portable players, which may mean that Starbucks is bypassing a large and growing segment of the music business.

Starbucks is taking a big risk in counting on a brand-new business as a major source of growth in the coming decades. Schultz understands the challenge. "Great companies are defined by their discipline and their understanding of who they are and who they are not," he says. "But also, great companies must have the courage to examine strategic opportunities that are transformational—as long as they are not inconsistent with the guiding principles and values of the core business."[23]

Starbucks is a fascinating company with a set of powerful customer connections that is experimenting in an imaginative, innovative attempt to create new ones. In the end, it is the customers who will decide whether expanding Starbucks into a music business is "not inconsistent" with the company's powerfully appealing brand image. What will they decide? Stay tuned.

YOUR BIG AHA'S

Starbucks is making an unusually far-sighted move in looking for ways to expand its customer connections into new business areas long before its existing model is fully mature. But creating a new business in a new arena is inherently challenging. Here are some of the lessons to be learned from the current state of the Starbucks saga.

The world's biggest brands are about more than just a great product. Just as Walt Disney recognized the limits to building a business on a cartoon mouse, Howard Schultz recognizes the limitations in building one on a simple cup of coffee. The challenge is figuring out what Starbucks stands for in the minds of its many avid customers and how to translate that same brand meaning into other products and services.

It takes time, money, and a willingness to gamble to expand into a brand-new business arena. As Starbucks has discovered, it's wise to expect missteps and mistakes when exploring new customer offerings. *Joe, Slate,* and book sales have all proved to be disappointing for Starbucks, while CD sales are struggling to take off. The company has wisely managed to control the amounts it has invested in these experimental ventures rather than "betting the business" on an untried new arena.

One key to success on a new business frontier may be buying the experience you need. For Starbucks to try to build up the expertise to succeed in music retailing from scratch would have been time-consuming and fraught with peril. Instead, the company purchased Hear Music, an innovative record chain whose intimate, personal style and ethos made a natural fit, and brought its savvy chief executive into the Starbucks hierarchy.

The perfect delivery system for one kind of product or service may or may not work for a different product or service. Starbucks coffee shops have developed a highly successful formula for pulling customers off the street for a brief break over a favorite drink. Can the same formula be applied to the very different

market for music CDs? Early reports are variable—some Hear
Music Coffeehouses report steady sales, while others often
stand empty. Don't assume that the delivery system you've
honed for one product or service will automatically work for
another.

There comes a time in the life of almost every organization—
whether it's a for-profit company, a not-for-profit group, or a government agency—when it must expand its products or services. The
reasons are varied, from the need to increase revenues to the desire to
provide clients with benefits they can't enjoy anywhere else. As the examples in this chapter illustrate, extending your brand in this way isn't
always easy, and it certainly isn't foolproof. But if, throughout the process, you maintain an unwavering focus on the needs and desires of
your customers, you won't go far astray.

Because, in the end, the strength and depth of your customer connections is what it's all about.

A Challenge That Never Ends

As I hope this book has shown, the challenge of creating deeper, richer, more satisfying connections to your customers is the single most important task facing any manager in today's complex, rapidly changing world. In fact, it's job one for everyone inside practically any organization. It doesn't matter whether your main area of focus and responsibility is customer service or marketing, information technology or finance, human resources or public relations, research and design, or manufacturing. In the end, without a steady stream of customers, our organizations have no reason for existing, whether they're for-profit companies, not-for-profit groups, or government agencies. So creating and maintaining meaningful, lasting customer connections needs to be at the top of everyone's agenda, whether they interact with customers directly or indirectly.

This is a challenge that never ends. You may be able to come to closure on certain other management tasks: The design for a new product is completed and the product is successfully launched. A new facility (a factory, a store, a hospital, or a hotel) is designed and opened to general acclaim. A new IT system is installed and begins providing more accurate and timely data. Congratulations—you've done a great job and can afford to pat yourself on the back.

But when it comes to connecting with your customers, there's never a moment when you can truly declare, "Mission Accomplished." There are two main reasons for this. First, like other important relationships—friendships, marriage, family—your relationship with your customers is (or should be) a long-lasting, evolving, living entity. It's never enough simply to make today's sale or provide today's service. You also want your customers to come back tomorrow—to make another purchase, to give you another opportunity to help, or to recommend your goods or services to a friend or family member. If your organization is to survive and thrive, your circle of customers must be perpetually self-sustaining and expanding, and that requires continual attention and hard work on your part.

Second, customers—like all human beings—are always changing. The offerings customers raved about yesterday are taken for granted today, and tomorrow they are likely to appear positively boring. The next new thing—a hot new product or cool new service—is always emerging, whether from a competitor next door or a rival halfway around the world, and customers are quick to notice and abandon you if they like the new offering better. Therefore, the customer connection isn't like a mathematical equation you can solve once, for all time. It's more like a game or a dance, with partners who are continually developing new, surprising moves that demand quick and sensitive adjustments on your part.

So don't consider this book some kind of handbook about customer connections—a compendium of perpetual wisdom for the ages. Instead, think of it as a series of snapshots of today's state of play—a collection of ideas drawn from the current practices of some of the world's smartest and most successful organizations. My hope is that, in these pages, you've found one, two, or more exciting ideas you're eager to try in your own organization—new moves that may help you develop an even deeper and more mutually beneficial connection with your own customers, now and for years to come.

ENDNOTES

Chapter 1   What Happened to My Customers?

1. Cited in *Rx for New Product Success,* by Drew Davis, Northwestern University Media Management Center, www.mediamanagementcenter .org/publications/data/Rx%20for%20New%20Product%20Success .pdf.

2. Cited in "Get Creative!" by Bruce Nussbaum, *Business Week* (August 1, 2005), p. 61.

3. Bryan Eisenberg, cofounder, Future Now; quoted in "Companies Tap into Consumer Passion," by Georgia Flight, *Business 2.0* (October 2005), p. 84.

4. Interview for the PBS *Frontline* show "The Persuaders," http://www. pbs.org/wgbh/pages/frontline/shows/persuaders/interviews/atkin .html.

5. Michael V. Copeland, "How to Capture the Buzz," *Business 2.0* (June 2005), p. 94.

6. George Flight, "Companies Tap into Consumer Passion," *Business 2.0* (October 2005), p. 84.

7. Christopher Palmeri, "Toyota's Scion: Dude, Here's Your Car," *Business Week* (June 9, 2003), http://www.businessweek.com/magazine /content/03_23/b3836050.htm.

8. "Toyota Gets People Buzzing—But Not about a Car," *Advertising Age,* August 3, 2006, http://adage.com/print?article_id =110867.

9. "Whyville.net and Toyota Financial Services Announce Launch of 'Scion Solutions,'" press release, http://www.marketwire.com /mw/release_html_b1?release_id=144511.

10. "BzzAgent Product Overview," http://www.bzzagent.com/pages /Overview.jsp.

11. Paul Sloan, "Why Some Brands Can Stand Alone," *Business 2.0* (October 2005), p. 49.

12. "Consumers Rebel Against Marketers' Endless Surveys," by Jack Neff. Advertising Age, October 2, 2006, http://adage.com/print =article_id=112237.

13. David Kiley, "Shoot the Focus Group," *Business Week* (November 14, 2005), p. 120.

14. Gina Chon, "Chrysler's Made-Up Customers Get Real Living Space at Agency," *Wall Street Journal* (January 4, 2006), p. B9.

15. "Marketing Memes," http://www.ishkur.com/editorials./marketing .php.

16. Virginia Heffernan and Tom Zeller, " 'Lonely Girl' (and Friends) Just Wanted Movie Deal," *New York Times* (September 12, 2006), p. C1.

17. Randall Stross, "AOL Said, 'If You Leave Me I'll Do Something Crazy,' " *New York Times* (July 2, 2006), p. 3.

18. Bruce Nussbaum with Robert Berner and Diane Brady, "Get Creative!," *Business Week Online* (August 1, 2005).

19. Robert Berner, "Welcome to Procter & Gadget: The Consumer Giant Is Leading the Way in Building Brands with Mechanical Gizmos," *Business Week* (February 7, 2005), p. 76.

20. David Kiley, "Shoot the Focus Group," *Business Week Online* (November 14, 2005).

21. Spencer E. Ante, "The Science of Desire," *Business Week* (June 5, 2006), p. 98.

Chapter 2   Engineering the Total Customer Experience

1. http://en.wikipedia.org/wiki/McDonalds; http://www.mcdonalds.com /corp/invest/pub/2006_fact_sheet.html.

2. "In-N-Out Burger" in *Wikipedia,* http://en.wikipedia.org/wiki /In-N-Out_Burger.

3. Stacy Perman, "Fat Burgers," *Los Angeles Magazine* (February 2004), p. 36; Tom McNichol, "The Secret Behind a Burger Cult," *New York Times* (August 14, 2002), p. F1. Schlosser's *Fast Food Na-*

tion: The Dark Side of the All-American Meal (Boston: by Houghton Mifflin, 2001).

4. Carleen Hawn, "The In-N-Out burger," *Fast Company* (September 2003), p. 36.

5. See note 3; John Pomfret, "In Calif., Internal Lawsuits Served Up at Burger Chain," *Washington Post* (January 30, 2005), p. A3.

6. Daisy Nguyen, "West Coast Chain's Fans Go Bunless from Way Back," *Houston Chronicle* (March 28, 2004), p. 3.

7. Carl Van Fleet, "Burgers: In-N-Out Burger," *Restaurants & Institutions* (September 1, 2004), p. 50.

8. Pomfret, "In Calif., Internal Lawsuits Served Up at Burger Chain."

9. "The Converts: They saw the light. Now they're making sure everyone else does, too." *Inc. Magazine* (November 2006), http://www.inc.com/magazine/20061101/green50_converts_Printer_Friendly.html.

10. "Dell Computer Corporation—Chairman and CEO Interview," *CEO Wire* (January 6, 2006), http://www.accessmylibrary.com/coms2/summary_0286-12257300_ITM.

11. Conrad de Aenlle, "Is Dell a Buy for Consumers or Investors?" *New York Times* (September 3, 2005), p. C5.

12. "Dell to Expand On-Call Services Team," *Wireless News* (November 15, 2005), p. 1.

13. Interview with Tufts University President Lawrence S. Bacow (October 5, 2006).

Chapter 3   Reimagining the Sale:
Creating Customers Who Are Happy to Buy

1. See, for example, "The Harris Poll on Work" (July 5–11, 2006), http://www.pollingreport.com/work.htm.

2. "Sephora: Liberating Beauty Products," *Business Week* (January 25, 2006), http://www.accessmylibrary.com/coms2/summary_028612257300_ITM.

3. Paul Sloan, "Why Some Brands Can Stand Alone," *Business 2.0* (October 2005), p. 49.

4. Pallavi Gogoi, "Meet Jane Geek," *Business Week* (November 28, 2005), p. 94.

5. Chuck Salter, "Customer Service: Commerce Bank," *Fast Company* (May 2002), p. 80.

6. Cited in "Putting a 7-Eleven Spin on Brand Banking," by Matthew De Paula, *USBanker* (March 2003), p. 28.

7. See note 5.

8. Steve Bills, "Commerce Tracking Behavior," *American Banker* (October 31, 2005), p. 23.

9. See note 5.

10. Lauren Bielski, "Talk Is Cheap," *ABA Banking Journal* (March 2005), p. 33.

11. Howard J. Stock, "Commerce Bank: Ahead of the Curve," *Bank Investment Consultant* (October 1, 2004), p. 28.

12. "Into the Fold: Banks in America Are Seeking out People They Once Shunned," *Economist* (May 6, 2006), p. 76.

13. Jerry Andree, township manager for Cranberry Township, Pennsylvania. Quoted in "Lifestyle Centers Breathe New Life, Theoretically, into Retail Projects," by Tim Schooley, *Pittsburgh Business Times* (December 9, 2005), http://pittsburgh.bizjournals.com/pittsburgh/stories/2005/12/12/focus5.html.

14. ICSC definition quoted in "Shopping in the Great Outdoors," by Lorrie Grant, *USA Today* (August 3, 2004), p. B4.

15. Parija Bjhatnagar, "Not a Mall, It's a Lifestyle Center," *CNN/Money* (January 12, 2005), http://money.cnn.com/2005/01/11/news/fortune500/retail_lifestylecenter/.

16. Joseph Weber with Ann Therese Palmer, "How the Net Is Remaking the Mall," *Business Week* (May 9, 2005), p. 60.

17. Brannon Boswell, "Investors Want to Know: What Defines a Lifestyle Center?" *Retail Traffic* (December 1, 2002); Lorrie Grant, "Shopping in the Great Outdoors," *USA Today* (August 3, 2004), p. B4.

Chapter 4   The Hospitable Organization: Turning Customers into Guests

1. David Armstrong, "Reaching for the Stars: Kimpton Adding Luxury While It Doubles Hotels," *San Francisco Chronicle* (March 31, 2006), p. C1.

2. Monica Khemsurov, "Boutique Hotels on a Budget," *Business 2.0* (April 1, 2005), http://money.cnn.com/magazines/business2 /business2_archive/2005/04/01/8256026/index.htm.

3. Allan Richter, "Son of W," *Hotel Interactive* (June 6, 2005), http:// www.hotelinteractive.com/index.asp?lstr=jstewart@loews.com&page _id=5000&article_id=4601; "One Year after Launch, Starwood's Aloft Hotel Brand Proves to Be a Developer Favorite," *Hospitality Net*, http://www.hospitalitynet.org/news//4027666.html.

4. Charles Gandee, "Bohemian Rhapsody," *Travel & Leisure* (October 2006), p. 205.

5. Barney Gimbel, "Jerry Levin's High-Profile Retreat," *Fortune* (October 18, 2004), p. 54; Rachel Abramowitz and Stacie Stukin, "Psyche Spa Helps Corporate Titans Cool Their Jets," *New Orleans Times-Picayune* (November 4, 2005), p. C5.

6. Catherine Yang, "Another Case Entirely," *Business Week* (April 11, 2005), p. 64.

7. Julie Appleby, "Case Bets on Business to Heal Health Care System," *USA Today* (July 6, 2005), p. B3; Marianne Kolbasuk Mcgee, "Steve Case's 'Revolution' Acquires Health and Tech Companies to Flesh out Consumer Offerings," *Information Week* (October 5, 2005), http://www.informationweek.com/showArticle.jhtml;jsessionid =NZDISYA4HNVE2QSNDLRSKH0CJUNN2JVN=articleID =171203297&queryText=Steve+Case.

8. Kim Severson, "For Hospital Menus, Overdue Surgery," *New York Times* (March 7, 2006), p. F1.

9. Christine Sparta, "Sending in the Clowns Is Serious Business for Sick Kids," *USA Today* (January 28, 1999), p. 8D.

10. Yilu Zhao, "In the Bronx, an Ounce of Connection," *New York Times* (November 29, 2001), p. G1.

11. Edwin McDowell, "At Children's Hospitals, Friendly Designs," *New York Times* (November 17, 2002), p. 11.1.

Chapter 5   Home Away from Home: The Art of Welcoming Customers

1. "Lapidus of Luxury," *Metropolis Magazine* (January 2001), http://www.metropolismag.com/html/content_0101/ml.htm.

2. "Morris Lapidus Biography," in *Miami Beach History*, http://www .miamibeach411.com/History/bio_lapidus.html.

3. See note 1.

4. "Morris Lapidus Biography," in *Miami Beach History,* http://www
    .miamibeach411.com/History/bio_lapidus.html.

5. Leslie Petrovski, "Paco Underhill on Why We Buy," *Museum Store*
    (Fall 1999), http://www.envirosell.com/articles/Museum_Store.htm.

6. See note 5.

7. Robert La Franco, "It's All about Visuals," *Forbes* (May 22, 1995),
    p. 108.

8. Susanna Hammer, "Lessons from a Retail Rebel," *Business 2.0* (June
    2005), p. 62.

9. "Three Secrets to a Retail Rebel's Success," *Growth Strategies* (Octo-
    ber 2005), p. 2.

10. "Urban Outfitters Tie-Up Spins New Groove in-Store," *In-Store*
    (May 10, 2005), p. 6.

11. Polly LaBarre, "Sophisticated Sell," *Fast Company* (December 2002),
    p. 92.

12. Michael D. Cole, "The Apparel Top 50: A Rising Tide," *Apparel* (July
    2005), p. 24; "Financial Overview" on corporate web site at
    http://www.urbanoutfittersinc.com/financial/index.jsp.

13. "Three Secrets to a Retail Rebel's Success," *Growth Strategies* (Octo-
    ber 2005), p. 2.

14. Susanna Hammer, "Lessons from a Retail Rebel," *Business 2.0* (June
    2005), p. 62.

15. Warren Cohen, "Crisis Coverage Escalates to a Crawl," *Inside.com*
    (October 5, 2001), http://wjcohen.home.mindspring.com/insideclips
    /crawl.htm.

16. Erika Falk and Sean Aday, "Are Voluntary Standards Working? Can-
    didate Discourse on Network Evening News Programs," The An-
    nenberg Public Policy Center (December 20, 2000), http://www
    .annenbergpublicpolicycenter.org/02_reports_releases/report_2000
    .htm.

17. Peter Johnson, "Woodruff, Vargas to Replace Jennings," *USA Today*
    (December 12, 2005), p. D1.

18. Karen Lurie, "News That Sounds like Anything But," *PopPolitics.com,*
    http://www.poppolitics.com/articles.2003-01-06-tvlanguage.shtml.

19. Jacques Steinberg, "CBS Sets out to Revamp Its Evening News," *Houston Chronicle* (August 20, 2005), p. 10.

20. Jon Lafayette, "FNC Gambit: Less Is More," *TV Currents* (June 6, 2005), p. 3.

Chapter 6   Haven Wanted: Providing Security in an Unsafe World

1. Katherine Stroup, "Waiting for Takeoff," *Newsweek* (April 15, 2002), p. 57.

2. Blake Morrison, "Airport Security Failures Persist," *USA Today* (July 1, 2002),   http://www.usatoday.com/news/sept11/2002/06/30/airport -security.htm.

3. Jane Engel, "Now on Concourse 1: A Health Club, Clinic and an Aquarium," *Los Angeles Times* (February 15, 2004), p. L3.

4. Sarah Bernard, "The Perfect Prescription," *New York* (April 18, 2005), p. 60.

5. "Increase in US Medication-Error Deaths between 1983 and 1993," *Lancet*, 351 (1998), pp. 643–44.

6. Laura Heller, "Target to Bring Fashion to Pharmacy with Clear Rx," *Drug Store News* (March 21, 2005), p. 10.

7. Quoted in "Why Hackers Are a Giant Threat to Microsoft's Future," by Fred Vogelstein, *Fortune* (October 18, 2004), p. 263.

8. John Markoff, "At Microsoft, Interlopers Sound Off on Security," *New York Times* (October 17, 2005), p. C1.

9. Steve Lohr and Laurie J. Flynn, "Microsoft to Delay Next Version of Windows," *New York Times* (March 22, 2006), p. C1.

10. "Bill Gates Interview Transcript," *Financial Times* (February 15, 2006), http://news.ft.com/cms/s/3855568e-9ddc-11da-b1c6-0000779e2340 .html.

11. Adam L. Penenberg, "Microsoft vs. Computer Security: Why the Software Giant Still Can't Get It Right," *Slate* (January 9, 2006), http://www.slate.com/id/2133993.

12. Neil Fawcett, "Bug Hunt—Microsoft's Plan for Secure Computing," *Enterprise Times* (March 1, 2004), http://www.enterprisetimes.com /et/na_ent_09_2005_03.asp.

13. See note 10.

Chapter 7   Open-Door Policy: The Challenge of Transparency

1. Judy Rife, "New York State Toll Pass System Makes Website More Functional," *Knight Ridder Tribune Business News* wire feed (March 3, 2004), p. 1.

2. Jennifer Saranow, "States Prod Drivers to Use High-Tech Tolls," *Wall Street Journal* (December 13, 2005), p. D1.

3. Elizabeth Pariseau, "Registry to Test Drive-Thru Window," *Boston Globe* (January 3, 2002), p. B11.

4. California Department of Motor Vehicles, *DMV Gives the Gift of Time: Additional Branches Equipped with Queuing System During the Holidays* (December 13, 2005).

5. Eric L. Wee, "Coming Online: Virginia Driver's License Renewal," *Washington Post* (August 19, 1998), p. V1.

6. Michael Wilson, "A 311 Caller Who Knows How Potholes Are Fixed," *New York Times* (September 13, 2003), p. B1.

7. "About DOITT/311," on the Department of Information Technology and Telecommunications web site, http://www.nyc.gov/html /doitt/html/about/about_311.shtml.

8. Jennifer Steinhauer, "From Recycling to Poultry at Door, New York Has a Number to Call: 311," *New York Times* (April 23, 2003), p. B1.

9. Winnie Hu, "City's 311 Line Takes Big Step Past Potholes," *New York Times* (July 19, 2004), p. B1.

10. Thomas J. Lueck, "City's 311 Help Lines Plans to Add Data on Social Services," *New York Times* (November 1, 2005), p. B1.

11. Winnie Hu, "New Yorkers Love to Complain, and Hot Line Takes Advantage," *New York Times* (December 1, 2003), p. A1.

12. See note 11.

13. Keith Dawson, "Your Newest Competitor: Local Government," *Call Center Magazine* (March 2005), p. 6.

14. Donna Lamb, "Immigrants Urged to Dial 311 for Services," *New York Beacon* (December 16–22, 2004), p. 4.

15. "The City of New York 311 Citizen Service Center Client Information Privacy Policy," http://www.nyc.gov/html/doitt/downloads /pdf/311-privacy-polic.pdf.

16. Harvey Chipkin, "National Report," *Hotel and Motel Management* (September 19, 2005), p. 22.

17. Greg Lindsay, "Home Sweet Airworld," *Advertising Age* (October 17, 2005), p. 16.

18. See note 16.

19. Scott McCartney, "The Middle Seat: Beyond Orbitz: How to Find the Best Tickets: New Web Sites Help Fliers Track Down Hidden Fares and First-Class Upgrades," *Wall Street Journal* (July 5, 2005), p. D1.

20. Joseph Turow, *Niche Envy: Marketing Discrimination in the Digital Age* (Cambridge, MA: MIT Press, 2006), p. 71.

Chapter 8   One Size Does Not Fit All: The New Art of Customization

1. David Colman, "For the Man with a 15.95-Inch Neck," *New York Times* (November 18, 2001), p. 9.6.

2. Marcia Biederman, "A Bulge in Misses 8? Digital Scanners Resize America," *New York Times* (November 27, 2003), p. G8.

3. Jay Cohen, "Scanner Cuts Cost of Custom-Made Clothes," *Associated Press* writer. Available at the TC2 web site, http://www.tc2 .com/news/news_scanner.html.

4. Ray A. Smith, "In Search of the Perfect Fit: Retailers Are Pushing Made-to-Measure Suits; How Do They Measure Up?" *Wall Street Journal* (October 22, 2005), p. P4.

5. Marv Blousek, "Online Clothing-Design Orders Take off for Dodgeville, Wis.-Based Lands End," *Knight Ridder Tribune Business News* (October 17, 2003), p. 1.

6. Melynda Dovel Wilcox, "Clothes: Fitting Pretty," *Kiplinger's Personal Finance* (January 2003), p. 24.

7. Bob Tederschi, "A Lands' End Experiment in Selling Custom-Made Pants Is a Success, Leaving Its Rivals to Play Catch-Up," *New York Times* (September 30, 2002), p. C7.

8. Julie Schlosser, "Cashing in on the New World of Me," *Fortune* (December 13, 2004), p. 244.

9. Ibid.

10. Marcia Biederman, "A Bulge in Misses 8? Digital Scanners Resize America," *New York Times* (November 27, 2003), p. G8.

11. "US Postal Service's Citizens' Stamp Advisory Committee," information available at http://coins.about.com/cs/uspsinfo/a/033103

.htm; "Web Sightings: Put Your Personal Stamp on Postage," [Baltimore] *Daily Record* (August 27, 2004), p. 1.

12. "PhotoStamps: Terms and Conditions," http://photo.stamps.com/PhotoStamps/conditions.

13. Bob Tedeschi, "Before You Drop That Check in the Mail, Stamp It with a First-Day Issue of Your Own Smiling Face," *New York Times* (May 9, 2005), p. C6.

14. Jessica Mintz, "Custom Stamps Put Dogs and Dictators on Your Envelopes," *Wall Street Journal* (September 2, 2004), p. B1.

15. Joshua Glenn, "Stamping Out Crime," *Boston Globe* (May 1, 2005), p. D2.

16. See note 15.

17. See note 13.

18. Eric Wilson, "Vanity Postage," *New York Times* (December 22, 2005), p. G1.

19. See note 13.

20. "About Basic Brown Bear," company web site, http://www.basicbrownbear.com/a_aboutus.cfm.

21. Doris Hajewski, "Build-A-Bear Workshop Rolls into Summerfest," *Knight Ridder Business News* (July 2, 2005), p. 1.

22. Roger O. Crockett, "Hot Growth: Build-A-Bear Workshops," *Business Week* (June 6, 2005), p. 77.

23. Mary Jo Feldstein, "Build-A-Bear Hits the Big Time with NY Store," *St. Louis Post-Dispatch* (July 18, 2005), p. A1.

24. See note 23.

25. "The Art of Service," *Fast Company* (October 2005), p. 47.

26. See note 22.

Chapter 9   Let Me Introduce You:
Customer Communities in an Interactive World

1. Bhana Pande, "Harley's Fortunes Revived by Focus on Existing Clients," *Media* (January 30, 2004), p. 20.

2. Dale Boss, "Can Harley Ride the New Wave?" *Brandweek* (October 25, 2004), p. 20.

3. Andrea Kingsmill, "Road Kings: Harley Mystique Fuels Riders' Motorcycle Passions," *Houston Chronicle* (November 22, 2003), p. 1.

4. See note 3.

5. Dale Boss, "Can Harley Ride the New Wave?" *Brandweek* (October 25, 2004), p. 20.

6. See note 5.

7. Bhana Pande, "Harley's Fortunes Revived by Focus on Existing Clients," *Media* (January 30, 2004), p. 20.

8. Patricia Sellers, "eBay's Secret," *Fortune* (October 18, 2004), p. 160.

9. Adam Cohen, *The Perfect Store: Inside eBay* (Boston: Little, Brown, 2002), cited in "eBay" on Wikipedia, http://en.wikipedia.org/wiki/eBay.

10. Christine Tatum, " 'Junkies' Profit as eBay Thrives," *Knight Ridder Tribune Business News* (June 17, 2002), p. 1.

11. Glenn R. Simpson, "eBay to Police Site for Sales of Pirated Items," *Wall Street Journal* (February 28, 2001), p. A3.

12. Doug Bedell, "Expanding Universe of eBay Auction Site a Social, Economic Force," *Denver Post* (January 8, 2001), p. E1.

13. Amy Feldman, "eBay Gatekeeper," *Money* (October 2000), p. 135.

14. Boaz Herzog, "Meth Trade Finds New Portal: eBay," *Knight Ridder Tribune Business News* (September 17, 2005), p. 1.

15. See note 8.

16. Saul Hansell, "Meg Whitman and eBay, Net Survivors," *New York Times* (May 5, 2002), p. 31.

17. Verne Kopytoff, "eBay's New Way to Aid Sellers," *San Francisco Chronicle* (June 24, 2005), p. C1.

18. See note 8.

19. Brian Carroll, "Establishing Trust a Key Challenge for E-Tailers," *Furniture Today* (July 21, 2003), p. 25.

20. See note 16.

21. Oliver Prichard, "MySpace.com Carves out Internet Niche," *Knight Ridder Tribune Business News* (December 11, 2005), p. 1.

22. See note 21.

23. Lorne Manly, "This Is Not Spinal Tap: A Concert Film by Fans," *New York Times* (January 19, 2006), p. E1.

24. Michelle Theriault, "Students Plug in to Web Sites," *Knight Ridder Tribune Business News* (January 15, 2006), p. 1.

25. Thomas K. Arnold, "The MySpace Invaders," *USA Today* (August 1, 2006), p. 4D.

26. See note 23.

27. See note 25.

28. Jessi Hempel, "The MySpace Generation," *Business Week* (December 12, 2005), p. 86.

29. "Marketing on MySpace: ForBiddeN Fruit," *Economist* (July 29, 2006), p. 60.

30. Chris Gaither, "For Musicians, MySpace Is Site to Be Seen and Heard," *Los Angeles Times* (July 5, 2005), p. C1.

31. David Brooks, "They Bond, Let It All Hang Out," *Atlanta Journal-Constitution* (January 10, 2006), p. A9.

32. Thomas K. Arnold, "Niche Competitors Crowd Into MySpace," *USA Today* (August 1, 2006), p. 1D.

Chapter 10   High-Tech Goes High-Touch: Using the Internet to Go Global and Go Local

1. Daniel Mark Scroop, *Mr. Democrat: Jim Farley, the New Deal, and the Making of Modern American Politics* (Ann Arbor: University of Michigan Press, 2006), p. 134.

2. Adam Nagourney, "Politics Faces Sweeping Change via the Web," *New York Times* (April 2, 2006), p. A1.

3. New Politics Institute, "Mastering New Media Trends: A Strategic Check-List," (February 9, 2006), www.newpolitics.net/node/83.

4. Robert D. Putnam, *Bowling Alone: The Collapse and Revival of American Community* (New York: Simon & Schuster, 2000).

5. Jesse Holcomb, "Community.com," *Sojourners* (May 2004), p. 9.

6. Sean Dodson and Ben Hammersley, "Feed Back: The Web's Candidate for President," [Manchester, England] *Guardian* (December 18, 2003), p. 23.

7. Matea Gold, "Politics: Where Political Influence Is Only a Keyboard Away," *Los Angeles Times* (December 21, 2003), p. A41.

8. Edward Cone, "The Marketing of the President 2004," *Baseline* (December 1, 2003), p. 32.

9. See note 6.

10. Jeanne Cummings, "The E-Team—Behind Dean Surge: A Gang of Bloggers and Webmaster," *Wall Street Journal* (October 14, 2003), p. A1.

11. Brian Faler, "Dean Leaves Legacy of Online Campaign," *Washington Post* (February 20, 2005), p. A12.

12. Tom Baxter, "Old-Time Politics Meets New Strategy," *Atlanta Journal-Constitution* (December 29, 2003), p. A1.

13. Jill Zuckman, "Democratic Presidential Candidates Spin Web of Support on Cybertrail," *Knight Ridder Tribune Business News* (December 3, 2003), p. 1.

14. Matea Gold, "Politics: Where Political Influence Is Only a Keyboard Away," *Los Angeles Times* (December 21, 2003), p. A41.

15. See note 13.

16. Yana Bey, "Net Effect Is a 'Meet-Up,'" *BusinessLine* (Chennai, India, April 5, 2004), p. 1.

17. Statistics from www.truthlaidbear.com; cited in *Emergence of the Progressive Blogosphere: A New Force in American Politcs* by Chris Bowers and Matthew Stoller (Miami, FL: New Politics Institute, August 10, 2005).

18. Jeff Daniel, "Meet and Match," *St. Louis Post-Dispatch,* "Everyday Magazine" (November 21, 2004), p. E1.

19. Brian Faler, "Dean Camp's Tactics Applied to Colorado; Web Site Aims to Organize Liberal Activists," *Washington Post* (October 9, 2005), p. A05.

20. Adam Nagourney, "Politics Faces Sweeping Change via the Web," *New York Times* (April 2, 2006), p. A1.

21. See note 20.

22. See note 12.

Chapter 11   Everyone Is Welcome:
The Challenges of Customer Diversity

1. C. K. Prahalad, *The Fortune at the Bottom of the Pyramid: Eradicating Poverty through Profits* (Upper Saddle River, NJ: Wharton School Publishing, 2005).

2. Statistics from the Selig Center for Economic Growth, Terry College of Business, University of Georgia, 2005, cited in "Protecting Your Brand: Service Diverse Customers."

3. Lee Smith, "Facing Diversity," *Fortune,* special section, www.timeinc.net/fortune/services/sections./fortune/corp/2004 _10diversity.html.

4. See note 3.

5. Gerry Lupacchino, *Protecting Your Brand: Service Diverse Customers* (Boston: Novations Group, 2006).

6. Kim Severson, "For Hospital Menus, Overdue Surgery," *New York Times* (March 7, 2006), p. D1.

7. Kristen Matejka, "Guest-Specific Marketing Enhances the Venetian's Appeal to Different Segments," *Hotel Business* (May 7–20, 2005), p. 46; "Meet the Cohorts," on the Cohorts web site, www .cohorts.com/meet_the_cohorts.html.

Chapter 12   Your Best, and a Little Bit More: Offering Something Extra to Your Customers

1. Jacques Barzun, "Paradoxes of Publishing," in *Jacques Barzun on Writing, Editing, and Publishing* (Chicago: University of Chicago Press, 1971), p. 101.

2. Jeffrey Trachtenberg, "Book Publishers Build Buzz Early, Hollywood Style," *Wall Street Journal* (December 1, 2005) p. C1.

3. Claudia H. Deutsch, "Book Publishers Are Selling Words with Pictures," *New York Times* (August 2, 2006) p. C10.

4. "At 100, Art Museum Looks Inwards and Outward," *Denver Post* (February 6, 1993), p. 7B.

5. Laurel Graber, "Does an Educational Exhibition Have to Be Dryly Serious? Fuggedaboudit," *New York Times* (August 8, 2006), p. E3.

6. M. Hunt, "The Grand Generation: Folklore in Aging," *The Journal of Museum Education,* vol. 9, no. 4, pp. 15–16; cited in "Museum Marketing and Strategy: Directors' Perception and Belief," Jin-Tisann Yeh and Chyong-Ling Lin, *Journal of American Academy of Business* (March 2005), p. 279.

7. Ellen Hoffman, "The Fine Art of Dining," *Business Week* (August 15, 2005), p. 86.

8. Alison Arnett, "Not Just for Ladies Who Lunch: MOMA Has Elevated the Museum Restaurant. Can Boston Do the Same?" *Boston Globe* (May 11, 2005), p. E1.

9. Lisa Jennings, "Puck Group Taps Cultural Venues for New-Market Growth Opportunities," *Nation's Restaurant News* (June 13, 2005), p. 4.

10. Cathy Hainer, "Museum Restaurants Please the Art Lover's Palate," *USA Today* (November 13, 1998), p. 10D.

11. See note 7.

12. See note 9.

13. Greg Beato, "Cups of Pith—Starbucks Tries (Again) to Elevate Its Customers," *Las Vegas Weekly* (December 22–28, 2005), http://www.lasvegasweekly.com/2005/12/22/popculture.html.

14. Richard A. Martin, "Say It Ain't So: After Three Issues, Starbucks and Time's Jointly Published Joe Grinds to a Halt," *Seattle Weekly* (February 16, 2000), http://www.seattleweekly.com/news/0007/features-martin.php.

15. See note 13.

16. Stanley Holmes, "Strong Lattes, Sour Notes," *Business Week* (June 20, 2005), p. 58.

17. Dorian Lynskey, "Stir It Up: Starbucks Has Changed the Music Industry with Its Deals with Dylan and Alanis," [Manchester, England] *Guardian* (October 6, 2005), p. 18.

18. Melinda Newman, "Starbucks Digs Deeper into Digital with New Hear Music Stores," *Billboard* (December 24, 2005), p. 24.

19. Alison Overholt, "Listening to Starbucks," *Fast Company* (July 2004), p. 50.

20. See note 17.

21. See note 19. Moore's book, *Crossing the Chasm* (New York: HarperBusiness, 1991).

22. See note 16.

23. See note 19.

INDEX